A REGION IN TURMOIL

CONTEMPORARY WORLDS explores the present and recent past. Books in the series take a distinctive theme, geo-political entity or cultural group and explore their developments over a period ranging usually over the last fifty years. The impact of current events and developments are accounted for by rapid but clear interpretation in order to unveil the cultural, political, religious and technological forces that are reshaping today's worlds.

SERIES EDITOR
Jeremy Black

In the same series

Sky Wars: A History of Military Aerospace Power
David Gates

Britain since the Seventies
Jeremy Black

War since 1945
Jeremy Black

The Global Economic System since 1945
Larry Allen

A REGION IN TURMOIL
SOUTH ASIAN CONFLICTS SINCE 1947

ROB JOHNSON

REAKTION BOOKS

This book is dedicated to Hannah and Tom

Published by Reaktion Books Ltd
79 Farringdon Road
London EC1M 3JU, UK

www.reaktionbooks.co.uk

First published 2005

Copyright © Rob Johnson 2005

Printed and bound in Great Britain by CPI/Bath Press, Bath

British Library Cataloguing in Publication Data
Johnson, Robert, 1967–
      A region in turmoil: South Asian conflicts since 1947. –
      (Contemporary worlds)
      1. Insurgency – South Asia – History – 20th century
      2. Insurgency – South Asia – History – 21st century
      3. Postcolonialism – South Asia – History – 20th century
      4. Postcolonialism – South Asia – History – 21st century
      5. South Asia – History – 20th century 6. South Asia – History – 21st
      century 7. South Asia – Politics and government – 20th century
      8. South Asia – Politics and government – 21st century
      I. Title
      954'.04

ISBN 1 86189 257 8

Contents

Preface

South Asia, a region that stretches from the Hindu Kush to the Malay Peninsula, and from the Indian Ocean to the Himalayas, has endured decades of conflict since the Second World War. Some of these are the result of legacies inherited from the colonial and even the pre-colonial eras, but most have sprung up because of issues that have arisen since 1947. Whilst many scholars have analysed each of the disputes in detail, there have been relatively few attempts to bring together the conflicts in a coherent whole. This is a pity, for there are striking parallels and patterns within them. Moreover, a regional study offers the chance to gain a clearer picture of the contours of instability, the causes of conflicts, and their resolution.

A regional study enables us to make some general comments about the nature of conflict. The term 'conflict' has been selected deliberately, not because of a problem with the definition of war in any legalistic sense, but because the number of deaths caused by politicized violence in 'unconventional' settings often far exceed those that occur during inter-state or 'conventional' fighting. Conflicts embrace armed confrontations, insurrections, communal rioting, insurgencies and episodes of terrorism, as well as wars. Nevertheless, and perhaps inevitably, the limitations of the available space do not permit inclusion of non-politicized conflicts, such as organized and violent crime, or the vast number of civil conflicts that do not necessarily degenerate into violence.

In writing this book I should like to offer my thanks to Professor Jeremy Black for his inspiration to take a wider perspective on warfare. Surely, his prolific and penetrating studies, which examine conflict from a global perspective on the macro scale, and, at the same time, continue to stress the importance of the individual, local and regional level, command our attention. Many of my ideas are but dim reflections of Black's original brilliant theses located in a South Asian context. I would also like to thank a number of South Asian scholars, including Professor Chris Bayly, Dr Vernon Hewitt and Dr Ian Talbot for allowing me to consult them or read and cite their work. I am also grateful to Peter Dent, a former Commissioning Editor at Reaktion, for supporting the publication of this book. To the reader I offer my thoughts on South Asia with humility, especially since I am conscious of the sensitivities of the issues in this subject and how difficult the nature of the sources can be in contemporary history. I have tried to be objective, but acknowledge that this is a Sisyphean task and apologize for any errors that have occurred as a result.

Chapter 1

The Significance of Conflicts in South Asia

A bungled terrorist attack on the Indian parliament buildings in December 2001, coming so soon after the shocking events of September that year in New York and Washington, DC, drew attention to the fact that Jihadist terror was indeed a global phenomenon. Combined with appalling attacks in Bali, Kenya, Aden and Saudi Arabia, which were specifically designed to maximize casualties, it was clear that South Asian states would be compelled to respond to the new threat. These developments, however, which have dominated the West's military reorientation after the Cold War, are but a new layer of complexity in a region that has experienced insurgency conflicts for decades.

Indeed, South Asia is a region plagued by violence and a depressing number of human rights violations. Anecdotes of shocking brutalities and atrocities, caused by a potent cocktail of ethnic, sectarian or nationalistic antagonisms, should surely command the attention of the international community. Until recently, the Kashmiri Separatists detonated bombs in Srinagar on a regular basis, and the Indian Army responded with a tough policy of 'zero tolerance' to those it suspected of harbouring the guerrillas. Pakistan's Shiite and Sunni Muslims still clash in Karachi, whilst Pushtun fighters, often imbued with a deep conviction in their own militarized brand of Islam, joust with government troops.[1] In Sri Lanka, the so-called Tamil Tigers carried out suicide bombings on the crowded streets of Colombo and their remains were graphically portrayed to the world via the Internet.

Ethnic groups on the periphery of Burma-Myanmar raid, and are raided by, the Burmese regular army with great brutality. Occasionally, these conflicts have drawn in the West. Tourists are a potential target for hostage-taking in the region. Terrorist attacks on diplomatic staff and Christian church-goers in Pakistan have been a reaction to, or have caused responses from, Western governments. Nevertheless, in an era where there is growing concern about the proliferation of weapons of mass destruction, 'rogue states' and international terrorism, South Asia is curiously overshadowed in Western scholarship. This may be for the legitimate reason that the Middle East is of far greater concern for the international community following recent conflicts in Israel and Iraq and the terrorist attacks on the United States in September 2001. Nevertheless, both India and Pakistan are now 'nuclear powers' with a history of escalating smaller conflicts. Most of these have rippled outwards from the epicentre of Kashmir, and, until there is a lasting settlement, this dispute still threatens to destabilize the region.

India now possesses an army of some 1,100,000 men, the world's second largest, which is divided into five regional commands with four field armies. In 1992–3 its defence budget stood at $6.75 million, or, put another way, 15 per cent of its total budget. In 1993 the Pakistan Army stood at 510,000, but since the imposition of military rule some 30 per cent of the total budget goes on defence, representing 8 per cent of GDP. Thus 131 billion rupees are devoted to national security, when only 1.6 billion rupees go on education and 3.2 billion is spent on health. Although recent escalations in defence spending seemed to suggest a greater precariousness in relations between these two states, the economic weaknesses of the countries have limited the ability of the armies to conduct sustained operations. Nevertheless, a severe economic crisis in one or other of the two powers could cause a fatal rupture in relations and lead to conflict.

These factors alone mean that it is imperative to gain a better understanding of conflicts in South Asia. It is equally important that a contextual analysis is made from a South Asian perspective as well as a Western one. India and Pakistan have at times been singularly unsuccessful in influencing or coercing neighbouring states and satellites, but that has not stopped them trying. What is at stake is a collection of economic, cultural, political and strategic issues vaguely called 'national interests'. Yet the very concept of national identity is at the root of the problem. Both India and Pakistan face considerable divisions internally from significant minorities who feel marginalized or alienated from their national governments. Similar political inequalities have inspired conflicts in Sri Lanka, and prompted military dictatorships in Pakistan, Bangladesh and Burma. Even India's civilian government, which has remained free of military control, has periodically imposed its will on dissident groups within the subcontinent, as exemplified by Indira Gandhi's Operation Bluestar against the Sikh Separatist movement in Amritsar in the 1980s.

What is immediately apparent in conflicts between states in South Asia is that domestic and foreign issues are indivisible. The partition of the Punjab in 1947, for example, cut across the ethnic distribution of the Sikhs, and, despite a massive migration of peoples, left significant minorities of Hindus and Muslims on the 'wrong side' of the new border. Further north, the failure to resolve the fate of Kashmir peacefully in 1947 generated a conflict about sovereignty and national identity that lay between and also within the states of India and Pakistan. Significant numbers of Tamils in southern India were affected by the struggle between the Sinhalese and Tamils of neighbouring Sri Lanka, a conflict that eventually drew in India as a 'peacekeeper'. But perhaps the classic example of internal conflict escalating into an inter-state war was in 1971, when East Pakistan broke away from the political domination of Islamabad to become Bangladesh. More recently, Pakistan's desire to prevent the formation of a separate 'Pushtunistan' was one of the reasons for its clandestine intervention in the Afghan civil war. It backed the Pushtun-dominated Taliban until 2001, but still faces regional conflict with the peoples of the Federally Administered Tribal Areas (FATA) of the North-West Frontier Province and Baluchistan.

The South Asian conflicts are the products of legacies from earlier periods, mixed with internal divisions and external (and sometimes superpower) influences. India, for example, has regarded itself as the hegemonic power of South Asia because of its size, strength and strategic location. It has frequently found itself restricted, however, by the real powers of the region, namely the United States, China and, until recently, the Soviet Union. They have influenced the direction of South Asian politics and will, it seems, continue to alter the trajectory not just of the individual states but also of the region as a whole. This fact is best illustrated by the conflicts between India and Pakistan in 1965 and 1971. Both states developed strategies based on the speed of external intervention, but the cause of the war of 1965 was, although ostensibly a border dispute, chiefly the result of China's victory over India in 1962 and the conclusion by the Pakistan armed forces that there was an opportunity to strike a decisive blow. Emboldened by an alliance with China, Pakistan expected an easy victory against India. Despite the negative impression of external intervention, setbacks for both India and Pakistan led them to call for foreign support, and both have tried to utilize foreign military and economic aid whilst at the same time try-ing to shut out intervention from the West, China, the USSR and the UN.

The United States National Intelligence Council (NIC) report 'Global Trends, 2015' suggests that external influences will continue to play a crucial part in strategic thinking in all the countries of the region. Tariq Mahmud Ashraf believes that India's economic and conventional mili-tary advantages will give it even greater advantages on its neighbours in the future. Indeed, Ashraf fears that the precedent of the United States-led operations in Afghanistan in 2001 and Iraq in 2003 means that India will be tempted to make pre-emptive moves of its own to neutralize threats before they become too serious.[2]

THEORIES OF CONFLICT

The idea of conflict, as opposed to war, is designed to avoid some of the difficulties of classification that threaten to distort any analysis. Jeremy Black has frequently drawn attention to this problem and argues persuasively that many Western interpretations are narrow and limited by their own terms of reference.[3] Conflict thus refers to a number of forms of politicized violence, inter-state war, insurgency and guerrilla war, terrorism, and sectarian or communal rioting. The flexibility offered by this definition means that it is possible to make a far more comprehensive analysis of the causes of fighting in South

Asia. In addition, the nature of that bellicosity can also be determined more accurately. When it comes to peace-making, only a broad interpretation of conflict could explain, for example, why Kashmir continued to form the locus of Indo-Pakistan confrontation for almost 50 years, even when traditional inter-state negotiations could have settled the dispute through diplomatic channels.

In considering the causes of conflict in South Asia, Black offers a useful interpretation. Instead of merely stacking up the causes of war as a series of factors, upon which scholars might usefully debate and prioritize, he argues for a consideration of the triggers 'within a context that notes . . . the terms of a cultural world that focused on conflict – in other words, bellicosity'.[4] That is not to say that wars are planned and executed when based on entirely rational, aggressive calculations. Black is right to note that there is a vast difference between the intended conflict and the one that so often develops. This was certainly the case for India when it confronted China in 1962. Archival research reveals a series of hesitations, contingency plans and considered opportunities, but the tendency to rationalize decision-making after the event creates the impression of order where they may be none. Memoirs, even well-intentioned ones by South Asian statesmen and soldiers, also fall into this category. Even broad policy lines or 'national interests' may be subject to interpretation and review in light of unfolding events.

Perhaps the problem with bellicosity within cultures is that statesmen are sometimes confronted by a threat they did not foresee or desire. India, despite the fighting against Pakistan in 1948, neglected its armed forces to some extent in the 1950s. Most units were short of equipment and transport, whilst essential technology, such as radio communications, was lamentably deficient. Armoured vehicles, combat aircraft and even artillery were in danger of obsolescence. India's military performance in the early 1960s was, unsurprisingly, disappointing as it struggled to defend itself against new threats from China and Pakistan, as well as Assamese insurgents on the north-east frontier.

In fact, what seems to characterize the decision-making in South Asian conflicts, be they conventional wars or insurgencies, is that political and military elites based their calculations on subjective perceptions of 'threat'. This would be applicable to those adopting a defensive as well as an offensive strategy. Thus Pakistan, which regarded India as a menace to its very existence, would contemplate pre-emptive strike as well as defensive operations. Concerned that Delhi was integrating Kashmiri Muslims into the political economy of India, Pakistan used proxy separatist insurgents to destabilize the province and remove the threat of losing this area for good. In a similar way, India has long perceived Pakistan as a threat and has deployed the bulk of its armed forces in a position to resist any incursions. When, in 1971, it felt threatened by separatist, left-wing groups sympathetic to the idea of an independent Bangladesh, India acted to ensure that there was a friendly government in Dacca and thus no question of a destabilizing insurgency spilling over into Bihar or Uttar Pradesh.

The perception of a threat, whether that threat is real or imagined, can generate the culture of war. Perhaps more often labelled 'militarism', the militarization of political and religious groups can help to explain the development, for example, of Jihadist Islam in Pakistan, Iran and Afghanistan, as well as elsewhere in the world.[5] Al-Qaeda frequently refers to the 'threat' posed by Jews and Christians to the holy places of Saudi Arabia because of the stationing of American troops there since 1991. In addition, Islamist extremists talk of the victimization of the Muslim world, citing attacks on civilians and states from Algeria to Chechnya, and from Kosovo to Indonesia.[6] These fears and anxieties are not confined to terrorist groups. State governments respond to perceived threats and this has the effect of escalating conflicts, turning small border incidents in, say, Kashmir or the Rann of Kutch into major operations.

There are significant patterns in India–Pakistan relations, and in the conduct of their counter-insurgency operations.[7] Although minimum force has often been the initial guiding principle, insurgencies have encouraged them to form and deploy large numbers of paramilitary organizations. These have the advantage of being cheaper, easily enlisted and more heavily armed than the civil police, but there has been a risk that their tactics generate yet more resistance. Often less accountable than either the regular forces or the police forces, paramilitaries are nevertheless a significant element in the security of the two states. On the other side, many Asian insurgent movements have suffered from particular problems, ranging from a lack of finance to difficulties in mobilizing popular support. Kashmiri separatists have spent years trying to dislodge the Indian Army, but their campaign to erode confidence in the Indian political process seems to have failed. Even the Mukti Bahini, a guerrilla force backed by the overwhelming majority of the Bengali population in 1971, could not defeat the Pakistan Army. It is, in fact, often the presence of rival nation states that assists guerrillas to overthrow their enemies. It was India's support to the Mukti Bahini that was crucial in bringing the war of 1971 to a conclusion. Similarly it is Pakistan that has prevented the effective suppression of guerrilla forces in Kashmir. By contrast, the United States and its coalition allies were able to defeat the Taliban roundly in 2001, having ensured the cooperation of all of Afghanistan's neighbours, including the Taliban's former backer – Pakistan. This pattern has been repeated time and again in recent South Asian military history.

The region's conflicts have other patterns and parallels. South Asia has struggled with the absence of any tradition of democracy, and, at local level corruption, poverty and a lack of education have taken their toll. There has been a long history of intolerance (political and religious), recurrent episodes of civil unrest and, with the exception of India, military intervention in government. South Asia is a region of great diversity, but division and conflict are common. In some quarters, one still hears reference to the colonial legacy for this pattern. However, the importance of military rule, the cycle of interventions by military authorities and the emphasis on hierarchy, whilst perhaps attributable to the Raj, cannot explain their recurrence at different points in South Asian political history, especially when India has not succumbed to this pattern. Robert Bradnock confidently asserted that India's colonial inheritance was 'a record of ninety years' systematic exploitation of the internal divisions of South Asia as a tool for sustaining imperial power'.[8] After 50 years of independence, the accusation that all of South Asia's divisions and conflicts are, in some degree, the fault of the British seems less and less convincing. Whilst there has been an attempt to shift the blame to nebulous concepts like globalization, Gandhi himself was probably more accurate when he remarked: 'The rot began with the alien government. We, the inheritors, have not taken the trouble to rectify the errors of the past.'[9]

South Asia is a region of immense diversity and great population density, which cause ethnic tensions. The close proximity of many peoples of different linguistic, cultural and ethnic backgrounds makes the success of Indian democracy remarkable, but there are significant problems. On the north-eastern frontier, for example, Mizo and Naga tribesmen resent the influx of 'foreigners' into border regions and especially their economic inferiority. Tribal lands are jealously guarded and, traditionally, trespassers were ambushed and decapitated: severed heads were posted up as a warning to others. In the south of India, many Tamils distrust the central authority of New Delhi, and particularly the chauvinist policies of the recent BJP government on the question of languages and education. In Pakistan, many provincial tribal groups resent or actively resist the Punjabi-dominated government. In the last decades there have been serious conflicts in Baluchistan, Waziri lands and, most famously, in the former East Bengal, now Bangladesh (1971).

Religion remains a potent source of conflict in South Asia, a fact often underestimated in the West. The destruction of a mosque at Ayodhya in 1992 by a group of 500 Vishwa Hindu Parishad (a wing of BJP) led to rioting in Bombay and other cities, thousands of dead and the defiant destruction of Hindu temples in Pakistan and Bangladesh. A group of Hindu extremists called Shiv Sena ('Shiva's Army') called for adoption of a policy of Hindutva ('Hindu-ness'). In Pakistan, Muslim fundamentalism has spawned a militant brand of Islam and provides thousands of recruits for movements like the Taliban and even al-Qaeda. Ramzi Yousef, for example, the bomber against the World Trade Center in 1993, was not an Iraqi as first believed, but a Pakistani (his real name was Abdul Karim Rind). The Markaz Dawa Al Irshad ('Centre of Preaching') of Pakistan (to which Osama Bin Laden contributed 10 million rupees) supports its own militant organization, Lashkar-e Toiba, which has carried out terrorist operations in Kashmir and in India itself (against perceived 'infidels' who 'oppress' Muslims). The Lashkar is now Pakistan's biggest Jihadi organization and has regular contact with a certain 'Abu Aziz', which is considered a 'Kuniat' or code name for Bin Laden.

National or sub-national identity is the key to many of the region's disputes. Since independence in 1947, both India and Pakistan have been eager to assert their sovereignty and people's will. Ironically, both are opposed to the idea of Kashmiri independence. Indeed, across the two countries there are minorities who favour either autonomy or independence, but so far only Bangladesh has achieved this (with India's assistance – hence Pakistan's fears). The Sikhs of the Punjab, for example, hankered after greater autonomy in the 1980s and some still want full independence, especially after Mrs Gandhi's crack-down in Operation Bluestar in Amritsar. In Pakistan, many Pushtuns of the North-West Frontier Province seek an independent Pushtunistan, an aspiration supported by the Afghan government of Najibullah (until he was overthrown by the Taliban). In Sri Lanka, the LTTE or 'Tamil Tigers' waged a bitter guerrilla and terrorist campaign to be free of the Sinhalese authorities, and in Burma, tribal guerrilla forces like the Mong and Karen continue to oppose the far left government in Rangoon.

The legacy of previous wars have been no less significant. The governments of India and Pakistan find it difficult to compromise over Kashmir because of the amount of blood that has been spilt. Pakistan, for example, has expended a great deal of effort (and money) in the support of insurgents and in campaigns in 1947–8, 1965, 1971 and 1999. So far it has not achieved a lasting strategic advantage. It sponsored the Taliban, only to see them ousted by a Western-backed coalition. It also armed the Militants in Kashmir, but it is no nearer seeing the creation of an 'Azad' (free) Kashmir beyond the Line of Control. These defeats, combined with a rise in militant Islam, may foster a feeling of bitterness and irredentism that makes conflict more likely in the future.

Many of the conflicts in South Asia are worthy of consideration on their own merit because they each have considerable long-term significance. The conflicts reveal, for example, interesting and important details about China's armed forces on the border of India and Tibet, and therefore the perpetuation of bad relations between India and Asia's only superpower. On the eve of India's nuclear tests in 1999, the otherwise moderate Defence Minister, George Fernandes, described China as 'India's Number One Problem'.[10] These powers are likely to remain economic rivals in the twenty-first century. The failure of the Soviet Union in Afghanistan had far-reaching effects beyond South Asia, whilst the long-term effects of guerrilla campaigns in Sri Lanka and the instability in Kashmir have yet to be fully realized.

Within the limits of the available space, this book attempts to analyse the foundations of modern strategic thinking in South Asia – including conventional, insurgency and counter-insurgency operations – in order to get a clearer picture of the capability and intentions of the protagonists. Many of the South Asian forces draw on their own military traditions, which have affected recruitment, training, a propensity to intervention in civilian government and attitudes towards casualties (both combatant and non-combatant). An outline examination of command and leadership, strategy, the quality of South Asian forces, some tactical issues, the military organization of the South Asian states, media and public opinion, and terrorism is set in the context of an assessment of operations in South Asia since 1947. There is an attempt to link these together in a comparative way, but also to make in-depth analyses of the most significant conflicts. The diplomatic aspects of the conflicts have been given a stronger emphasis than a purely military analysis in order to understand the causes of the conflicts and their resolution. The Cold War and the post-Cold War destabilization of the Middle East, which have had repercussions not just in the West, but also in South Asia, are given less coverage, since a detailed examination is beyond the scope of this study. However, these still merit further study in a South Asian context.

This book therefore tries to place the issues outlined above in a comparative and contextual analysis, without neglecting the importance of each conflict for its own significance. To do this, the book is divided into three sections. The first deals with three layers of South Asia's strategic situation: one, the military, political and economic context of the largest power, India; two, the regional setting of the conflicts though a brief overview of Pakistan, Sri Lanka, Nepal, Myanmar (Burma) and Bangladesh; three, the global dimension, examining the superpowers, the United Nations, globalization and, briefly, international terrorism. The second section of the book takes the most prominent conflicts in turn for a more in-depth examination, including Kashmir, the India-China Border War of 1962, the wars of 1965 and 1971 between India and Pakistan, which included the emergence of Bangladesh, and the wars in Afghanistan from 1979 to 2001. In the final section, there is a synoptic evaluation of the insurgencies of South Asia, with a further consideration of terrorism across the region and an assessment of the patterns of conflict in the region.

If one is to set aside issues of weapons and communications technology, which are developing rapidly at the beginning of the twenty-first century, the overall pattern of warfare in South Asia in the last 50 years gives a strong indication of the trajectory of future conflicts in the region at all levels. The global context of these conflicts has been important, and other powers outside the region have been instrumental in the process of peace-making. Above all, the globalization of terrorism is likely to have serious repercussions for South Asia and the wider world. It is surprising that there are so few studies that have attempted to draw together the conflicts of South Asia in the regional and global context. It is a situation that threatens to distort any perspective of the individual conflicts and could obscure a full appreciation of the interests of the Asian states: it is hoped that this work, in some small way, will redress that imbalance.

Chapter 2

Conflicts in India

'Long years ago we made a tryst with destiny and now the time comes when we shall redeem our pledge, not wholly or in full measure, but very substantially. At the stroke of the mid-night hour, while the world sleeps, India will awake to life and freedom.' The words of Jawaharlal Nehru, the leader of the Indian National Congress movement, and, from the 14 August 1947, the first premier of an independent India, seemed to encapsulate the excitement of a country on the verge of its independence from foreign colonial rule. It was, however, a celebration tinged with poignancy. Nehru later told his sister: 'I was hardly aware of what I was saying, the words came welling up, but my mind could only conceive the awful picture of Lahore in flames.' As the crowds of New Delhi stood in the torrential downpour waiting for the moment when 'India discovers herself again', all were aware that the transfer of power was marred by communal violence of unprecedented savagery in the Punjab. From July, thousands had been killed in Lahore: butchered in back streets, shot, beaten to death with *Lathi* sticks, burned alive; Muslim youths even laid wires across streets at night, pulling it to throat height to knock down Sikh cyclists. Arsonists turned areas of the old city into an inferno, the sparks silhouetting the gangs of knife-wielding rivals. The Muslims would advance chanting 'Allah Akbar!'; the Sikhs would counter-charge with 'Sat Sri Akal'; and both sides would beat drums to intimidate the other. Lieutenant-General Frank Messervy, the British Indian Army Commander-in-Chief of Northern Command, was struck by the endless rows of corpses he found in Sikh villages, 'laid out like pheasants after a shoot'.[1]

Within weeks India had been partitioned by its new rulers. It was a process accompanied by terrible atrocities. The South Asian states of India, West Pakistan and East Pakistan were spawned amidst conflict, and, despite the entreaties of Mohandas Gandhi for peace and tolerance, there was an undignified scramble by each side to assert its control of street, village, town and territory. Party militants in the Congress Party even called for a change to the party emblem that Gandhi had championed. They accepted the tricolour of saffron, white and green, but they rejected the spinning wheel – a 'woman's thing' – for the wheel that had adorned the shields of Asoka's warriors, the *dharma chakra*, symbol of strength and authority. The new wheel was to be flanked by lions representing force and courage. Gandhi's call for a rejection of industrialization, along with his appeal for a return to an archaic India, was treated with contempt. Perhaps it should be noted that Sikh symbolism was no less potent: amongst the five objects that each Sikh man had to wear was the *kirpan* (dagger).

Conflict in such a diverse society should not have been unexpected, and many British officials had long predicted catastrophe. The subcontinent was divided between 275 million Hindus (including 70 million low-caste 'Untouchables' ostracized by other Hindus), 35 million Muslims, 7 million Christians, 6 million Sikhs, 100,000 Parsees and 24,000 Jews. Yet within these groups there were other divisions: there were 15 official languages and 845 dialects. Even body language did not help: when a man of Madras nodded his head, he meant 'yes'; when a northerner did the same, he meant 'no'. Religious diversity was illustrated by the fact that 11 million claimed to be 'holy men'. The 20 million who could be classed as 'aborigines' included the tribesmen of Nagaland, who ambushed and decapitated unwelcome trespassers. Another 10 million South Asians were itinerants of various professions. Some religious groups exercised strict rules of peacefulness, others of violence and codes of honour that demanded revenge and perpetuated blood feuds for generations. Hindus, whilst recognizing several principal gods, actually worshipped three million deities, including their manifestation in trees, monkeys, cows and snakes. Symbols had long been important in South Asia. In Sind, in the subcontinent's oldest prehistoric village sites, representations of female goddesses, sacred bulls and the characteristic fig-leaf shape of the *Pipal* tree were found amongst the stone weapons. The symbolic use of the female goddess and the bull (later a representation of Shiva, the creator, for Hindus) can thus be traced back more than 4,000 years. In defence of these identities, war has been just as persistent. At Harappa, the oldest city-state of the region, the inhabitants were protected by walls 40 feet (*c.* 13 metres) thick and by the presence, it is thought, of a militant religious elite. In more modern times, the calls to defend religion or state identity have lost none of their potency.

In August 1947 ten-and-a-half-million people were uprooted by the partitions, four times the number forced to migrate after the Second World War in Europe and ten times the number made refugees by the creation of Israel. Many left voluntarily, others were thrown out. Muslim patients were sometimes ejected from hospitals, and 2,000 people at Kasauli hoping to get to Pakistan were rounded up, systematically robbed and told to walk to their new country. Buses, trucks and trains were commandeered. Amidst the human tide, gangs of killers were at work. Trains packed with refugees were set upon by mobs armed with guns, spears, axes and clubs. Thousands were hacked to death. A Kashmiri Hindu remembered his train being slowed just 14 miles from the Indian border. Sword-wielding Muslims cut indiscriminately about them, severing the head of a mother next to him. He recalled how her head, still connected by a few tendons, hung down towards the infant in her lap. The baby smiled at its mother's face, but before he could rescue the child, the Kashmiri was stabbed and fell to the floor of his compartment. As he passed out, he saw young women hurled from the windows of the train and their assailants leaping after them. As the trains of dead continued into India, Sikhs and Hindus reciprocated by slaughtering Muslims and sending a similar grisly cargo into Pakistan. One group of Sikhs at Amritsar, having killed the travellers on one train, posed as relief workers to root out the survivors, and then despatched them too.

The violence soon spread from the Punjab to the other main cities of India. On 31 August 1947 in Calcutta, two Muslim men were attacked by a mob of youths and had their heads split open by iron bars. Triumphant, the attackers exclaimed that the men had been killed to exalt the goddess Kali. It was the signal for the sacking of Muslim properties and brutal killings. Only by threatening to fast to death was Gandhi able to contain the worst excesses. But new disturbances flared up in New Delhi. Muslim railway porters were murdered, then an attack was made on Muslim traders in the heart of the commercial district. This was the prearranged moment for Hindu fanatics in white headdresses and Sikh Akalis in their bright blue turbans to launch an offensive across the city. Nehru himself was on the streets, cursing the rioters and ordering, often without success, the police to intervene. Hearing of the move, Sikhs captured a Muslim woman and doused her burqa in petrol and then set fire to her outside Nehru's residence in York Road. Bodies were strewn everywhere, from the Viceregal Lodge to the old city. On 4 September V. P. Menon, the Viceroy's assistant who had helped to draft the partition document, held a secret meeting with leading Indian civil servants and concluded that Delhi was ungovernable and that India as a whole was heading for collapse. They parted to the sound of machine-gun fire across the city.

For many Indians, robbed, beaten, their relatives butchered, Muslims were the enemy. In Pakistan, there was a widespread feeling that the holocaust being committed against their co-religionists elsewhere was part of a widespread attempt to destroy the new country at birth. The view was reinforced when the promised arms and equipment from the division of the old Indian Army failed to materialize (in fact, three trains did arrive containing obsolete rifles and useless stores) and the new government found itself running the country sitting outdoors on boxes with a handful of telephones and a radio set housed in a latrine.

The desire for revenge was common. Madanlal Pahwa, a Punjabi whose father had been severely wounded by a Muslim mob, was recruited by a Hindu fanatics' organization, the Rashtriya Svayamsevak Sangh. He joined in the murder of Muslims on trains, then organized his own gang in Bombay, which took to robbery, intimidation and murder. Embittered by Gandhi's message of reconciliation with Muslims in light of the Punjab massacres, it was one of Madanlal's trainees and followers, Nathuram Godse, who shot and killed Gandhi on 30 January 1948. The organization was temporarily dealt with by the police, and the assassin was executed, but the followers of the orange banner with its swastika motif pledged themselves to the destruction of Pakistan for decades after. Whilst Gandhi became an icon of peace and hope in a world threatened by conflict and even nuclear war, there are millions of Hindus who still put their faith in confronting Muslims and exacting revenge for the dead of 1947–8. Across the border, there are millions more in Pakistan who feel that their Islamic state is under threat, and, in self-defence, the *Jihad* is a justified response.

The immediate aftermath of Gandhi's death was marked by a sense of shock and a greater willingness to bring the communal violence to an end. Lord Louis Mountbatten, the outgoing Viceroy, when told of the assassination, had asked instantly 'who did it?', and cautioned that, had it been a Muslim assassin, the violence would have escalated beyond the control of any authority. As it turned out, Gandhi came closer to his objective of communal reconciliation in death than he had in his lifetime. His influence was also felt in other ways. Jawaharlal Nehru tried to embody some of the Gandhian principles in the new constitution and in his foreign policy.

Nehru's legacy was to blend the idealism of Gandhi with pragmatic leadership at home and abroad. His aims were essentially threefold. First, to create a nation state of integrated regions based on a democratic, secular political structure. In this task he was assisted by the legacy of the British administration and by the strong sense of unity generated by the movement for independence. Second, Nehru wanted to create the widest possible freedom of action in international and domestic affairs. He aimed to create an economy that was fully independent of all Western, or global influence, but he soon realized that this was not possible, particularly as the crushing poverty of India demanded rapid progress to avoid unrest. He therefore decided to retain as much freedom from foreign constraints as possible and, from an ideological perspective, he avoided any close association with either the Soviet bloc or the Western alliances of the Cold War era. Third,

Nehru aimed to defend India's territory and 'security interests' robustly by developing the armed forces and meeting any military threat.

In his first broadcast to Indians on 7 September 1947, Nehru proposed 'to keep away from the power politics of groups, aligned against one another, which have led in the past to world wars and which may again lead to disasters on an even vaster scale'.[2] He did not shun the outside world completely, though. He hoped to offer leadership to other nations that were in the process of freeing themselves from European colonial rule. India would provide the flagship of the 'non-aligned' nations and champion the cause of the oppressed. Yet despite the early hopes, India has failed to fulfil this idealistic element of its foreign policy and has been accused by its neighbours of pursing a line that is little more than national self-interest.

Nevertheless, despite the attention paid to the rhetoric of peaceful coexistence, Nehru adopted a pragmatic approach from the outset. He made no secret of the fact that India's interests would be protected by force if necessary.[3] Moreover, K. Subramanyam, a former foreign policy advisor, remarked that non-alignment was simply a 'moral stand'; it was itself a practical means to achieve independent action and therefore fulfil India's national interests.[4]

The attention paid to the apparent peaceful doctrine of India's foreign policy was partly the result of the *Zeitgeist* after the Second World War, for this was the period in which the United Nations was formed, charters on human rights were drawn up, and the two superpowers expressed a desire to see the end of European colonial rule. However, the emphasis was also due to Nehru himself. Acting as his own foreign minister, Nehru commanded a great deal of respect internationally. Geoffrey Moorhouse noted: 'Nehru gave India a place on the world stage through sheer force of personality'.[5] As the architect of the new India, Nehru's influence was clearly substantial, but his actual record in foreign affairs hardly amounted to a significant 'place on the world stage'. Stanley Wolpert pointed to another reason: 'He was India's royal figure and its matinee idol, that unique combination of brilliance, good looks and brooding isolation who endeared himself to admirers of both sexes and all ages throughout the land.'[6] He was, in other words, respected simply because he was independent India's first leader: 'the captain of its ship of state, as benevolent a despot as Ashoka or Akbar'. It meant that the more belligerent aspects of his foreign policy were, and often still are, overlooked.

When Nehru called the first Asian Relations Conference in the spring of 1947, it appeared that India was looking to provide leadership amongst 28 other African and Asian states. At a second conference in 1949, Nehru led the condemnation by fifteen Afro-Asian states of the Dutch 'police action' in Indonesia, but in the conference of 1955 at Bandung, he found that not all of the 29 nations represented were prepared to follow India: it was China that seemed to offer the chance of a powerful alternative to Western hegemony in Asia. Nehru's celebrated 'five principles', or Panchsheel, announced after the Sino-Indian trade deal over Tibet in April 1954, may, in fact, have been laid down by the Chinese and not Nehru at all, but Nehru got the credit.[7] The principles asserted: mutual respect for each other's territorial integrity and sovereignty; non-aggression; non-interference in each other's internal affairs; equality and mutual benefit; and peaceful coexistence. The deal was celebrated in the slogan 'Hindi Chini bhai bhai' ('Indians and Chinese are brothers'). In fact, it signalled a free hand for the Chinese in Tibet in return for the improved security of India's northern frontiers – or so they thought. In 1962 China overran India's borders completely and inflicted the greatest humiliation in the sub-continent's post-war history.

India's critics have also pointed to the 'hypocrisy' of the Panchsheel, citing interference in the affairs of its neighbours as evidence. As the largest state, India is intimidating. Moreover, much of the intervention has been military in nature and includes the incorporation of Hyderabad; operations in Nepal, 1950; Goa, 1961; East Pakistan, 1971; Sikkim, 1974; Sri Lanka, 1971 and 1987–9; Maldives, 1988; Nepal, 1988–9; and, the on-going dispute, Kashmir. India defends its record by claiming that in all cases intervention has been a request of the governments concerned and that, in the case of East Pakistan and Kashmir, its own territory was attacked. Nevertheless, all the incidents show that India is prepared to fight to defend what it regards as its national interests. What supports this view is the reactive nature of India's foreign policy. Despite the ambitious sentiments, many of the conflicts that India has become embroiled in have been forced upon it. There is little evidence of long-term planning. K. Subramanyam, in his capacity as the Director of the Institute of Defence Studies, noted that, during the crisis with China in 1962, 'what struck me was the absence of an integrated view of international developments at various levels of government in spite of Prime Minister Nehru's own uncluttered perception of them'.[8] R. Litwak pointed to the way that India tended to purchase arms only as a response to 'a major acquisition of weaponry by Pakistan'.[9] Such an approach to its foreign policy, particularly when influenced by the heady admixture of nationalistic public opinion, is a worrying one given the unresolved nature of the Sino-Indian border and the running conflict over Kashmir with Pakistan, especially when India, China and Pakistan are all nuclear powers.

THE INDIAN ECONOMY

The formulation of foreign policy is often subject to the pressures of domestic factors and the Indian armed forces have suffered as governments placed the emphasis on economic development. For India, the overriding consideration was the state of the economy and the enormous pressure put upon it by population growth – running at about 2 per cent, or five to six million per annum. As an intellectual socialist, Nehru championed the concept of centralized planning and nationalization. There were an estimated 360 million Indians in 1950, but the loss of the wheat basket of the Punjab and the arrival of thousands of temporarily unproductive refugees in the early years added to the burden on the available food supply. Many millions were undernourished, living on such a low calorific and protein level that diseases of malnutrition, such as tuberculosis, were common. Tuberculosis alone claimed about half a million lives per annum. The first Five Year Plan of 1951, modelled on Soviet central planning, was limited in its objectives, and any increase in agricultural production was absorbed by the population increase.[10] The target for industrial production was an increase of 11 per cent, or the equivalent in goods and services of $18–20 billion. India, however, was forced to import four million tons of wheat from the United States and remain a 'food deficit nation' for two decades, facing its biggest crisis in the famines of 1952 and 1953, and again in the late 1960s. Of the $3.7 billion dollars of government spending, $3 billion went on stimulating the consumer goods industries dislocated by wartime production. Repairs to communications also accounted for much of the costs, although infrastructure remained poor across the country. Just 7.6 per cent of the capital outlay went on mining and 11 per cent on energy generation. Agricultural reform, perhaps the most important of all the measures introduced by the government, foundered on mismanagement, rural conservatism and superstition.

The Second Five Year Plan (1956–61) spent three times the budget of the first and increased food yields to 80 million tons. Mining and power-generation got the largest slice of the capital too and enjoyed a corresponding success, but once again population growth offset the success of the plan. More radical politicians called for greater control of the richest in Indian society, but Nehru resisted their demands, counting on his own appeal and the laurels of Congress after independence to maintain direction. The Third Five Year Plan (1961–6) appeared to be a great success and was broadcast as such: giant leaps in mining, industrial production, electrical power, and 90 million tons of food. Yet without the additional $5 billion granted by a consortium of nations called the Aid to India Club (the United States, Great Britain, France, West Germany and Japan) and additional technical support from the Soviet Union, the plan would never have enjoyed the success it did. It seemed that non-alignment had enabled India to benefit from both sides of the bipolar world created by the Cold War, but there could be no disguising the massive increase in urban poverty caused by migration from the land, the continuing inequality of land distribution and the destitution of millions of rural Indians. India may have advanced in the league tables of industrialized nations, but that was hardly any comfort to the Indian peasant.

In an effort to alleviate its fundamental economic problems, successive Indian governments have been forced to abandon any initial hopes for autarky espoused by Nehru, and look for support through greater global integration. In agriculture Green Revolution changes required a greater volume of petrochemicals and fertilizers, much of which had to be imported, adding to pressure on the balance of payments and therefore on the search for new markets.

Development needs, however, have also brought India into direct confrontation with other countries. The greatest need has been for energy. Since agricultural development required more electric pumps for land irrigation, particularly after the endless expansion of cultivable area (which initially increased at a rate of 1.2 per cent per annum between 1951 and 1971, and then 0.09 per cent thereafter), power needs in this sector increased dramatically. Yet commercial demand was even greater. Between 1971 and 1988, electricity generation increased from 61 billion KWH to 217 billion KWH, but the overall deficit in 1987–8 was 10.9 per cent nationally with some regions short by 30 per cent. The reality of developing world cities is that power supplies are rationed, greatly limiting commercial activity. The effect of energy deficiency goes beyond the immediate commercial arena, though. The burning of cow dung, a substitute fuel for many poor families, is regarded as a waste of vital land fertilizer, whilst forest clearance for wood fuel has already had catastrophic effects in the lower river basins such as the Ganges delta, where flooding is now far more common, potentially bringing India into confrontation with Bangladesh.

Given the huge energy needs, the Soviet Union stepped in to offer assistance in the construction of hydroelectric schemes such as the 2,400 MW station at Tehri, as well as financial support for a nuclear power plant. Western countries also initially offered support in nuclear power, especially the United States, Canada and Great Britain, but there was a distinct cooling of enthusiasm when India detonated its first nuclear device in Rajasthan in 1974. Canada cut off assistance, and the United States, especially President Carter, tried unsuccessfully to get India to sign the nuclear Non-Proliferation Treaty. Despite the international pressure, India continued with its nuclear programme, constructing its own plant at Kalpakkam, near Madras, in 1983. There were, however, significant operating problems that stemmed from the use of its own indigenous technology.[11]

Investment and aid have also had important implications for foreign relations. Central planning involved the strict regulation of foreign investment, and despite some optimism that the Janata government of 1977–9 would embrace a free market, George Fernandes, the Minister for Industry, tightened controls on investment, even banning Coca-Cola. Indira Gandhi, however, recognized the need to liberalize the economy in order to attract the volumes of investment needed for future and sustained development. There was a further streamlining of licensing requirements in Indian industry under Rajiv Gandhi from 1984–5. But it was not only private companies that benefited; the government encouraged joint ventures from overseas too. It should be noted, however, that many in India still aimed to avoid the sort of foreign dependence they perceived existing in many African states, and, according to many European and American businesses, India remains a difficult country to work with because of its burdensome red tape. Having said that, few of the richest nations could avoid the rate of growth of GNP in South Asia, some 4 per cent in India between 1976 and 1990.[12] Japan has assisted in car manufacturing and electronics, and the United States has also led on 'high tech' investment, mainly through the close links maintained by the 600,000 highly qualified Indians resident in America. In fact, the United States government has shown a lot less interest in South Asia than the high technology industries might suggest. In 1985 American investment in India was just $500,000, whereas Hong Kong attracted $2 billion and the Philippines $1.24 billion.[13] Nevertheless, there has been, since the greater liberalization of the Indian economy under Rajiv Gandhi, a significant improvement in this position, and since the late 1980s the United States has become the largest single investor country in India. However, controls and restrictions remain. In 1988 V. P. Singh laid down that foreigners should not own more than 40 per cent of any Indian company.[14] The effect has simply been to deter the kind of investment that is enjoyed by the free markets of countries like Taiwan (which attracts ten times the amount of capital that India does).

It was recognized from the outset that India faced a dilemma in trying to attract foreign investment without compromising its faith in centralized planning and independence in economic policies. Despite the adoption of socialist doctrine in planning, the Second Five Year Plan recognized that whilst certain crucial industries (such as capital goods) would remain directly under government direction, other private enterprises should be permitted. Whilst strict limits were placed on the degree of foreign influence over these private concerns, however, it was still hoped that foreign aid packages would be forthcoming. Indeed, by the time of the Second Five Year Plan, foreign aid was seen as essential. This offered other countries a degree of leverage over India that had strategic implications. Whilst the Organisation for Economic Co-operation and Development (OECD) countries of the West contributed 50 per cent of foreign aid and the Soviet Union only 5 per cent, the Soviets claimed that their funding was responsible for one third of India's steel and aluminium production, half of its power generation and mining plant, and 80 per cent of its metallurgical equipment.[15] Some of this investment was repaid in the form of barter agreements with the Soviets after an agreement in 1958, so it could be classed as trade rather than aid, whereas the United States PL480 programme offered capital and foreign exchange for urgent food needs or for consumption goods. Many Indian commentators with a distaste for American hegemony have tended to play down the benefits of US investment and aid whilst praising the Soviet Union's projects (which, in fact, had a heavy industry bias and were more recognizable as giving India 'progress' than the 'hidden' development of American capital).[16]

Since a peak in the Third Five Year Plan, aid has played a less important part in investment in India, reflecting the determination by Indian governments to break free of any foreign constraints. Indira Gandhi argued: 'No country should even think of using aid to make India change its fundamental policies. If any country has such ideas, it is nurturing wrong notions.'[17] Yet, despite the nationalistic rhetoric, India was completely unable to separate aid from constraints imposed by the International Monetary Fund (IMF), the World Bank and even individual countries: Britain's Westland helicopter deal, for example, was perceived in India as an aid package with 'strings attached'.[18] In an attempt to diversify the source of aid, India took an increasing share from the International Development Agency, and looked to countries like Japan and organizations like the European Economic Community. Nevertheless, the Soviet Union contributed the largest amount of all its aid packages to the developing world to India, even before it began to invest in India's energy programmes from 1986, although it should be noted that interest repayments (caused by imports, including arms) had hitherto exceeded the volume of aid.

The association with the Soviet Union failed to produce the lasting benefit the Indian planners had hoped for, and probably went a long way to deterring greater support from the United States. Western and international interests have been more concerned, however, with India's rate of development and the stability of their investments. In 1986 the IMF and the United States insisted on the devaluation of the rupee by 36 per cent. For those, like Mrs Gandhi, who had hoped to be free of foreign intervention, it must have been a stern 'reality check'.

The attempts to achieve greater diversity in investment were mirrored by a similar desire for Indian trade, again in order to reduce dependence. There was a rapid decline in Britain's share of trade with India after 1947, although there was some levelling out by 1960. In that year, of the 19 per cent of imports from the European Community, 16 per cent was from the United Kingdom alone. Nevertheless, the share of other countries was far greater, and the United States was the source of 30 per cent of India's imports. Ten years later the relative position was magnified still further: the United Kingdom's share had fallen to 8 per cent with the United States steady at 28 per cent. In the 1980s the British share had fallen still further to 5 per cent and the United States to 10 per cent, whilst the European Community had risen to 33 per cent. The Soviet Union, however, enjoyed the greatest portion of India's imports. In absolute terms, the volume rose sixteen times between 1970 and 1985, reflecting the closer diplomatic relationship.

In exports, India was only successful to a degree. Although the flow of engineering goods to the United States and the Middle East increased in the 1970s, the outbreak of the Iran–Iraq War in 1980 halted the export of goods to its chief importer, Iran. Yet conflict in the Gulf can only be partly to blame. Many countries complain that India's goods are uncompetitive compared with other Asian economies, and quality control is uneven by international standards. Gemstones and textiles, the latter always India's leading export commodity, are the mainstay of its export trade. India has tried to diversify its economy in recent years by the expansion of its service sector, but, once again, the quality of its services and quality control are inconsistent.

It is significant that India was not regarded as one of the 'Tiger' economies of the 1990s. Although GDP grew by 6 per cent annually over that decade, the average increase of income per person was less than 4 per cent because of the pressures of population growth. Within the states of India, fiscal deficits, a strong dependence on subsidies and the lack of progress on social reforms (such as education: literacy rates were between 68 and 74 per cent in 1998) hold back the whole country. Indeed, in some states, like Bihar, average incomes per person have actually fallen. Infrastructure development is at a standstill because of a lack of funds. Big firms have taken to building their own roads, power stations and ports. New Delhi has imposed tighter controls on state borrowing, but arrears to various domestic and foreign suppliers have permitted some states to bypass the discipline of central government.[19]

Despite the weaknesses of the Indian economy, the striking aspect of South Asia's situation is the relatively insignificant volume of regional trade – a legacy of regional conflicts. Before 1947 South Asia was an integrated economy, a position fostered by the British, who saw India as a crucial component not only in the Indian Ocean region, but also in a worldwide imperial system of trade. The Punjab, for example, supplied food to northern and central India, whilst the ports of Bombay and Calcutta serviced both a vast hinterland and acted as entrepôts to the rest of the world. The insistence on partition cut across the existing infrastructure and ruined the Punjab. Nationalistic rivalry continues to deny the fulfilment of the region's full potential. Since 1949 trade between India and Pakistan has virtually ceased altogether. The total of Pakistan's imports from India was valued at 100,000 rupees out of a total of 66.7 million rupees. India's imports from Pakistan were a negligible 500,000 rupees.[20] The fear felt by India's neighbours at the economic giant on their doorstep is also manifest at grass roots level, further hindering development. In Bangladesh, soon after the declaration of independence that India had assisted, Indian traders were subject to intimidation because of fears that they would dominate the commercial activity of the new country. In Sri Lanka in 1990 there were threats against any trader selling Indian goods – a political as well as an economic protest about intervention and domination in the region.

The trade figures for India do not include the flow of arms from Eastern Europe and the Soviet Union in the same period and would, if included, inflate the degree of orientation of India towards the Eastern Bloc until its demise in 1990. Easy terms and cheap credit made arms deals attractive to India, just as they were to many developing world countries during the Cold War.[21] Although India detonated its own nuclear device in 1974 and test fired its own Agni intermediate-range missile, it has long been dependent on foreign arms. The British sold India two aircraft carriers, *Vikrant* and *Viraat*, as well as Jaguars and Sea Harriers. The Soviet Union, though, was still the greatest source of weaponry, supplying about 65 per cent of its total. Some of the arms included the Soviet Union's most advanced Mig29 and Mig31 aircraft. Such weapon systems, even at discounts of 50 per cent, according to the CIA, still totalled $4,200 million, although much of that was paid for in goods rather than in cash. Nevertheless, one has to question the wisdom, given India's dire economic and fiscal difficulties, of such a large arms purchase programme. Furthermore, the reliance on Soviet weapons created an even stronger link with the Eastern Bloc and called into question the whole concept of non-alignment. Certainly this was the way the United States interpreted India's stance in the 1980s. Such a large proportion of the Indian Army dependent on the supply of Soviet weapons implied a strategic dependence too, but the demand for weapons from the cheapest source makes more sense against the background of India's fundamental economic problems outlined above.

India plays a small part in international economic forums, such as GATT and UNCTAD, but it is hardly influential in global terms. From a regional perspective, India is the strongest power economically, but this only creates further tension with its smaller neighbours, and, given its record of military intervention, there is a distinct unwillingness to cooperate. There can therefore be little doubt that conflict in South Asia is a major obstacle to India's future economic development. Equally, in the past the absence of a robust Military Industrial Complex led to the neglect of the armed forces and consequently impaired performance. Clearly military power and economic strength are inextricably linked. What is interesting for India is that its economy has grown faster in the last five years than in the previous forty. In 2003-4 India's growth rate was 7 per cent per annum. Following exchange deals with the United States over nuclear and space technology, India clearly has the potential to develop economically and militarily faster than its South Asian neighbours.

INDIA: REGIONALISM AND DIVISION

Partition and secession are something of an obsession for the governments of South Asia, with new threats of sub-division appearing every decade after 1947. In a region of such diversity strong centrifugal forces are understandable, and, as economic problems or central government direction become unbearable, there are calls for separate states to be created. The legacy of partition, ethnic divisions, fears for the survival of a particular identity and threats to the homogeneity of the nation state have generated conflict in pockets across the region. From the beginning, however, India has used military force to neutralize these demands. In the weeks before independence, the Princely States, which had never been incorporated directly under British rule (but which had recognized Britain as the 'paramount power' over their affairs), were informed that they must join either the new India or Pakistan. Junagadh, a small state in the Saurasthra peninsula of Gujarat, hesitated in its decision, but the Muslim ruler was bundled into an aircraft and sent to Pakistan after an economic blockade and a takeover by an 'army of liberation' of Hindu émigrés who had been armed by India. Pakistan protested and refused to recognize the Indian action as legal, but it was unwilling to take the matter further.

Nevertheless, the far larger state of Hyderabad was a more serious issue. The Nizam and his court were Muslim, but the state population was overwhelmingly Hindu, and, given its geographical position in the heart of the subcontinent, there was every expectation that Hyderabad would join India. Nevertheless, the Nizam's advisors hoped that independence might be an option, a not unreasonable notion given the long history of the state. Nehru and Vallabhai Patel, the chief negotiator for Congress, decided to give Hyderabad a year's grace to decide, but it is clear they expected only one outcome. In September 1948 Indian troops crossed the border in a 'police action'. Unlike the situation in Kashmir, where separatist forces had taken the Indian Army by surprise and seized part of the state, the Indian forces had had time to build up an intelligence picture of Hyderabad and its strength, assisted by the Hindu population, who were eager to join India formally. The aim was to execute a rapid operation to avoid interference from outside (such as gunrunning) and to minimize the loss of life. In just four days, two Indian divisions crushed all resistance in Operation Polo, and the Nizam capitulated.

Once again Pakistan complained, but it was really still preoccupied by the fighting on its immediate border over Kashmir. With three-quarters of the population Muslim, Pakistan felt that India must recognize that the state belonged to them. Yet India, which had condemned the Nizam of Hyderabad's quest for independence as the 'whim of an autocrat', was prepared to accept the decision of the Maharajah of Kashmir to join India. Indian troops were airlifted to resist the Muslim irregulars that had tried to seize control, leading to the first war on the borders of India and Pakistan. The state has been mired in an Indo-Pakistani confrontation ever since, with three major outbreaks of fighting since 1947.

The communal violence and the disputes over Junagadh, Hyderabad and Kashmir in 1947–8 highlight the divided nature of the subcontinent. Indian governments have tried hard to build a sense of national identity over strong regional and religious loyalties. Religious loyalties have proved one of the most poignant for India since Pakistan was built on a shared Muslim faith. In 1947, 40 million Muslims remained in India, and today the figure is well over 100 million, so it was clear to Nehru and to subsequent leaders that India had to be a secular state with a foundation of religious toleration. Such a sentiment is enshrined in the Indian constitution, but that did not stop the Bharatiya Janata Party (BJP) from advocating the creation of a Hindu state, and from trying to 'reclaim' Hindu temple sites where Muslim mosques now stand. In Ayodhya, there was a call for the mosque of Babri Masjid to be razed so that a temple to Rama could be reconstructed. Mob attacks on the mosque in 1992 left more than 1,000 dead across the country. In education, too, the BJP has tried to push a stronger Hindu line. At times this has taken on racial overtones. BJP-approved textbooks advocate a history where superior 'Aryan' northerners overthrew the civilization of 'Tamil' southerners. Romila Thapar has pointed out that archaeological evidence does not support racial divisions along these lines or such a simplistic chronology.[22] Today, Hindu nationalists argue that there was no invasion, but that Aryan civilization was indigenous – the so-called Hindutva ideology. As Thapar notes: 'the amended theory [is] axiomatic to their belief that those for whom the subcontinent was not the land of their ancestors, or the land where their religion originated, were aliens'. Similar caricatures are applied to epochs of invasion, thus the Hindu period is a 'golden age', the Muslim Mughal period is a 'dark age', and the British Raj 'alien and oppressive'. Such views make the definition of alien, and therefore 'enemy', far easier, especially amongst illiterate or less well-educated people.

It is not just Hindu chauvinists who cause neighbouring states concern, for India has a record of military intervention even when Indian leaders profess to be pursuing a peaceful ethic in foreign policy. Nehru exercised just such a policy in 1961, sending troops to take over the Portuguese colony of Goa in a 'police action'. It says much for Nehru's international standing, and antipathy towards colonial rule, that protests were muted. There were quite different responses to Indonesia's 'police action' against East Timor and Saddam Hussein's operations against his neighbours in the last decade of the twentieth century. In 1962, however, clumsy diplomacy rather than aggression led India into a border war with China that ended in a rout of Indian forces. The Chinese withdrew, but relations were permanently damaged and the whole question of India's security, particularly after the outbreak of another war with Pakistan in 1965, returned to the top of the government's agenda.

When Mrs Gandhi came to power in January 1966 she did so initially in the hope that peace would be the hallmark of her administration at home and abroad. In fact, within weeks, Mizo tribesmen in the north-east of India had exchanged gunfire with the Indian Army in possibly the worst uprising of the country's history. The situation in central India was no less acute, with millions threatened with starvation following the failure of the monsoon in 1965. Despite the arrival of American aid and grain supplies, the devaluation of the rupee damaged the government's popularity: strikes and riots became commonplace. In the Punjab, militant Sikhs called for their own *suba* (state) within India, but the campaign was only partially successful before it was called off as another war with Pakistan broke out. Criticisms of the Congress Party escalated, and for the first time it lost its hold on several crucial states. To recapture lost voters, Indira Gandhi appeared to endorse a more socialist programme, abandoned any semblance of 'appeasement' to Pakistan and argued for an independent nuclear capability. She stated: 'We must be satisfied that we have what I might call a credible guarantee for our security.'[23]

In 1969 the Congress Party split on the policy line that Mrs Gandhi was pursuing, but it seemed only to strengthen her position. She ordered the army to support East Pakistan's bid for independence, and on 9 August 1971 she signed a Treaty of Peace, Friendship and Cooperation with the Soviet Union, which many believed had brought non-alignment, the bedrock of Nehru's foreign policy, to an end. Launching the Fifth Five Year Plan, Gandhi placed the emphasis on alleviating poverty in light of further famines, but it was the test firing of a nuclear weapon that caught the headlines. Gandhi herself tried to argue that India was interested in atomic power only to solve its energy needs – but it was an unconvincing argument.

Against accusations of corruption in the elections, and outbreaks of communal violence, Gandhi ordered the arrest of hundreds of political opponents, culminating on 26 June 1975 with the declaration of a 'state of emergency'. Immediately suspending civil liberties, opposition parties were banned; new radical programmes were announced; and there were great propaganda efforts to broadcast Indira's principal messages. Yet, despite some tangible economic progress, Gandhi was ousted by the Janata Party after new elections in 1977 and the state of emergency was ended. Nevertheless, at 62, Indira campaigned afresh and won back power in 1980, proving how potent her appeal had been.

The Emergency Rule had created a greater determination amongst Sikhs for their own state, and a new militancy characterized the pressure for change. In May 1984, led by Jarnail Singh Bhindranwale, a group of Sikhs took control of the Golden Temple in Amritsar, the holiest location for Sikhs, initiating months of violence across the Punjab. Stung by criticisms that she was unwilling to act decisively, Mrs Gandhi swung to the extreme of launching a military operation, codenamed Bluestar, to destroy the separatists' stronghold. In two days and nights of fighting, more than 100 soldiers and an unknown number of Sikhs were killed. The priceless library of Sikh culture was incinerated, and it incensed the population of the Punjab. Twelve months later, Indira Gandhi was assassinated by two Sikh bodyguards. Why had she ordered such a drastic operation? Colleagues felt that she had become fatalistic about opposition to her rule, and spoke of 'enemies lurking everywhere'. It has also been suggested that she used divisions for her own ends, giving notice to all potential separatists by her actions and splitting Sikhs into those clearly for or against the Congress Party.[24] The decision certainly split the nation and communal violence worsened after her murder: Delhi was the scene of three days and nights of rioting and terrible atrocities against Sikhs. The official death toll was 1,000, but several witnesses believe that the figure was much higher.

Rajiv Gandhi's new administration was initially greeted with a great deal of hope. He liberalized the economy, ending many of the old trading restrictions of his predecessors and looking towards world trade as a solution to India's economic backwardness. However, accusations of corruption continued to dog the 'first family'. In the Bofors Scandal, many leading members of Congress were thought to have accepted bribes as the Indian Army sought to acquire a new type of Swedish heavy artillery. Nevertheless, it was the lack of progress in resolving the Kashmir dispute, or unrest in Punjab, that tarnished Rajiv Gandhi's reputation. Sikh separatists threatened to shoot those that attended national elections, rendering a much publicized accord worthless. In the north-east, too, hopes of a settlement to the communal violence between tribesmen and 'foreign' immigrants (Hindus, Muslims and Christians from further west) soon faded, and by 1990 the Indian Army was forced to deploy to the area.

The most dramatic military intervention of the period, though, was in Sri Lanka. Ethnic antagonism, stemming from the determination of the Sinhalese to suppress the Tamils, escalated into a 'civil war'. With thousands of Tamils in southern India secretly supplying or at least sympathizing with the 'boys' across the water, there was a distinct threat that the unrest would generate 'nationalistic' sentiments in southern India. In 1986, therefore, Rajiv Gandhi tried to bring both sides to the negotiating table. Having received an invitation from the Sinhalese government to despatch a peace-keeping force, the Indian Army had the thankless task of trying to disarm the Tamil fighters. Eventually, some 45,000 troops had been deployed, but the Tamil Tigers, the most militant of all the guerrilla groups, waged a terror war against all their opponents – Sinhalese and Indian. In 1991 Rajiv Gandhi himself was the victim of a Tigers bomb. A massive police crackdown then followed across southern India.

Since 1991 the conflicts in Kashmir, Punjab, Assam and Nagaland have continued. New separatist movements have also sprung up in Bihar and West Bengal, although to some extent these movements represent political expediency by regional leaders rather than genuine attempts to break away from India. Since the governments had to face the fact that the Soviet Union had passed into history and had to come to terms with the West, the currency exchange was adjusted to a more realistic level; some subsidies were abandoned in unprofitable industries (such as the railways); and more government restrictions on international trade were abolished. Regional trade is still small, however, and India's neighbours are wary of the South Asian giant. With no resolution to the disputes in Kashmir, the Punjab and the north-east, and no improvement in relations with Pakistan and China, India seemed destined to be hamstrung by these regional problems, which are detrimental to India's, indeed, South Asia's economic development. What is particularly worrying is the BJP's chauvinism in domestic affairs and India's failure to resolve its long-term economic problems. The rise of the BJP, supported by its paramilitary wing, the RSS, suggests that a spirit of nationalism is still developing in India. There is a significant risk, given the continued poignancy of the struggles with Pakistan or with separatists, that a militant nationalism will triumph. One can only hope that, amidst the passions of communal pride, more Gandhian counsels will prevail.

A superficial survey of the domestic conflicts in India and its foreign policy cannot do justice to the complexity of the problems governments face or the solutions they have attempted, but an overview offers the chance to read the broad economic and political contours of the region. It is evident that conflict is inherent within South Asia. This is partly historic, but there are acute problems that have exacerbated older rivalries in more recent times. There is also a great capacity for extremism and high passion in these disputes. Nationalism and strong religious loyalties have created a dangerous cocktail. The memory of past atrocities, humiliations and confrontations heightens the feelings of each side. When India test fired three nuclear weapons in the Rajasthan desert in May 1998 (in a move directed more at China than Pakistan), the Prime Minister Vajpayee boasted: 'Let the world know we have a very big bomb.' Pakistan, however, responded with the test firing of five of its first bombs, and Prime Minister Sharif remarked coldly: 'today we have paid them back – We would rather be beheaded than tolerate this insult.'[25]

At a lower level, the advent of militant Islam with its preference for suicide bombing and terror attacks against civilians creates the danger that conflicts of the future will be wars between peoples that statesmen will find increasingly difficult to control. The attack on the Indian parliament in December 2001 had the potential to precipitate a dangerous crisis with Pakistan. Mass movements mobilized by pandemics, by Islamic extremism, by separatism, or by economic catastrophe (India is rated 139th out of 172 nations in terms of quality of life, income, life expectancy and education: Pakistan was 138th) may cause significant conflicts in the future. Yet, there is also hope. If a civilization can produce the idealism of Gandhi, where peace is obtainable through reconciliation despite the wrongs inflicted by another, then politicians could obtain much mileage by invoking his memory. The only problem is that Gandhi, like history, is so often used in a partisan fashion to reinforce and justify a line of policy, and we should not forget that Gandhi was assassinated by one of his own countrymen, convinced that India, as a nation, was being betrayed.

Chapter 3

Conflicts in Pakistan, Bangladesh, Sri Lanka, Nepal and Myanmar

Pakistan hardly had a promising future in 1947. It had few natural resources, little in the way of manufacturing capability and it was a nation divided by 1,600 kilometres of Indian territory. East Pakistan, on which the country depended for its chief exports of tea and jute, in fact had little in common with West Pakistan, except religion. Following the communal violence of partition, six million *Mohajirs* (refugees) had arrived to burden the new state, and there were still 10 million Hindus resident in East Pakistan who represented a potential 'fifth column'. Few could forget that India, a giant rival power, was its neighbour. But there were significant tensions in the concept of Pakistan as a state that had nothing to do with external enemies. Bengalis, who made up half of the population, objected to the imposition of Urdu as the official language, as did the speakers of the other four main languages in West Pakistan: Pashto, Sindhi, Moharjir and Baluchi, not including all the other dialects of tribal areas. If Pakistan was difficult to define linguistically, ethnically it was just as diverse. In West Pakistan, the Punjabis are still the majority, with Pushtuns from the North-West Frontier Province the second most numerous. There are quite distinct differences between these groups and the Baluchis, Sindhis, the Barhuis of Baluchistan, and the range of Tibetan-Mongol descendants in Baltistan. The Chitralis, Gilgitis and Hunza tribesmen and Kashmiris too are distinct from their northern and western neighbours. Significantly, the army is almost exclusively Punjabi, and many believe that it has been the instrument for projecting Punjabi-oriented policies on the rest of the country[1]

Before partition, Kashmir had been an independent state under a Maharajah that recognized British suzerainty, whilst the Punjab had been ruled by the British directly. By contrast, Sind, Baluchistan, Chitral and the North-West Frontier were controlled by temporary military occupation, punitive military expeditions and monitored by British political officers. As a result the tribesmen had a long tradition of military resistance to the authorities of the plains and regarded themselves as independent.

Even in religious terms, Pakistan is diverse, and sadly violence is all too frequent. Although 97 per cent are Sunni Muslims, there are Shias in the northern provinces, and Christians and Parsees in the big urban centres like Karachi and Hyderabad. Sectarian rivalry between Shias and Sunnis erupted into gun battles in Gilgit in 1988 and 100 people died: a problem that resurfaced in 1989 and 1991. Shias there believe that Islamists from outside the area have orchestrated a deliberate campaign. In recent years, competition for jobs has fuelled violence between Sindhis and Mohajirs, but it is the growth of militant Islam that has attracted international attention. Grenade attacks on Christian worshippers, car bombings and street violence are not tolerated by the military government, but there is a worrying trend of increasing terrorism in the country.

Officially, Pakistan is a secular state in accordance with the wishes of its founder, Mohammed Ali Jinnah. Jinnah died of tuberculosis in September 1948 so it fell to his successor, Liaquat Ali, to endorse the secular position. The decision angered religious leaders, the influential mullahs, and Liaquat was assassinated in Rawalpindi in 1951. Without firm leadership, there were years of argument about the direction the country should take. There was no constitution until March 1956, and two years after the decision to adopt a parliamentary democracy, the President, retired Major-General Iskander Mirza, imposed martial law and abolished political parties. Some believe that this was a pre-emptive strike against those, especially Bengalis, who criticized

Pakistan's alignment with the West. The army leaders maintained their action was to safeguard the territorial integrity of Pakistan (which was threatened by parochialism) and to protect the country from self-serving politicians. Mirza's rule did not last, because his Prime Minister, General Muhammed Ayub Khan, replaced him in a *coup d'état*. A new constitution, favouring strong leadership, was announced in 1962, but stability seemed to be more attractive than political rights to many voters and there was not widespread opposition. At home, Ayub favoured modernization and economic development. In foreign policy, in return for a water rights settlement with India, Ayub secured huge funds from the World Bank. The money supported the construction of two dams, the Mangla and the Tarbela, on the Jhelum and the Indus. The United States offered military support in the form of weaponry and generous financial aid. Furthermore, when India and China clashed in 1962, Ayub moved quickly to ally Pakistan with Beijing. The Chinese occupation of northern provinces (dating from the Chinese takeover of Tibet in the years 1950–55) was settled and a strategic road, the Karakoram Highway, was constructed to link Chinese and Pakistani territory. Emboldened by these successes and thinking it had American and Chinese support, Pakistan launched a disastrous war against India in 1965. It achieved nothing.

Pakistan was so internally divided that a further partition was perhaps inevitable. Following an attempt on his life, Ayub stepped aside in March 1969 in favour of General Agha Mohammed Yahya Khan, the army commander-in-chief. Yahya immediately reimposed martial law and ended the autonomy of the hill states in the north, sending a strong signal that he intended to centralize the state. Nevertheless, in an attempt to widen the base of support, limited political activity, the so-called Basic Democracy, was permitted again in 1970 and elections were held. After years of being denied real political power, and faced by economic hardship, the Bengalis were angry with West Pakistan. In light of a terrible cyclone in East Pakistan, which caused thousands of deaths and made millions homeless, Sheikh Mujib, the leader of the Awami League, won an overwhelming victory. In West Pakistan Zulfikar Ali Bhutto, head of the Pakistan People's Party, was simply unwilling to permit constitutional change. The division of the country was now clear. Fearing yet more political bickering and the secession of East Pakistan, Yahya suspended the assembly. This only provoked a general strike in East Pakistan. When the army went in, it initially crushed the unarmed opposition, but, as 10 million civilians fled the fighting into India, thousands of young Bengali men joined resistance groups. Soon the regular Pakistan Army found itself bogged down in a bloody guerrilla war. India intervened, and a general war broke out along the borders of both East and West Pakistan. Unable to defeat its giant neighbour, Islamabad sued for peace in a matter of weeks. Bangladesh was thus independent, and Bhutto replaced the humiliated Yahya in Pakistan.

Despite the promise of reform, Bhutto's decision to sack the regional government of Baluchistan in February 1973 merely provoked another uprising. It is estimated that as many as 10,000 died in the fighting, but Bhutto was determined that this was not to be a repeat of the East Pakistan fiasco. Air strikes were used to quell the tribesmen and new security measures were imposed in the capital. Nevertheless, rioting broke out in Lahore, Karachi and Hyderabad as accusations of corruption flourished. Martial law was reimposed once again. The only real achievement seemed to be talks with India over Kashmir where both sides had agreed to respect the 'Line of Control', a cease-fire line following the fighting of 1965 and 1971. But this was the final straw for the Pakistan Army: the 'appeasement' of India illustrated the weakness of the Bhutto government abroad, and the civil unrest at home suggested that the army needed to restore order and stability.

As a result, General Zia ul-Haq staged a bloodless coup on 5 July 1977 and ruled for just over seven years as dictator. Bhutto was tried and hanged on the ambiguous charge of murder. Political parties were banned, but Zia courted popularity by introducing aspects of Shariah law into the judicial system. He argued that he favoured a more radical Islamic state with personal piety and scriptualism above social liberalism, although there is every indication that this was political expediency to legitimize his administration by pleasing the clerics. Indeed, Zia used his faith to define his nationalism. He told an International Islamic Conference: 'I will tell you what Islam and Pakistan means to me. It is a vision of my mother struggling on, tired, with all her worldly possessions in her hands, when she crossed the border into Pakistan.'² He also stated: 'the preservation of that [nationalist] ideology and the Islamic character of the country was . . . as important as the security of the country's geographical boundaries'.³ Unrest in the 1980s between the Sufis of Sind, who followed a humanistic and spiritual branch of Islam, and the mainstream Sunni Muslims was typical of the heightened sectarian tensions caused by the religious emphasis of the military government. This generated unforeseen consequences. Many Sufis played a crucial role in demanding a restoration of democracy. As a result, Pakistan still threatened to tear itself apart on the issue of national and religious identity. The question was: was Pakistan to be a modernizing, secular state or the cradle for the rebirth of Islamic traditionalism?⁴ 'Islam in danger' is still the rallying cry of the Muslim League, and, after the setbacks of 1971, the traditionalists have continually advocated the supremacy of their atavistic programme over the modernists.

In December 1979 Pakistan was suddenly thrust into the frontline of the Cold War by the Soviet invasion of Afghanistan, and the United States began sending generous shipments of arms to bolster Pakistan, which in turn assisted the Mujahideen and helped pay for the four million refugees who flooded across the North-West Frontier. Nevertheless, Zia was still dependent on the bayonets of his army to rule. Bhutto's widow and Western-educated daughter, Benazir, led the outlawed PPP (Pakistan Peoples' Party) on a civil disobedience campaign in 1983 in the hope of restoring democracy. Zia responded with a military crackdown and thousands were killed, the heaviest toll being in Sind. Finally, under international pressure, Zia relented and permitted the restoration of political parties, under strict limits, in 1985. Benazir toured the country to rapturous acclaim, but she was imprisoned and the momentum for a full return to democracy was lost. Only the mysterious death of Zia and several other leaders in a mid-air explosion caused a change of direction.

At first there was optimism. Benazir won the resulting election. One prominent newspaper, *Dawn*, declared: 'The long night of authoritarianism is over and the warm sunshine of a new dawn of democratic renewal bathes the national horizon and lights the path ahead'.⁵

Benazir quickly made enemies of the drug traders, however, and local governments often scotched social and economic programmes at provincial level. More importantly, she exercised little authority over the army.

The army has remained independent and influential despite the advent of civil rule, but more importantly it has caused a degree of 'de-politicization' because martial law removes the experience of democracy.[6] The army has successfully protected its own financial interests against other legitimate demands on the country: some $8 per head was being spent on the armed forces in the 1970s. By recruiting on such a narrow basis from the Punjab and pushing such a strong 'nationalist' line, it has alienated many Pakistanis outside the Punjab from politics and actually weakened the process of integration. The accusation that the army manipulates the political system does not stop there. Many army personnel have, it is claimed, secured for themselves cheap land and the top jobs as captains of industry, although this may be an exaggeration. What is not in doubt is that the influence over the electoral process in the 1970s created a precedent for intervention, and the army decides to act in what it perceives as its own or the 'national' interest with impunity.

Pakistan military intelligence, the ISI (Inter Services Intelligence), aided its own favoured factions after the Soviet withdrawal from Afghanistan 1989, and there have been widespread accusations that the same organization fuelled guerrilla activity in Kashmir that provoked an Indian Army campaign of suppression later that year. The Pakistan Army remained critical of the Bhutto government, and it was joined by much of the press and rival political parties. Indeed, Ian Talbot suggests that the ISI created the Islami Jamhoori Ittehad alliance and plotted the downfall of the government.[7]

With little legislative progress and plagued by the legacy of Zia's divisive 'Islamization' policy, fighting broke out between Sindhis, Pashtuns and Moharjirs in Karachi and Hyderabad and hundreds died in political terrorism. Kidnapping was rife in Sind, and rural banditry suggested that Pakistan was slipping into anarchy. The army regarded limited operations in Sind as a waste of time and advocated a return to martial law. It has even been suggested that, having made deals with each party to leave the army sacrosanct from reform, the generals feared that the PPP could no longer guarantee the arrangement.[8] In August 1990, at the army's prompting, Benazir Bhutto's government was deposed by the President in favour of Zia's old colleague and Chief Minister of the Punjab, Nawaz Sharif.

Sharif's government was faced with an immediate crisis when the United States refused to continue its $564 million economic and military aid programme. The Americans were concerned that Pakistan was developing a nuclear weapons arsenal. With civil unrest worsening across the country, the survival of any civilian government looked unlikely. To make matters worse, torrential monsoon rains in 1992 led to massive flooding in all the major river valleys. Thousands were killed and more than a million were made homeless. Whole areas of agricultural land were ruined when river defences were breached to save dams on the lower Indus. Seventy per cent of Pakistan's exports are agricultural goods, especially rice and cotton, and they account for a quarter of the GDP. Farms are often small, however, and their yields are amongst the lowest in the world, a situation perpetuated by the stifling and conservative controls of wealthy *zemindars* (landowners). Even before the floods of 1992, irrigation schemes had reduced two-thirds of the arable land to saline sterility or left it permanently waterlogged. Much of Pakistan's industry is orientated towards agriculture, so the floods of 1992, in which as much as 50 per cent of the crops were destroyed, also affected this sector.

The energy sector was at risk too. With two-thirds of its oil coming from Kuwait, the Iraqi invasion of 1991 had already hit the country hard, and Pakistan still suffers the same energy shortages as India. In Chitral, the town is effectively divided in two. On alternate evenings, traders open up stalls in one half whilst the other remains in a lonely gloom. The invasion of Kuwait also hit the country's other great earner, namely the incomes sent back to Pakistan by migrant workers in that country. Pakistan was thus dependent on the $2 million it received from the World Bank, the IMF, the Asian Development Bank and individual donor states like Great Britain, but, with a quarter of all its export earnings being spent on servicing foreign debts, it was not enough.

Bhutto led further protests in light of the unfolding economic disaster, but Sharif, despite trying to revive the popularity of his government by playing the 'remember Kashmir' nationalist card, was removed by the army.[9] Whilst the United States had abandoned Pakistan once the Soviet Afghan threat had subsided, it saw new reasons to cultivate its old association after the terrorist attacks of 11 September 2001. Tracing the roots of al-Qaeda to Osama bin Laden, a guest of the ruling Taliban (which Pakistan regarded as a protégé), the United States offered to support General Musharaff's regime in return for cooperation against the Taliban. In fact, thousands of Pushtun fighters crossed the border of the North-West Frontier once they had tasted the effects of American bombers. Today, Jihadist organizations threatens more violence and further destabilization in Pakistan and Afghanistan, unless, perhaps, American dollars are able to restore long-term economic stability.

BORN OUT OF CONFLICT: BANGLADESH

The partition of India in 1947 was a disaster for Bengal. The British had established Calcutta (now Kolkata) as one of the most important centres for commerce, education and culture in the subcontinent. The city was the point from which Bengal's major cash crop, jute, which was produced in the hinterland to the east, was processed and exported. Calcutta was dominated by the Hindus and so on partition it was carved away into India, leaving the Muslim-dominated hinterland without a major commercial port. Many Bangladeshi historians blame the British for a legacy of dictatorial agricultural policies through their promotion of the semi-feudal *zemindar* system.[10] They argue that support for the landowners and the emphasis on cash crops drained the region of its wealth and distorted the social structure. Moreover, they believe that the British deliberately pursued a policy of divide and rule between Muslims and Hindus. In fact, religious rivalry ran far deeper than the era of the British Raj, and it has to be said that the British period merely emphasized old rivalries. The minority Hindus tended to collaborate with British rule, entering British educational institutions and studying the English language, although, ironically, they became the focus of resistance in the last two decades of the Raj. The Muslim peasants grew angry at the landowners system and incensed by Hindu moneylenders, and they rioted when crops failed. The association of inter-faith rivalry with their respective economic situations was the source of later antagonism.

In 1947 East Bengal effectively became the client state of West Pakistan. With all the crucial government and military posts in the hands of personnel from West Pakistan, and few other similarities except Islam, there was a growing sense of injustice. This, in turn, led to the growth of Bengali nationalism. When the West Pakistan government declared that Urdu would be the sole national language, the Bangla-speaking Bengalis felt an even stronger sense of separate identity. The drive to reinstate the Bangla language gradually metamorphosed into calls for self-government. Victory for the Awami League, the Bangla nationalist party, in the elections of 1970 seemed to stiffen the resolve the West Pakistan president, General Yahya. He postponed opening the National Assembly and plans were laid for the suppression of the Bengalis. Riots and strikes broke out and Sheikh Mujib declared that Bangladesh was on the road to independence. It was the signal for Yahya to crush the 'insurrection'.

The Bangladeshi War of Independence was one of the shortest and bloodiest in South Asian history. The Pakistan Army, in a lightning crack-down, occupied all the major towns and cities by May 1971, but it found controlling the countryside far harder. Full-scale offensives were launched forcing terrorized civilians to flee the country into India. Air strikes were made more effective by the use of napalm against villages, and there were widespread reports of slaughter and rape in rural areas. Bangladeshis still refer to Pakistan's tactics as 'genocide' or 'Holocaust'.[11] India, however, swamped by refugees, felt that it could not avoid inter-vention. Border skirmishes between Pakistani and Indian troops broke out, particularly when Indian-trained Bangladeshi guerrillas re-crossed the border. When the Pakistani air force made a pre-emptive attack on Indian forces over the frontier in the west on 3 December 1971, a general war broke out.

Strategically the situation was hopeless for Pakistan, which faced a war on two fronts with little prospect of being able to reinforce the garrison of East Pakistan. Indian troops attacked from all points of the compass, the guerrillas took possession of the north and east, whilst the civilian population exacted its revenge at every opportunity across the country. The fighting was over in just eleven days and thus Bangladeshi independence was assured with India's support. Sheikh Mujib became the new country's first Prime Minister in January 1972.

The devastation caused by the war led to famine in 1973-4 and in the unrest that followed martial law was imposed. Mujib was assassinated in 1975, illustrating the sort of political instability that has led to successive military coups and political murders since. In 1979, however, Bangladesh moved towards democracy under the leadership of the popular President Zia. Zia established good relations with the West and the oil-rich Islamic countries, raising hopes of a new prosperity for the country, but he was assassinated in 1981 and a military government was reinstated. Periodically for the next ten years there were vague announcements to the effect that elections would be held 'soon'. The Bangladeshi media were enthusiastic about each of these statements, but there was no progress before 1991. That year the military dictator General Ershad was forced to resign after civil disobedience by an unprecedented popular coalition movement led by the Bangladesh Nationalist Party and the Awami League. Democracy was thus re-established with Begum Khaleda Zia as the new Prime Minister.

Despite some initial successes in domestic and foreign policy, the democratic experience foundered again. The economy at first enjoyed a growth rate of 4.5 per cent. Links with the West were strengthened when the government sent troops to assist in the Gulf War, and deployed units as peacekeepers in the American invasion of Haiti and the war in Bosnia. In just three years, however, many at home had become disenchanted with the Begum Khaleda Zia government and the erosion of democratic freedoms. Despite election promises, the Special Powers Act of 1974, which enabled the government to imprison anyone without trial for 120 days, had never been repealed. The powers were soon being used again against political opposition, and the army and police were deployed against the rallies of rival groups. Furthermore, there were claims that the government had rigged by-elections. Opposition parties called for a general strike and the civil service refused to support the Begum Khaleda Zia administration. A general election was held in February 1996, but, fearing further corruption and intimidation, the opposition parties did not participate. Only 5 per cent of voters turned out in protest. Nevertheless, there were widespread claims of result rigging. Certainly heavy-handed tactics against anti-government protesters raised grave doubts about the legitimacy of Zia's leadership when re-elected.

Opposition parties campaigned against the election result, and, after much protest, Zia stood down on 30 March 1996 in favour of a caretaker government under Muhammad Habibur Rahman. Elections, which were generally free of voter intimidation, were held in June that year and a coalition government headed by Sheikh Hasina Wazed of the Awami League was formed. In October 2001 the Bangladesh Nationalist Party won the parliamentary elections, and, ironically, Zia was sworn in as Prime Minister.

Bangladesh, like Pakistan, regards India as a potential threat because of its geo-strategic location, but equally India is anxious that internal unrest in Bangladesh could affect the Muslim population of West Bengal, or threaten to destabilize the sensitive border region of Assam. Just as in other regions, Bangladesh is both subject to, and able to influence, its South Asian neighbours. Indian analysts fear that Bangladesh may be a sanctuary for Jihadist terrorists, where they can receive funding and training. Subhash Kapila fears that Bangladesh-based extremists have been responsible for the setting up of a 'host of Islamic Fundamentalist organizations in the Assam State of India's North East'.[12] He claims that al-Qaeda affiliated groups, such as al-Haramanian Islamic Foundation, regularly meet in Dacca and that Abu Nasir, a Bangladeshi who has links with al-Qaeda and – more surprisingly – with Pakistan's ISI, has established contacts with Jihadists in Thailand. These fears of widespread networks may be exaggerated, but the detonation of a bomb during the visit of the British High Commissioner to Hazrat Shah Jalal shrine on 21 May 2004 had all the hallmarks of al-Qaeda: Jack Straw, the British Foreign Secretary, certainly regarded it as such in his condemnation of the blast, which left two people dead and fifty more injured. Moderate groups in Bangladesh have spoken out against the extremists and have even established an alliance called

South Asia Peoples Union Against Fundamentalism and Communalism. In their inaugural meeting of 24 May 2004 they protested in the strongest terms against extremists' intimidation tactics in Rajshahi District and the execution of eighteen people in Islamist 'Extra Judicial Courts'. Such pressure is likely to prevent what India fears most – the 'Talibanization' of a neighbouring state.

FROM PEACE TO CIVIL WAR: SRI LANKA

The legacy of British colonial rule in Ceylon was certainly mixed. The former Crown Colony embraced parliamentary democracy and the transfer of power was a peaceful one; many believed it a model of decolonization. English was accepted as the *lingua franca* for the majority Sinhalese population and for the Tamil labourers from southern India whom the British had brought in to work the coffee, tea, cinnamon and coconut plantations, and who had subsequently settled in the country. Ceylon enjoyed good relations with Britain and it remained within the British Commonwealth after its independence in 1948 (becoming Sri Lanka in 1971). However, there was a definite change in direction in the post-colonial period. The new government adopted socialist social and economic policies, introducing welfare reforms whilst maintaining the strong export economy. More controversially, the Sinhalese-dominated government disenfranchised the 800,000 Tamil plantation workers.[13] Furthermore, the Sinhalese nationalist leader, Solomon Bandaranaike, who was elected in 1956, introduced legislation that made Sinhalese the national language. The intention had been to redress the imbalance of power between the Sinhalese majority and the Christian-educated, English-speaking, elite. Whilst it gave more Sinhalese access to power, however, it enraged the Tamil Hindu minority who began pressing for a federal system of government, with significant autonomy for the areas with a Tamil majority in the north and east.

Sri Lanka's fault lines, however, were not limited to Tamil-Sinhalese differences. In 1959 a Buddhist monk assassinated Bandaranaike when he attempted to reconcile the two rival communities. His widow, Sirimavo, was elected as Prime Minister, and, avoiding the Tamil-

Sinhalese issue, she continued her husband's socialist policies. Suffering the stagnation typical of centralized planning, however, the economy performed badly. Against a background of economic unrest, the Sinhalese Maoist JVP (Janatha Vimukthi Peramuna) Party launched an ill-judged uprising in 1971. Thousands died in the fighting that followed.

The division in Sinhalese politics, and government decisions over religion and education, revived the discontent of the Tamil minority. In 1972 Buddhism was enshrined as the state's primary religion in the constitution, relegating the Hindu faith of the Tamils. Moreover, the numbers of places at university for Tamils were reduced. Such was the magnitude of the civil unrest that resulted from these announcements that a state of emergency was declared in Tamil areas. The Sinhalese security forces fought against more and increasingly well-organized Tamil groups, who now demanded an independent homeland. In another attempt at reconciliation, Junius Richard Jayewardene, who was elected in 1977, promoted Tamil to the status of a 'national language' in Tamil areas. He also gave Tamils greater powers in local government, but it failed to quell the violence.

When the most militant group, the Liberation Tigers of Tamil Eelam (LTTE), ambushed and wiped out an army patrol in 1983, Sinhalese mobs killed several thousand Tamils in revenge in just two days, burning and looting property as they went. This was the turning point. There was widespread violence, and even massacres of civilians on both sides. What followed was a South Asian version of 'ethnic cleansing', since the immediate impact of the violence was that thousands of Tamils moved north into Tamil-dominated areas, whilst a similar counter-flow of Sinhalese began to leave the areas around Jaffna. In fact, this made it easier for Tamil secessionists to claim the northern third of the country and the eastern coast as their own. Whilst they were clearly in the majority in the north, however, they were proportionately equal to the Sinhalese and Muslims in the east. Apart from these political developments, the conflict produced a number of socio-economic effects. By 1985, 50,000 Sri Lankans were living in refugee camps, whilst a further 160,000 Tamils were in exile in the Indian state of Tamil Nadu. The economy suffered as a result of the widening conflict. Tourism, one of the country's biggest earners, dwindled. To make matters worse, tea prices slumped and foreign aid donors threatened to withdraw support because of human rights violations. Nevertheless, by now the Sri Lankan government was convinced that only a military solution would save the country.

When government forces pushed the Tamil Tigers back into Jaffna city in 1987, Tamil unrest in Southern India compelled the Indian government to consider intervention. After some negotiations, Jayewardene reached a compromise with Rajiv Gandhi whereby the Sri Lanka Army would pull out of Tamil areas and an Indian Peace Keeping Force (IPKF) would restore order in the north and disarm the Tigers. As the first 15,000 troops were deployed, however, Sinhalese and Muslims in the south protested against the Indian 'occupation' and the 'sell out' to the Tamils in the east of the island. Rioting broke out, and by 1989 it had developed into a full-scale rebellion. Behind the violence, the JVP coordinated a series of strikes and political murders. The government, led by Ranasinghe Premadasa, tried to persuade the JVP to rejoin the political process and abandon its campaign, but it failed. Once again, force was applied. Premadasa unleashed paramilitary squads that killed JVP terror suspects and unceremoniously dumped their bodies. The reign of terror lasted three years and claimed the lives of 30,000 people.

The Sri Lankan government swung between political concessions and military operations to find a solution, but neither brought the terrorism to an end for long. In the north, there was an increasing number of terrorist attacks by the Tigers and retaliatory IPKF operations. Despite the difficulties of its task, however, the IPKF compelled the Tigers to reconsider negotiation as a solution to the conflict. The Tigers agreed to a cease-fire, and the Indian Army withdrew from Sri Lanka in 1990.

One branch of the Tigers refused to accept a mutilated peace. They declared an independent *Eelam* (homeland) and vowed to continue the armed struggle. Premadasa was assassinated by a Tamil suicide bomber, one of the so-called Black Tigers, in 1993, just two years after Rajiv Gandhi had been killed in similar circumstances in southern India. By now, however, there were changes on the political landscape. Chandrika Bandaranaike Kumaratunga became Prime Minister in August 1994, when the People's Alliance Party defeated the United

National Party in the elections. The following year Chandrika was elected President, and, for the second time since 1959, her mother Sirimavo Bandaranaike became Prime Minister. New attempts were made at negotiations, but the truce of 1995 was broken by the Tigers in fresh terror attacks. The government therefore responded with a huge military operation that swept into the Jaffna Peninsula and drove the Tigers as well as much of the Tamil population out of the city. Once in occupation, the government introduced initiatives aimed at winning over the Tamil population and there were hopes that peace was within their grasp.

The Tigers, however, reorganized, retrained and appeared more determined than ever to continue the conflict. They were estimated to be made up of 8,000–10,000 combatants, with a trained core of fighters numbering between three and six thousand. The LTTE acted as a hybrid of terrorist cells and a more 'conventional' guerrilla army. The terror wing, including the suicide squads of the Black Tigers, were led by Velupillai Prabakaran, whilst the 'conventional' forces, clustered in the Eastern Province, came under Vinayagamoorthy Mualeetheran, who is better known as Colonel Karuna. In addition to their fighters in Sri Lanka, the LTTE could call on fundraisers, propagandists and weapons procurement specialists overseas, where they could also use the Tamil communities as cover for the work. Some of the LTTE lobbied the UN and foreign governments, recruiting supporters in Europe, North America and Asia. The LTTE also owns a fleet of ships, registered abroad, which it uses for the smuggling of arms and ammunition. In 1993 the Indian navy intercepted an LTTE ship, which it believed had been supplied with its illegal cargo by Pakistan's Inter-Services Intelligence (ISI) to the LTTE-controlled area in Sri Lanka. The guerrillas scuttled the vessel to prevent its capture. Kittu, a senior member of the LTTE, chose to commit suicide by going down with the ship. Other Tigers taken, however, told their Indian interrogators about the origins of the arms consignment.

Despite the conviction of many analysts that LTTE has had no contact with other globalized terror groups, there is some evidence of cooperation and emulation. In 1995 the LTTE helped the Abu Sayyaf group of the southern Philippines by smuggling a consignment of arms and ammunition given by the Harkat-ul-Mujahideen (HUM) of Pakistan, which was at that time training and arming the Abu Sayyaf and the Islamic Liberation Front (the HUM was then known as the Harkat-ul Ansar). In return, the HUM and the Abu Sayyaf presented to the LTTE a consignment of anti-aircraft weapons, which it badly needed. The HUM and the Abu Sayyaf are now members of bin Laden's International Islamic Front. Despite the obvious parallels in suicide bombing, however, there appears to have been little contact (although, by their nature, globalized terrorists need only to be affiliated, or show support for 'allies', to be 'linked'). If these links were not unsavoury enough, however, the LTTE recruitment policies were ruthless in the extreme.

The LTTE's recruitment of children is one of the most tragic aspects of the whole conflict. Several factors pushed young people into the movement. First, a sophisticated LTTE propaganda machine regularly ran special events designed to appeal to children: the promotion of Tigers heroes, parades of LTTE fighters, public displays of military equipment and weaponry, rousing speeches and videos specially designed for broadcast in schools. Families of LTTE 'martyrs' were afforded special respect, and children were drawn to the prestige these accorded them. Second, children who witnessed or suffered abuses by Sri Lankan security forces often felt driven to join the Tigers. The abuses included internment, interrogation, brutalities, and even abduction, execution and rape. A study of 1993 of adolescents in Vaddukoddai in the north found that one quarter of the children studied had witnessed violence personally. Third, poverty and lack of educational opportunities often fuelled recruitment, particularly among Tamils of the eastern districts, where families were typically poorer and considered of lower status than Tamils in the north. Enlisting in the Tigers was perceived as a positive alternative to the bleak economic choices available to them. Finally, coercion pressured Tamil families to provide a son or daughter for 'the cause of Eelam'. If a family resisted, they were often subject to intimidation. In many cases, children were simply taken by force to remote Tigers hide-outs.

The initial grouping of child-soldiers into the 'Baby Brigade' was later abandoned and child-soldiers were integrated into other units.

Amongst the most committed was the 'Leopard Brigade' (Siruthai puligal), which consisted of orphaned children. UNICEF estimate that, of all the children in the LTTE, about 40 per cent are girls. The LTTE claims that the recruitment of girls and women is a way of 'assisting women's liberation and counteracting the oppressive traditionalism of the present system' and also claims that sexual abuse of female soldiers is rare, although there are no means to verify this. What is clear is that children of both sexes have been used in some of the fiercest battles of the conflict. At the battle of Elephant Pass in 1991, in which the LTTE attempted to capture an army base, most of the 550 LTTE casualties were children. Indeed, Human Rights Watch estimate that, in the decade of the 1990s, some 40 to 60 per cent of all Tamil Tiger casualties were children under 18. A United Nations study on the impact of war on children found that young people were used for 'massed frontal attacks' in major battles, and that children between the ages of 12 and 14 were used to massacre women and children in remote rural villages. The study also cited reports indicating the use of children as young as 10 as assassins.[14]

In mid-1996 the LTTE were sufficiently organized to be able to launch a series of raids on government troops in northern Sri Lanka. At the same time they carried out terrorist attacks in Colombo, which killed civilians indiscriminately. A large number of women and girls were used as suicide bombers because the LTTE calculated that they were less likely to be searched. The terror campaign, which continued until 2000, convinced many Sinhalese that peace with the Tamils was impossible. Even the government seemed vulnerable. Chandrika Kumaratunga won a second term in office in the elections of December 1999, keeping her People's Alliance coalition in power, but just days before the election she had been the target of a LTTE suicide bomber, and in the attack she lost the sight of one eye. In June 2000 the Industry Minister, C. V. Goonratne, was assassinated. There seemed to be no end to the killing. The massacre of 26 unarmed Tamil prisoners by a mob of Sinhalese in the town of Bandarawela in the interior in October 2000 illustrated that even the relatively peaceful central part of the island was not immune from the communal struggle. Tamils retaliated by slaughtering Sinhalese civilians.

The struggle was epitomized by the fighting around Elephant Pass, a Sri Lanka Army encampment that dominates the route into the Jaffna Peninsula. In 1991 the LTTE had made a frontal attack on it, but withdrew with heavy losses. The Sri Lanka Army extended its entrenchments and built new fortifications to protect the main camp, but in April 2000 the Tamil Tigers launched a series of attacks from their own positions nearby. In six days of intense fighting, much of which resembled the tactics of the Western Front of the First World War, the Sri Lanka Army abandoned the Elephant Pass. In September the area was subjected to a counter-attack as part of a general offensive on five separate fronts. Multi-Barrel Rocket Launchers (MBRL) purchased from Pakistan, heavy artillery and MIG 27 aircraft from Ukraine were used in the assault, but the losses were heavy: 114 killed and 766 wounded. The LTTE losses were unknown, but the Sri Lanka Army handed over 36 bodies for burial, many of whom were girls, although it wasn't clear if these were fighters, or civilians caught in the battle. The fighting caused renewed fear amongst the local people. The International Red Cross estimate of refugees that year totalled 160,000. Whilst the strategic value of the pass had determined the location of such intense fighting, the timing was perhaps influenced by a variety of factors. The LTTE and the Sri Lankan government had aimed to influence the voters of the 2000 elections scheduled for that autumn, and both sides had been proactive in acquiring weapons from foreign sources prior to the offensives that year.

However, foreign intervention of a quite different kind started Sri Lanka back on the road to peace. Norway attempted to broker peace talks between the government and the Tigers in November and December 2000, and delegates from both sides agreed to meet to discuss their positions. Twelve months later, Ranil Wickramasinghe, the leader of the United National Party, became Prime Minister and he seemed eager to continue the negotiations. The Norwegians suggested a one-month cease-fire, which began on 24 December 2001 (the first one in seven years), and this was renewed in January 2002. Sri Lanka's government also lifted its trade embargo on LTTE-controlled territory. Peace talks between the government and the LTTE have continued to raise the hope that, despite high inflation, high unemployment, poor infrastructure, the deep divisions caused by the civil war, and now the devastation of the 2004 Tsunami, Sri Lanka may flourish in the future.

THE DOMESTIC CHALLENGES FACING NEPAL

For a century, the Ranas, the royal dynasty of Nepal, had ruled as autocrats from the capital Kathmandu, but the British withdrawal from India brought to an end the Ranas' chief support. Factions within the royal family argued for a more liberal or a more centralized polity, but it was difficult to prevent the rise of the Nepali Congress Party, under B. P. Koirala, when it was supported by the giant neighbouring power of the Indian National Congress. Moreover, the victory of the Chinese Communists and the invasion of Tibet in 1950 brought another ideological element to Nepali politics. In fact, the Nepalese had long been tributaries of the old Imperial China (although it was regarded as little more than diplomatic courtesy by both sides), so there was a possibility that China would seek to interfere in Nepal's affairs. With increasing unrest and greater support for revolutionary parties, King Tribhuvan fled to India, only to return the following year as the nominal head of a democratic system. Although the Ranas' autocracy had been broken and the Nepali Congress Party dominated the legislature, progress towards a fully democratic system was slow. King Tribhuvan died in 1955, but it was another four years before the first election was held. Then, in 1960, King Mahendra (Tribhuvan's son) decided that a 'party-less' *panchaayat* system of councils would be more appropriate for Nepal: he had the government arrested. The king selected the Prime Minister, the Cabinet and appointed 16 of the 35 members of the national assembly, effectively returning the country to royal dictatorship.

By the 1970s there was growing discontent with the cronyism and corruption of the royal government. In 1979 the anger turned to rioting in Kathmandu, and King Birendra, the ruler from 1972, agreed to a referendum on the survival of the *panchaayat* political system or the restoration of political parties. Koirala, who had spent much of his time in gaol or in exile, campaigned unsuccessfully for reform and so the *panchaayat* system continued.

Foreign influences, however, began to play a part. Although lucrative international aid was siphoned away from the people of Nepal by the royal government, India imposed a trade embargo in March 1989 (ostensibly to obtain more favourable rates for Indian goods), which crippled the economy. There were shortages of petrol, kerosene, firewood, sugar and salt, and the government was forced to impose rationing and control prices, attracting further criticism. That year, a new popular protest called the Jana Andolan or 'People's Movement' challenged the façade of democracy perpetuated by the *panchaayat*. Although there were elections and there was freedom of assembly, no political parties were permitted. Freedom of speech was meaningless when newspapers were censored and the Indian press was banned. As protest meetings were called, the government responded with tear gas, mass arrests and then with live ammunition. Beatings of those in detention were common. Violent clashes left between 50 and 300 people dead: no sources agree on the exact numbers. But strikes, riots and pressure from aid donors finally persuaded the king to relent. He dissolved the Cabinet, legalized political parties and invited the opposition to form an interim government, promising free elections in 1991. The *panchaayat* system was finally abandoned, but there can be no doubt that the way that India had flexed its economic muscle with its blockade had strongly influenced Nepal's domestic politics.

The challenge to the two major parties, the Nepali Congress Party and the Communist Party of Nepal, has been similar to that of the governments of so many other South Asian countries. Establishing a workable democracy from shifting coalitions without the long experience of parliamentary system can be difficult. A weak economy, unemployment, illiteracy, ethnic division, religious antagonism and a rapid growth rate in the population have further exacerbated the problem of political harmony.

The fissures in the political landscape in Nepal were exposed in June 2001 by the massacre of King Birendra and most of the royal family by Crown Prince Dipendra.[15] Civil unrest erupted again in Kathmandu, and a curfew was imposed to quell street violence. Prince Gyanendra, the brother of Birendra, ascended to the throne, but there was a great deal of suspicion about the role he had played in the murders.

The most recent conflict in Nepal is the Maoist rebellion against the government, which has claimed thousands of lives since 1996. Angry at conditions on the land and neglect of the poor, the Maoists have used terrorist bombings and kidnappings to destabilize the country. In common with other terror groups, the aim appears to be to discredit the existing government, forcing it to over-react and claiming that it is incapable of dealing with civil unrest, which, the Maoists believe, only they can resolve permanently.[16]

The first round of peace talks between the rebels and the government took place in August 2001 and a cease-fire was declared, but it ended just as abruptly. The government was determined not to be deflected from its proposed land reforms and economic programmes. From exporting rice in the 1970s (following Green Revolution improvements to yields), Nepal is now a net importer of food and population pressure annually increases the burden. Foreign aid, which supports approximately 35 per cent of the country's hard currency, pressures the government to find a solution acceptable to an international audience. Equally it is eager to find an answer to its political problems so as to retain Nepal's appeal as a tourist destination (17 per cent of foreign exchange receipts are from tourism), and avoid the fate of Kashmir.

In early September 2001 an alliance of ten left-wing political parties emerged, and there were calls for a united government of representatives from all political parties, including the Maoist rebels. Significantly there were also demands for further changes to the constitution. Hopes of a peaceful solution were dashed with a series of coordinated bombings and kidnappings by Maoist rebels in November 2001. Then, with all the political parties in dispute about the way forward, the king suspended the constitution of 1990 and the country was governed through selected ministers. In the absence of any political solution, it was inevitable that the Maoists attacks would continue with greater intensity.

Sher Behadur Deuba, Nepal's Prime Minister in 2004, admitted: 'Nepal is in a deep crisis. The number one challenge is resolving the Maoist conflict.' From 2002 the Royal Nepal Army was given a greater role in combating the guerrillas and the number of counter-insurgencies operations was increased. American, British and Indian military advisors were brought in to assist in the retraining of the security forces. Yet resolving the crisis requires more than a purely military solution. Every party is divided and there are serious policy differences between each of them. The Nepali Congress Party, for example, is split vertically and the two sides do not seem to be able to cooperate. The UML (United Marxist Leninist) Party has too many leaders at the top who argue endlessly on almost every issue. Worse, the political elites of all the democratic groups seem more eager to seek offices under any circumstances than to find a lasting solution that benefits the country. As a result many Nepalis have nothing but contempt for politicians, who rarely leave the Kathmandu valley. Many party workers in the countryside have no choice but to go along with the Maoists. Indeed, a large number have been killed for not conforming to the dictates of the rebels.

The Maoists have certainly profited by the divisions and weaknesses of democratic politics in Nepal. As long as the parties remain at logger-heads, and the monarchy continues to believe that it has a right to intervene in the democratic process at will, the Maoists can make progress. The dissolution of parliament in 2002, and the selection of approved premiers, gives the impression that the king would really prefer to return the country to a *panchaayat* system. On the other hand, it may simply be that the king believed he had no other options, given the impasse in parliament and the growing strength of the Maoist insurgents. The fact is that the monarchy is perhaps the only unifying emblem in a country of great religious, political, linguistic and ethnic diversity. Whether this means that the monarchy should be any more than a symbolic and constitutional system is a moot point. The problem, at least in the short term, of insisting that the monarch restore the constitution of 1990 is that these enshrine considerable powers for the king.

There are other problems in trying to create a new political dispensation. Attempts to include the Maoists in a parliamentary system will mean having to accommodate their demands for a dominant position for them in the political system. They would certainly call for the incorporation of their own 'People's Liberation Army' in the regular forces. They would also put pressure on a weakened polity to demand an abolition of the monarchy.

The Maoists have made no secret of their desire to abolish the democratic system and to establish Nepal as a base for 'world revolution'.

Comrade Prachanda (alias Pushpan Kamal Dahal), the leader of the Maoist movement, admitted that negotiations with the government was merely 'a revolutionary tactic advanced in a conscious and balanced manner after drawing lessons from the same negative experience in Peru'. In other words, like the Sendero Luminoso, talking to the government was a useful way of keeping the security forces in abeyance whilst building up resources for attacks on the regime: there was no intention to reach a negotiated settlement.[17] Prachanda envisaged 'Nepal as a base area of world revolution, internationalist in content and national in form' with 'close solidarity with the struggles of other countries'.

Despite the difficulties that would attend the holding of elections (not least the intimidation and murder of democratic candidates by the Maoists) and the restoration of the constitution, a policy of drift is clearly not an option. Perhaps only a concerted improvement in law and order, in economic development, in political alliances and a willingness by the elites to grant concessions can offer a solution, but none of these in any way guarantees a secure future in the kingdom.

THE DIVIDED STALINIST STATE: MYANMAR (BURMA)

In 1947 the British and General U Aung San, the nationalist leader who had fought the Japanese occupation, reached agreement on the independence of Burma (renamed Myanmar in 1989). Most of the non-Burman peoples, namely the Shan, Kachin, Kayin, Kayah and Chin, supported the agreement, although their support proved short-lived. Despite the assassination of Aung San in July 1947, Burma became an independent republic on 4 January 1948. It did not join the Commonwealth, but its constitution established a bicameral legislature and cabinet government based on the British model. To cater for the ethnic diversity of the country, non-Burman areas were given a degree of autonomy.

The government, controlled by the socialist AFPFL, was immediately faced with insurrections of Communist rebels and of Karen tribesmen, the latter demanding a separate Karen nation. The situation was made more critical by the need to oust Chinese Nationalist troops who had been forced across the border by Mao's Communists in 1950. Not only were the Chinese Nationalists making raids into China, but also they occupied part of Burma's sovereign territory, and organized drug smuggling and extortion from rural areas to fund their campaigns. The Burmese Army carried out several military operations, but the government was forced to take the matter to the United Nations. In 1953, against the background of increased Cold War tension during the Korean War, the Chinese Nationalists were ordered to leave their bases on the Kengtung frontier.

In foreign affairs Burma was in favour of non-alignment, and Prime Minister U Nu made high-profile visits to both Washington and Moscow, and tried to cultivate good relations with other South Asian states, but Burma refused to join the Southeast Asia Treaty Organization and was one of the first countries to recognize the Communist government in China. Moreover, its centralized planning and the emergence of its own Stalinist government soon convinced international observers of Burma's real sympathies.

Profiting from the increased price of food during the early 1950s, Burma's economy grew rapidly and the country was settled enough for elections to be held. In 1951 the AFPFL triumphed and confidently announced ambitious welfare reforms. Antagonism with the non-Burman peoples, however, disrupted the timber trade, oil and mining, and American aid dried up when the Chinese Nationalists were expelled. Yet those with faith in Communist economic programmes insisted that industrialization was the key to success, and there was no investment in agriculture at all. A sharp fall in rice prices added to the growing economic crisis. In 1958 the governing AFPFL split into two factions over charges of corruption and the issue of national stability. The situation in the provinces was also deteriorating. Karens turned to a guerrilla war when they were unable to obtain independence, and there were demands from the Arakanese and the Kachins for secession too. As civil unrest spread, U Nu invited General Ne Win, the commander-in-chief of the army, to take over the government in October 1958 to restore order. Civilian government was soon restored, but after the elections of 1960, which were won by U Nu's faction on an anti-corruption platform, unrest amongst the minorities continued. There was considerable opposition to U Nu's plan to make Buddhism the state religion, and the country once again descended into civil disorder.

In March 1962, conscious of a threat to national unity, General Ne Win staged a military coup. He discarded the constitution and established a Revolutionary Council made up of military leaders who ruled by decree. Freedom of speech was brought to an end. While the federal structure was retained, a hierarchy of workers' and peasants' councils was created. A new party, the Myanmar Socialist Programme Party, was the only legal political organization permitted. Behind the slogan of 'the Burmese way to socialism', the Revolutionary Council nationalized the industrial and commercial sectors of the economy and imposed a policy of international isolation.

However, insurgency continued to be a major problem of the Ne Win regime. Pro-Chinese Communist rebels – the so called White Flag Communists – were active in the north of the country, where, from 1967, they received aid from Communist China; the Chinese established links with the Shan and Kachin rebels as well. The deposed U Nu, who managed to escape from Myanmar in 1969, also used rebels from the Shan and Karen minorities to organize an anti-Ne Win movement. Nevertheless, in 1972 U Nu split with rebel leaders over their demands to secede from the country.

By the early 1970s the insurgents controlled about one third of the whole state. Ne Win and several other leaders resigned from the army in 1972, but they continued to hold power. The Revolutionary Council was disbanded and Ne Win was installed as president. A new constitution, providing for a unicameral legislature and one legal political party, took effect in March 1974, but it was regarded as little more than window-dressing to its critics. Economic problems and more ethnic tensions throughout the 1970s and '80s led to the growth of a democracy movement, bringing together hundreds of thousands of students, ordinary citizens and even soldiers. They poured onto the streets to protest against autocratic rule and there were serious anti-government riots in 1988, which caused Ne Win to resign from office on 23 July that year. The governments that followed also failed to restore order, despite a wave of brutal beatings and killings, so the military seized control under the name of the State Law and Order Restoration Council (SLORC).[18]

In elections held in May 1990, the National League for Democracy (NCD) won a large majority, 80 per cent, of assembly seats. The SLORC, however, declared the election results invalid and arrested many leaders, including Aung San Suu Kyi. Suu Kyi, the daughter of the assassinated Aung San, commanded a popular following, but she had already been placed under house arrest in 1989. Although she was awarded the Nobel Peace Prize of 1991 for her courageous non-violent struggle, she remained under arrest until 1995 and was subsequently subjected to further severe restrictions. Nonetheless, she has stayed in the country, continuing to write and speak in favour of the restoration of democracy and political liberty. She has since been placed in house arrest, from September 2000 to May 2002, and again from May 2003.[19]

While maintaining a firm grip on political power and suppressing opposition to its rule, the SLORC saw economic failures as the main reason for the uprising of 1988 and abandoned rigid central planning soon after it took power that year, liberalizing the economy and opening many sectors to foreign investment. Aung San Suu Kyi, however, who has international standing, has appealed to foreigners not to invest in the Burmese regime. To end the internal disruption to the economy, the SLORC has managed to strike cease-fire agreements with most of the guerrilla armies that have fought the government. For example, the drug baron Khun Sa, seen as responsible for about half of Burma's annual opium crop of more than 2,000 tons, surrendered to the government in January 1996 along with thousands of his Mong Tai (Shan State) army fighters.

There have been signs, however, that military rule might be ended. In 1992 General Than Shwe became head of the military junta and assumed the position of Prime Minister. Many political prisoners were released; some of the martial law decrees were lifted; and plans to draft a new constitution were announced. In addition, Burma rejoined the non-aligned movement, the first sign that it was prepared to emerge from its diplomatic isolation. Nevertheless, there was little evidence that the army was prepared to return the government to full civilian control, and, even if it did, it is likely that it would insist on a constitutional 'leading role' in Burmese politics, as it did in 1989. A UN General Assembly committee unanimously condemned the Myanmar military regime for its refusal to surrender power to a democratically elected parliament.

It seems less valid, 50 years after the end of British colonial rule, to assert that regional conflicts are a legacy of imperialism. It is perhaps more valid to argue that failed socialist economic and social policies have been just as responsible for generating unrest. The rapid demographic growth of India and Nepal has created new tensions, whilst older ethnic divisions within Myanmar, Pakistan, Bangladesh and Sri Lanka have periodically flashed into violence. Perhaps it would be true to say that the long era of British rule, which was to some extent dependent on military power, encouraged the military forces of Pakistan, Bangladesh and Myanmar to intervene in the political process, but the argument seems less persuasive when examining India and Sri Lanka. In all South Asian states, Military Aid to the Civil Power (MACP), as the deployment of troops in civil disturbances is euphemistically entitled, is evident, and even in India and Sri Lanka the army has been used to further a political goal.

It is clear that there is an inter-connection between the policies of South Asian governments and the conflicts that have taken place, and therefore the deployment of military forces, or even the advent of military rule. Sectarian or communal strife has been a more consistent and prominent theme than any colonial legacy. As South Asian governments have struggled to administer their states centrally, they have had to confront, overrule or suppress a variety of ethnic, linguistic and religious differences. The long history of autonomous or independent polities, maintained even during the British period, has not been obliterated by the creation of new states since 1947. Old fissures have resurfaced and traditions, however they are perceived, have been jealously preserved. Against these forces, whether represented in a democratic political system or not, successive governments have relied on the executive arm of the state: the armed forces. Faced by economic weaknesses and fragmented political systems, there are clearly plenty of instabilities both within and between the South Asian governments of the future.

Chapter 4

Global Influences on South Asian Conflicts

STRATEGIC CONCERNS IN THE REGION

On 14 December 1971 the US carrier *Enterprise* and a flotilla of powerful warships known as Task Force 74 passed through the Malacca Straits en route to the Bay of Bengal. The approach of the fleet was much publicized. President Nixon and his National Security Adviser, Henry Kissinger, later claimed that this was designed to forestall Soviet support for India, as its troops crossed the border into Pakistan, America's ally. In fact, by the time the Task Force reached the Bay of Bengal the following day, the Indian Army had already closed in on Dacca and the offensive in the west was drawing to its conclusion. As the fleet sailed instead for Sri Lanka, Nixon believed that he had demonstrated support for his ally Pakistan and had shown the Chinese, also allies of Pakistan, that their *détente* with Washington was justified. Certainly the evidence suggests that Nixon intended a general 'show of force', but that did not prevent Indians from seeing the move as 'nuclear gunboat diplomacy'. Indeed, the Indian government tried to obtain assurances from the Soviet Union that, if the Americans launched their war planes against Indian targets, the USSR would respond. It was a critical moment in South Asia's relations with the Cold War superpowers, and illustrates just how delicately balanced the region was in the 1970s.

Although it is clear that many of the conflicts in South Asia have been generated internally, it is also evident that global influences have had a profound impact. Each of the states of South Asia points to pressing security issues, and these dominate the region. The cause of this insecurity and instability is geopolitical. India, for example, is regarded as the military and naval giant of the region. For Pakistan, and to some extent for Bangladesh and Sri Lanka, the sheer size of the Indian armed forces is a cause for concern when there are so few 'strategic frontiers' on the political borders of the country. Other than in the mountainous north, Pakistan's border with India provides no natural defences. Bangladesh is enveloped by Indian territory and Sri Lanka cannot command the seaward approaches against the Indian navy. The record of interventions in the internal affairs of other South Asian states by India adds to the concern. But diplomacy, which would appear to be the obvious solution, has been deflected from time to time by unresolved religious, ethnic and territorial disputes.

Moreover, although India is clearly the most powerful of the South Asian states, it shares the same anxieties about security as its neighbours. In the region as a whole, it is China that has caused India the most concern since 1947, largely because of its proximity, size and nuclear capability. It is also the only country in the region that has defeated India in war: India's forces were routed by the Chinese in the border war of 1962. Nevertheless, within the region, India's main preoccupation is with the relatively well-equipped, if small, army of Pakistan. Having fought in 1948, 1965 and in 1971, these concerns seem well justified. The Indian Army was also drawn into the Kargil conflict in 1999 in Kashmir, which, although a border skirmish, did involve the exchange of fire from heavy weapons and threatened to escalate. The alignment of Pakistan and China, which was arranged in 1965, means that India has to defend 15,000 kilometres of border against the two states. It has to be said that, for the most part, the border is mountainous and easily defended, but military setbacks and the nuclear arsenals of its two rivals make the situation far more grave for the planners in New Delhi. Intervention in other South Asian states to avoid threats to India's internal security, and a strong desire to defend its borders robustly following four major conflicts since

1947, seem more understandable when viewed from the Indian perspective.

Pakistan's efforts to forge a national identity based on Islam, and its relationship with neighbouring Muslim states to the west, forced India to create closer ties of its own with the Middle East. Appadorai and Rajan believed that geo-strategic considerations were the primary factor in India's foreign relations with the Gulf States and Israel.[1] Concerns about the attitude of India's Muslims *vis-à-vis* Pakistan and the Middle East created a further complex internal dimension to the issue. Furthermore, the oil crisis of the 1970s added another incentive to foster good relations with the Middle East. Since the Iranian revolution of 1979 and the growth of a militant Islamic fundamentalism, there are good reasons to continue this policy. With such pressure within the South Asian region, and the series of border wars with China and Pakistan mentioned above, it was in India's interests to further Nehru's policy of not aligning with the superpowers in the Cold War. Yet, although India sought to avoid alliances and commitments, it could not remain immune from the global confrontation of the Soviet Union, China and the West.

THE COLD WAR

Stalin had little interest in what he termed 'bourgeois India'. It may have been the social structure of India that Stalin found distasteful, or perhaps the long association with Great Britain, but the Soviet press condemned Nehru as 'the running dog of imperialism' and his administration as 'an Indian variant of bourgeois pseudo-democracy'.[2] India was certainly a low priority in Stalin's strategic concerns in 1947, and pre-war attempts to infiltrate the Communist Party of India had been thwarted. Khrushchev, however, felt differently. The supply of American arms to Pakistan in the 1950s appeared to be an attempt to open up or perhaps extend a second, southern front against the Soviet Union. India, for its part, saw an advantage in Soviet support when the Kashmir dispute was raised at the United Nations and Western powers had not supported Delhi's position. In late 1955 Bulganin and

Krushchev made the first official Soviet visit to India. With the development of the Chinese-Pakistani axis and attempts by Nixon and Kissinger to forge closer relations with China, India moved closer to the Soviets as a counterweight to these threats. In 1971 they signed the Indo-Soviet Treaty of Peace and Friendship, which, to outside observers at least, marked the end of India's non-alignment. It was the culmination of years of moving closer. Referring to India's antagonism with China and the developing relationship with the Soviet Union, Chawla argued that 'for all practical purposes India's non-alignment posture was meaningless after 1962'.[3]

Indira Gandhi, however, was forced to reconsider the treaty of friendship after the Soviet invasion of Afghanistan in 1979. Although the Indian government gave a muted reaction to the aggression, earning universal disapproval in the United Nations, there was some concern that the 'mutual consultation' clause of the treaty had been ignored. When Mrs Gandhi returned to office in 1980, she made it clear that the Soviet occupation of Afghanistan was not in India's long-term interests. Russian troops in Afghanistan effectively made the Soviet Union a South Asian power, and it was unlikely that the West would ignore the situation. Indeed, Pakistan soon enjoyed much closer support from the United States in arms and money. A strengthened Pakistan was seen as a threat to India, showing just how far the superpowers could destabilize a region, or change the balance of power well beyond the territories to which their policies were directed. Gandhi repeatedly argued for a Soviet withdrawal from Afghanistan with Brezhnev and Grmyko, but it had little effect. Nevertheless, in the public domain, India's criticisms of the Soviet Union were limited.

India, however, did maintain an independent stance in spite of its 'friendship' with the Soviet Union.[4] Brezhnev hoped that India would join an Asian security pact, but anxieties about China's reaction persuaded New Delhi not to sign. India also refused to attend an Asian security conference called by Mikhail Gorbachev at Vladivostok in 1986, and it turned down a tentative suggestion from the Soviets that India might provide naval bases for a Russian fleet. India's apparent lack of cooperation suggests that the Soviet Union was something other than a strategic partner. For India, the association with the

Soviets was largely economic. From 1978 Soviet oil supplied India, and by 1985 amounted to some 70 per cent of its exports. A further 15 per cent of its total exports consisted of machinery and precision tools, and, latterly, the means to generate nuclear power. In return, India exported agricultural produce, such as cereals, as well as a range of raw materials and consumer goods. Although the Indians were unhappy about exchanging their goods on a barter system for 'obsolete technology', Indo-Soviet trade increased fivefold from the 1970s.

A new diplomatic offensive was launched by the Soviets in 1986, when Gorbachev visited India and promised a substantial increase in military and financial assistance. The Soviets also offered support on nuclear power, petro-chemicals, civil aviation, and scientific and technological development. Given the economic problems that Gorbachev faced at home, the generosity of the offer suggests that the Soviet Union put great store on its relationship with India. Peter Duncan has argued that the move was prompted by fears in Moscow of a thaw in Sino-Indian relations and damage caused by the continued Soviet operations in Afghanistan.[5] On India's side, improvements in Soviet relations with China also alarmed those who felt that there was a risk of isolation. Gorbachev did little to reassure this group, telling the Indian press that the Soviet Union was unlikely to provide military assistance to India in the event of a war with either Pakistan or China, a view that was in line with his policy of fostering international cooperation and a diplomatic solution to disputes. The Delhi Declaration on Principles for a Nuclear-Weapon-Free and Non-Violent World, signed on 27 November 1986, was interpreted as something more than just an idealistic desire for world peace. The press recognized that the Soviet Union's drive for greater international cooperation would leave India without the kind of military support it wanted for national security. Consequently, in 1988, when Gorbachev returned to India, his visit was greeted less enthusiastically.[6] It was the collapse of the Soviet Union, however, that really transformed the situation. An international realignment was essential, and fortunately Rajiv Gandhi's liberalization of the Indian economy had already created better links with global markets and therefore with the West. In fact, the improved performance of the Indian economy after the severance of the link with the Soviets suggests that the Indian governments had simply been looking in the wrong direction when it came to both economic and security issues.

In 1947 India regarded itself as the natural leader amongst Asian and African states struggling for, or that had just achieved, independence. Mahatma Gandhi and Jawarhalal Nehru were hailed as icons for many movements demanding the end to European colonial rule, and Congress was regarded as a model for anti-colonial movements in the developing world. India joined the United Nations, where it initially played an active role, and it remained within the Commonwealth, joining other countries in statements that championed civil liberties and racial equality. By 1960, however, India's position had changed. African liberation movements tended to look to their own leaders or to pan-African idealists like Kwame Nkrumah, whilst Asian neighbours regarded India with suspicion. The United Nations too was critical of India's policy over Kashmir in the 1950s and condemned its seizure of Goa in 1961. It was against this background, and in the same year, that India joined the Non-Aligned Movement.

The existence of a bi-polar world in the 1960s was a threat to the independence of action that Nehru had sought as the mainstay of India's foreign policy. Alignment to one superpower bloc or the other threatened to reduce India to satellite, and even client status. Moreover, leading the Non-Aligned Movement gave India the chance to assert itself regionally, free of superpower influence. Furthermore, it offered the opportunity for India to act as a bridge between the developed and developing world, giving it considerable diplomatic leverage. Willaim Barnds offered other reasons for India's non-aligned stance.[7] He argued that India needed to concentrate on internal development and could not afford to waste its resources participating in a Cold War confrontation that did not directly concern it. Connected to this was the need to develop national unity, which was threatened by taking sides with one or other of the superpowers. Moreover, Barnds maintained, India's powerful position regionally meant that it had no need for external support.

Bradnock, whilst agreeing that India's priority was to maintain its freedom of action, argued that there was also genuine belief in a peaceful foreign policy.[8] Dating from Nehru's years as both Prime Minister and Foreign Minister, Bradnock felt that Indians were deeply hostile to the Cold War confrontation and favoured peaceful cooperation, decolonization and the achievement of full independence through economic development and political liberty. This was symbolized by the attitude of India's first ambassador to the United Nations, Mrs Vijayalakshmi Pandit, who opened with a strong criticism of South Africa's treatment of its Indian residents. India has accepted the humanitarian resolutions adopted by the Non-Aligned Movement, but the lack of practical application of those resolutions gives the impression that they are not much more than self-serving rhetoric. Mrs Gandhi, for example, seemed eager to retain India's prestige and apparent regional leadership in the Non-Aligned Movement in 1983. Three years earlier, when Indira Gandhi had regained office, she announced that India recognized the legitimacy of the new regime in Kampuchea (which was backed by Vietnam). However, recognizing that this was so unpopular with many South-East Asian states that they might boycott the New Delhi meeting of the Non-Aligned Movement, she deliberately omitted to invite the government of Kampuchea.

International criticism, however, far from deterring India from further participation in international forums, has apparently made it more determined to assume a role of regional leadership. In 1988, for example, at the height of the imbroglio with Sri Lanka's guerrillas, Rajiv Gandhi despatched 1,600 Indian paratroopers to stop a *coup d'état* in the Maldives. Sri Lankan Tamil mercenaries had tried to seize control of the country, but India's timely intervention forced the fighters to flee. They left behind 14 dead and 40 wounded. Just 100 kilometres off the coast of Sri Lanka, an Indian frigate intercepted the mercenaries, but found that several of their hostages had been killed. Rajiv Gandhi's action was supported in the Commonwealth and by the United Nations. Nevertheless, the actions of the Indian peacekeepers in Sri Lanka itself, or the activities of internal security forces in Kashmir, have been criticized internationally.

The United States was never comfortable with the South Asian states' stance of non-alignment, as it tended to view those countries that rejected American overtures as either hostile or even pro-Soviet. Peter Duncan has argued that the American approach was to encourage countries to join security alliances, whilst the aim of the USSR was to discourage them from doing so, even if that meant not concluding a treaty favourable to the Soviet Union. There were, of course, variations in the American stance. Eisenhower was more prepared to accept non-alignment as 'equidistance' between the two superpowers, but this was perhaps a misreading of the South Asian perspective. India rejected the whole concept of a bipolar confrontation since it regarded it as a threat to its freedom of action and a situation likely to endanger its security *vis-à-vis* neighbouring powers like China and Pakistan. Given the Treaty of Friendship with the Soviet Union, however, the Reagan administration was far more critical of India and the 'façade' of non-alignment. India's acceptance of Soviet weapons merely confirmed the Americans' suspicions.

America's policy towards South Asia has been rather sporadic and lacking in strategic definition. Other than containing the Soviet Union and the tide of Communism in South-East Asia, South Asia offered the United States the chance to establish a firm base on the southern flank of the USSR. With a strong presence in Japan, the Philippines and on the Indian Ocean island of Diego Garcia, and with allies in Europe, Turkey and the Middle East, Pakistan eventually came to represent a vital link in the chain around the Soviet empire. India too seemed to have the potential to attract American support. India was the world's largest democracy; it had been freed from its imperial rulers; and the majority of its population rejected Marxist ideology. Many Indians migrated to the United States, some 600,000 by 1990, creating human links between the two powers. Moreover, the war with China in 1962 prompted President Kennedy to send arms to India, and the Americans sent generous donations of aid throughout the 1960s. However, the United States relationship with Pakistan, and, according to Raju Thomas, the improved relationship with China in the Nixon era, may have been the critical factor that encouraged India to sign the Treaty of Friendship with the Soviet Union.[9] India simply feared that any super-power alignment with either of its two chief enemies was a major threat. Credence is given to this argument when one considers the chronology. Mrs Gandhi had been offered the Treaty of Friendship by the Soviet Union in 1969, but it was the war with Pakistan, which coincided with an improvement of Soviet relations with Islamabad in 1971, that changed her mind.

India's relations with the United States deteriorated proportionately to the improvement of its relations with the Soviets, but the Bangladesh War of Independence in 1971 revealed the fundamental differences in policy of the two countries. The Americans condemned the Indian intervention in Bangladesh as a deliberate move to break up Pakistan. The concern in Washington was that India would come to dominate the entire subcontinent. Its association with the Soviet Union meant that, by extension, the Soviets would be able to influence the whole region. The United States, however, felt that it was losing its influence over Pakistan at precisely the moment it needed to bolster its position in the subcontinent. To send a warning to India, an American fleet was sent into the Bay of Bengal in December 1971. The Indian public were outraged, but the Indian government had already secured a promise from the Soviet Union that, in the event of American naval action, India would get Soviet military support.[10] If India had sought to avoid entanglements in the global superpower confrontation, it had clearly failed: with fighting between India, Pakistan and Bangladeshi guerrillas, it was perhaps the closest South Asia came to a general war in the post-colonial period.

After 1971 relations between India and the United States did not improve. The Soviets were relieved when the crisis over Bangladesh passed, because it would not serve their interest to be engaged in a war in South Asia. Nevertheless, the promise of military support suggests that the Treaty of Friendship was far more than its title implied. From an American viewpoint, Indira Gandhi seemed to be in the Communist sphere. Although arms deals were considered in 1974, President Ford's visit to Delhi was cancelled by the Indian government in 1975. Mrs Gandhi was openly critical of American involvement in Vietnam; she supported Hanoi and she accused the United States of trying to undermine her government. The latter claim was absurd, but served a political purpose in Indian domestic politics in that it deflected the criticisms aimed at the Gandhi administration. Patrick Moynihan, the American ambassador to India (1973–5), investigated the claims and discovered only two cases of involvement in Indian politics. In both cases, money had been passed to a political party, but that party was Congress and Mrs Gandhi had, in fact, been one of the recipients of American financial support. Moynihan believed that, since Mrs Gandhi was no longer receiving American dollars, she simply assumed that it must have been going to her enemies.[11]

When India detonated its first nuclear device in 1974, it stood in contravention not only of the internationally acclaimed Non-Proliferation Treaty (NPT), but also of the United States, which was closely associated with it. India ignored the international critics. In the late 1970s the question of how India intended to use its heavy water reactor at Tarapur further dogged relations with America. President Carter gave up trying to limit supplies of uranium to India in return for the signing of the NPT, such was India's entrenched stance. Non-Proliferation was criticized in Delhi because it divided the world into 'haves and 'have nots', thereby perpetuating a second-rate status to countries that aspired to greater international influence. Moreover, the nuclear capability of China, and later, of Pakistan, were seen as major threats to India's security. Therefore, in spite of a UN resolution, and the urgings of Gorbachev before his demise, India still refused to sign the NPT. When Pakistan detonated its own bomb, the decision of the Indian government to go ahead with the test firing of more nuclear weapons was immensely popular with the Indian general public. Considerable American and UN pressure to deter India from further nuclear testing failed, and India has still not signed the NPT, but the American-led condemnation was resented in India.

The alignment of India with the Communist Bloc therefore seemed to be reinforced by hostility to the United States, criticisms of the West and by its nuclear policy. The Soviet Union supported Mrs Gandhi's state of emergency policy and continued to offer financial support, and it looked as if America's relations with India were unlikely to improve. But the Indo-American relationship seemed to change when the Jananta Party won the election of March 1977. The new Foreign

Minister, Atal Behari Vajpayee, warmed to the Carter administration in Washington and applauded its expressions of peaceful idealism. Nevertheless, the Janata government made no secret of its intention to court the Soviet Union as well, and Moscow reciprocated. Then, just two years later, the political landscape in India changed again. The Janata Party was defeated in 1979, the same year that the Soviet Union invaded Afghanistan.

The Indian government believed correctly that America would assist Pakistan so as to contain any further Soviet moves in the region, and to act as a base from which to supply the Mujahideen guerrillas. The American moratorium on arms sales to Pakistan (imposed after the military coup of 1977) was therefore brought to an end, even though it was known in Washington that there was a significant risk of an arms race between India and Pakistan. Sure enough, the Indian and Pakistani governments acquired arms as a safeguard against each other. In the 1980s Indira and Rajiv Gandhi warned the Americans of the effect that their support for Pakistan was having, but Washington was unsympathetic to a country that had so often defied and criticized the West. In fact, Carter's military aid to Pakistan, valued at $400 million, was regarded as too little by the military dictator of Pakistan, General Zia.[12] President Reagan therefore increased the financial and military support to Pakistan, although it has to be said that he was determined to undermine the Soviet occupation of Afghanistan: the purpose of the policy was not to intimidate India. Indeed, America went on supporting favoured factions in Afghanistan even after the Soviets had withdrawn and, in this latter period, the United States began to take far more control of arms supply and distribution from the Pakistan Army.[13] It did not take long, however, for the situation to deteriorate in Afghanistan as rival warlords and ethnic groups vied for power. Continued involvement in the Afghan civil war did not serve any American interests, and therefore the need to support Pakistan was less pressing.

Despite the diminished American involvement in Afghanistan, which potentially could have cleared the way for better relations with India, there was little effort on either side other than high-profile visits by Indira and Rajiv Gandhi (in 1982 and 1985). Stephen Cohen, in giving evidence to a Congressional Committee in May 1985, stated:

> I don't think we can treat South Asia on an intermittent basis. The disasters of the past, and I would include Afghanistan, have been due to American forgetfulness in South Asia . . . government operations should flow from policy and policy should be based on interests, but rarely have I seen this actually occur in American policy towards South Asia.[14]

Yet, there was some consistency in American policy that Cohen himself reiterated: support for South Asian states against Soviet and Chinese threats; support for common democratic systems (with the exception of Pakistan, although America was pleased to see the restoration of civilian, democratic government under Benazir Bhutto and then Nawaz Sharif from 1989); and support for the mass migration of skilled and professional Indians to the United States. In addition, America was concerned about the smuggling of drugs, mainly opium, from Pakistan to the West and the possibility of further nuclear weapon development by Pakistan and India. Since the Memorandum of Understanding between Delhi and Washington in 1985, there was an improvement of relations between the two countries. The final collapse of the Soviet Union assisted the process of reconciliation, but, despite a massive increase in American investment in India, there were still criticisms that the transfer of technology was slow. American companies, including Pepsi Cola, were allowed to operate in India again from 1989 as the Soviet assistance dried up and Delhi cast about for financial support.

After the appalling terrorist attacks of '9/11', India and the United States shared a concern about the rise of militant Islam. Before 2001, it was hoped that President Clinton would address the problems that the Indian government faced in Kashmir sympathetically, especially after his efforts in Israel and Northern Ireland. Yet there was no commitment from the American administration to become embroiled in what was widely regarded as a matter for the UN. The attack on America by al-Qaeda, and the tracing of that organization's headquarters to Afghanistan, changed the situation. Soon after the announcement by

George W. Bush that America was to launch a 'War on Terror', Indians quickly pointed to the terrorist attacks of Islamic groups in Kashmir as a similar problem. Following the American-led Coalition operations in Afghanistan in 2001, an attack on the Indian parliament by Islamic terrorists was condemned as an attack on the principle of democracy itself. The Indian government was eager to demonstrate that America's apparent ally, Pakistan, was sheltering Jihadist terrorists, and even supplying and equipping extremists to fight in Indian Kashmir. India, however, will try to retain its stance of non-alignment, and with fresh talks with Pakistan in 2004 it holds out for a resolution of the Kashmir dispute without international interference if possible.

INTERNATIONALIST ALIGNMENTS

As part of its Non-Aligned status and concerned by the escalation of the arms race during the Cold War, in which it could not compete, India mentioned the prospect of turning the Indian Ocean into a 'Zone of Peace' at the Cairo conference of 1964. The concept was advanced more formally in 1970 at the Non-Aligned Movement's conference in Lusaka and it was adopted as a UN resolution, 2832. Yet the idea of excluding the nuclear powers from the Indian Ocean was unrealistic from the outset, particularly since India's neighbours regarded the declaration as an attempt to turn the Indian Ocean into India's 'lake'. It was probably for this reason that Sri Lanka objected to Indian demands for the removal of the American military and naval presence at Diego Garcia. Moreover in 1981 Pakistan insisted that the declaration in favour of an Indian Ocean Zone of Peace should apply not just to the Indian Ocean and its islands, but also to the littoral states. In other words, India too would have to be a nuclear-free country. India's view was that Pakistan, and indeed other states, might use the IOZOP concept deliberately to limit India's naval influence in the region. In taking this view, it failed to appreciate just how concerned its neighbours were at India's military and naval power. These concerns seemed legitimate when India flexed its muscles by despatching troops to Sri Lanka in 1985 and the Maldives in 1988.[15]

The IOZOP proposal thus foundered not only on the unwillingness of the superpowers to cooperate (especially since they regarded access to the Gulf states as strategically important), but also on the divisions about the purpose of such a scheme by the regional powers. India particularly seemed to want the reduction of the American naval presence at Diego Garcia in order to increase the power of its own fleet. The Americans were unimpressed and noted that Indian objections to their presence on the islands were in stark contrast to their silence about the aggressive Soviet occupation of Afghanistan. The case seemed to be a simple one of India promoting its own national interests whilst disguising them as the internationalist cause of world peace.

The United Nations has been an important forum for the region, especially in brokering peace between India and Pakistan. With UN observers (but not peace-keepers) on the Line of Control in Kashmir, and UN condemnations of nuclear testing, all countries in the region have to acknowledge its influence. Yet the UN also holds out the prospect of economic advantages for South Asia. India has been eager to promote UNCTAD, the UN Conference on Trade and Development, as a means to redress the inequalities of wealth between developed and developing nations. Whilst India does not suffer the kind of crippling international debt of some African and Latin American states, the global recession of the 1980s and high price rises in oil gave it renewed interest in UNCTAD. The fact remains, however, that India's lobbying has had little effect on the leading industrial nations, which, in times of economic downturn, have tended to protect their own interests more determinedly than ever. Despite this failure, India continues to offer some leadership in calls for monetary reform and argues strongly in favour of the benefits of global economic interdependency.

Those countries once under British rule have another forum for informal contact with the West in the shape of the Commonwealth. Although Nehru was initially hesitant about joining this 'colonial club', the Commonwealth has developed beyond the role that its architects envisaged in the 1940s, and it is now a point of contact and solidarity for many developing states. On the whole, the Janata Party of India has been more enthusiastic about this aspect of the Commonwealth than the old Congress Party, and it was Moraji Desai who called, in conjunction with Malcolm Fraser, Australia's Prime Minister, for Commonwealth Heads of Government Regional Meetings in 1977.

What has been popular with all Commonwealth members is the statement of clear aims over racial and human rights matters. Expulsions have been endorsed against Commonwealth members that flout these sensitive issues. President Zia ul-Haq's leadership prompted Pakistan's exclusion until 1989, when India's Rajiv Gandhi made much political mileage by calling for Pakistan's readmission – a move designed to signal a willingness for reconciliation with its neighbour. The years of South African Apartheid attracted strong condemnation from India. It called for, and succeeded in setting up, a working group on the question of sanctions against South Africa. There was a strong reaction when Britain refused to join the rest of the Commonwealth in a condemnation of South Africa in the 1980s. South Africa was certainly a cause that India could champion in line with its general ethos on foreign affairs, but there can be little doubt that the presence of more than three-quarters of a million settlers of Indian descent in the country had a part to play, particularly when the Indian media took such a strong interest in the subject. The general media line was that Britain was insincere in its protestations of multiracial equality, and, although the Commonwealth was no longer a 'British' institution, it was certainly seen that way by millions of Indians. Indeed, such a view is not totally anachronistic: the British monarchy continues to provide a continuity with the past even though the constitutional arrangements of the Commonwealth recognize a totally 'free association' of nations.

The link between South Asia and the United Kingdom has changed considerably since 1947–8. Despite the successful transfer of power without the kind of bitter anti-colonial war that the French experienced in Indo-China and Algeria, and despite the emergence of the Commonwealth, the closeness of the partnership between Britain and its former colonies and dominions has diminished. Nevertheless, of all the Western powers, it is still Britain that enjoys the strongest ties, which is the result, to some extent, of a thriving Asian British community and a cultural exchange popular with younger generations. The nadir of Britain's relations with India was in the 1960s and '70s, when new immigration policies appeared to discriminate against South Asians. Although Britain has been at pains to explain the need to limit and absorb large numbers of immigrants from all over the world, there was outrage about the treatment of Indian and Pakistani visitors to Britain, which was widely reported in the South Asian press. There were many in India who felt that Britain was becoming a safe haven for terrorists – Sikh extremists and Pakistani Islamic Jihadists – where money could be raised and arms acquired. The fears were exaggerated and were raised only during the unrest of the 1980s, but the failure of an extradition treaty with Britain (in contrast to a similar proposal with Canada, which succeeded) did not improve relations.

Economic ties with the United Kingdom were far more significant than political ones. Despite the decline of British control of Indian industry after the colonial era, in 1985, 47 per cent of all foreign-owned assets were in British hands. British companies, which were the largest group in all foreign companies that had Indian subsidiaries, also handled some 12 billion rupees of India's stocks and shares (the United States, by comparison, had just four billion rupees). Since the 1980s, the trend of decline has continued. Of the share in all new foreign investments, Britain's was one of the smallest and far less than Germany or Japan. In trade, too, although Britain's volume of trade with India increased, its share of the total was in decline. This has little to do with underperformance in either country; rather it is the result of greater diversification in partners by both Britain and India.

For South Asian states generally, the end of the colonial period simply meant that they were free to take up new economic arrangements, if, of course, the governments of those countries were prepared to do so. It is really only since the ministries of Rajiv Gandhi that India has been proactive in seeking inward investment from the West, which in turn has stimulated the demand for high-tech products and engineering goods. As far as Indian products and services are concerned, however, there is not always universal satisfaction in the West. Research in the mid-1980s revealed that of all the British private companies that had entered into contracts with Indian businesses, about half felt that the results were 'unsatisfactory'. Bell and Scott-Kemmis concluded, however, that this result also reflects how unrealistic British planners were in their targets and assessments of costs and timescales rather than the fault of Indian companies.[16] The recent move towards Indian personnel by many British firms that rely heavily on telecommunications and service/call centres demonstrates that Indian labour (especially educated and English-speaking) is regarded as cheap and attractive, but there are continuing differences in expectations about quality assurance standards. Lingering bureaucracy and fear of corruption have also been deterrents to further investment and engagement by Western businesses.

South Asia's relations with the Middle East have also taken on far more importance since the oil price rises of 1973 and 1980. Economic cooperation with Iran was essential to pay for its increased oil imports, and the export of sugar, cement, iron ore and engineering goods increased until the Iranian Revolution of 1979. The Iran–Iraq War also disrupted trade into the region, but India has tried to continue its good relations and Indians have sought employment opportunities throughout the Gulf. Pakistan's relationship with the Middle East has been far more significant. If, as it has been suggested, Pakistan's scientists were working to provide Iraq with the technical knowledge to make a nuclear device, then a whole new dimension would be added to our understanding of Pakistan's position (but according to recent evidence Saddam Hussein feared an American 'sting' and turned down the Pakistan offer). There are several Islamist Shi'ite groups that favour the Iranian Revolution, and there is no doubt that Sunni extremists in Pakistan actively supported the Taliban in Afghanistan: the Intelligence Services were not entirely devoid of connections in that regard either. Rivalry between the Sunni and Shi'ite sects in Pakistan erupted into violence in 1999, and the American-led 'War on Terror', which has manifested itself in military operations in Afghanistan and Iraq, has renewed tension with the West. Both India and Pakistan have been forced to reassess their foreign policy position with regard to the Middle East on several occasions in the last ten years.

Despite the potential for economic growth within South Asia through greater regional cooperation, there has been great reluctance by the South Asian states to engage in SAARC (the South Asian Association for Regional Cooperation). The concept of sharing political and economic goals was first put forward by Zia ur-Rahman, the President of Bangladesh, in 1979, but a series of ministerial meetings took place before SAARC was officially recognized at Dhaka on 8 December 1985. Rajiv Gandhi hoped that SAARC membership would lead to improved relations with Pakistan. Soon after the agreement was signed, he signed a mutual 'no first use' clause with General Zia regarding the two countries' nuclear arsenals. The organization, however, is hampered by mutual distrust. The growth of India's economy makes the neighbouring states fearful of any long-term economic commitment and regional trade remains very low. By contrast, Mrs Gandhi always feared that India's neighbours would collaborate to block India's interests and the 'freedom of action' it needs. The SAARC charter, on India's insistence, has excluded the consideration of contentious bilateral issues: thus, at a stroke, it has removed the very *raison d'être* of its existence. However, if SAARC could be used to build closer economic ties, this might, in turn, encourage dialogue on a raft of 'contentious' issues. Since 1987 the Secretariat of SAARC has been based in Kathmandu. In August 1988 King Birendra of Nepal, in addressing the ministers present, admitted that SAARC had not yet 'become a palpable reality'.[17] Typically, the conference failed to reach any agreement on the future of Afghanistan and whether it should be admitted to the organization. With India's economy still out-performing those of its neighbours, Hindu–Muslim antagonism in India, and continuing tension over Kashmir, it is likely that SAARC will remain an aspiration rather than a reality.

A far more important aspect of South Asia's relations with the rest of the world concerns China. Chinese relations with India have been poor ever since the outbreak of the border war of 1962, in which Indian forces were effectively routed. Nevertheless, it was the possibility of a Pakistani-Chinese collaboration that prevented any reconciliation across the Himalayas. Typical Indian assessments of Chinese objectives were expressed by Girilal Jain, editor of the *Times of India*:

China looks upon Pakistan as a proxy for creating problems in India. China wants to deny us what we regard as our legitimate place in the sub-Himalayan region at least, if not in the larger region which could include the Gulf . . . the problem with China is not mainly the border dispute, it's China's perception of India's role in South Asia.[18]

Although India felt that China's refusal to participate in the Indo-Pakistan War of 1971 was evidence that India had faced down its former adversary, the reality is that China has shown remarkably little interest in affairs beyond its sensitive borders. It has proven many times that it is prepared to fight to defend what it regards as its territorial limits, its spheres of influence and its legitimate claims, including North Korea, its waters around Taiwan, Tibet, Myanmar, its borders with Vietnam and its Himalayan frontiers, but the Soviet Union and the United States were greater concerns than India in the same period. This opened the way for the Janata government's more peaceful overtures in the late 1970s.

In fact, both states have sought regional allies on the basis of the mutual antipathy in the 1960s. As India moved closer to the Soviet Union after 1971, so China and Pakistan drew together, and Beijing looked to foster better relations with Nepal, Bangladesh and Sri Lanka. The Aksai Chin, the disputed plateau on the Indian border, is still regarded as strategically important to the Chinese since it provides a southern link to the remote Xinjiang province of Western China. Nehru had signed an agreement with China in 1954 in which he believed that the border between the two countries was based on the Macmahon Line laid down in 1914, and therefore he was happy to recognize Chinese sovereignty of Tibet in return. The Chinese, who had never recognized the British line, believed that the border ran through the foothills of the Assam hills, and they were not prepared to give up a road they had constructed across the Aksai Chin between 1954 and 1957. Threats from the Indian government could not, as it turned out, be matched by military preparedness, and the Chinese recognized the opportunity to inflict a small, if humiliating defeat on Delhi.[19] The war was short-lived and relations were severed until 1976, but the boundary was impossible to settle on the basis on the Macmahon Line anyway since the British surveys had never been completed. As a result, periodic and perhaps pointless disputes arose. Neville Maxwell suggested that it was fear of a domestic backlash that prevented any Indian government from risking acceptance of the *status quo* and therefore the appearance of 'weakness' in foreign affairs. This also made it impossible to agree to the Chinese proposal, tabled as early as the 1950s and reiterated in the 1980s, that India should give up its claims to the Aksai Chin in return for the western portion of Arunchal Pradesh.

Rajiv Gandhi provided something of a breakthrough in India-China relations in 1988. His highly publicized visit of December that year did not address the border issue directly, but there was a growing consciousness that the border line itself was not the priority. India had to engage with China because of its proximity and its relationship with Pakistan. The Indian government realized, especially after the completion of the Karakoram Highway, that China was a power that could intervene in South Asian affairs through its support of Islamabad. Whilst building up its frontier defences, India has sought to avoid antagonism with Beijing. From a military perspective, there is an awareness of China's nuclear capability, but faith in the concept of a trans-Himalayan deterrence and greater optimism about the performance of Indian troops on the borders. Nevertheless, any aggressive stance by India across the mountains is unlikely. Both China and India have a vested interest in reducing, not escalating, military budgets. India has even turned a blind eye to Chinese human rights violations in Tibet, even though Tibetan refugees shelter within its territory. The likelihood is that no formal arrangements will be reached for some time on the actual borders, but there will be a mutual recognition of the relative geo-strategic interests of both sides. As public opinion in India is less troubled by the issue of the Chinese border (since there is more concern over Kashmir), Indian governments will be relieved of that burden in forging better relations with the remaining Asian superpower.

GLOBAL COOPERATION AND THE WAR ON TERROR

The international community certainly has a crucial role to play in containing or resolving conflict in South Asia, from stressing the need for nuclear non-proliferation, to the offer of the 'good offices' of the United Nations. Given the extended period of the conflict in Kashmir, however, one should be conscious of the limitations of imposing a settlement externally: a more successful scenario might be the encouragement of the South Asian states to negotiate between themselves and the provision of the intermediaries, as Norway was able to do for Sri Lanka in the 1990s.

Of course there are occasions, particularly when conflict has already broken out, where firm measures have been more appropriate. In 1971 the United States suspended its military support of India (which had begun in 1962 after the border war with China) and despatched a fleet into the Bay of Bengal. The extremity of this measure may have accelerated the end of the conflict, but it also caused enormous resentment. Moreover, it should be noted that President Carter's threats to limit uranium to India failed to persuade India to sign a Nuclear Non-Proliferation Treaty. Indeed, cutting off military aid cannot guarantee compliance, since the supply of arms can be made by other powers (such as the Soviet Union in the 1970s, and perhaps 'rogue' states in the twenty first century). Moreover, whilst high-tech weapons may be limited and thus starve the protagonists of their ability to conduct conventional operations, it is far harder to influence insurgency in this way.

The international community needs to be conscious that, in light of the humiliation of colonial rule, India and Pakistan are eager to assert a fully independent line of diplomacy even at a high cost. Ever since Nehru's ministry of 1947–65, there has been a strong emphasis on the non-aligned nature of India's foreign policy, and this tradition makes it harder for the West to pressure Indian and Pakistani governments. Equally, although the testing of nuclear weapons in the 1990s was strongly criticized in the West, and India and Pakistan appeared to be defiant, the sheer cost of the testing programmes generated criticism at home. It is therefore the economic dimension that so often limits the military capabilities of the South Asian states. A likely new dimension in this regard will be the exploitation of oil in Central Asia. Pipelines will be needed to exploit the vast new reservoirs in and around the Caspian Sea. China is already negotiating a deal with Kazakhstan, but instability in the Caucasus makes it desirable to route new lines through Afghanistan, Pakistan, Iran or Iraq.

International intervention to prevent or resolve conflicts presupposes a will to intervene, but there is some doubt whether, after American-led operations in Afghanistan and Iraq, Western powers will be so eager to do so in other regions where it does not feel that its own interests are at stake. This has to some extent explained why there has been so little attention from the UN in areas such as Kashmir and Myanmar. If limited war escalates into nuclear confrontation, as in 1999, over the Kargil Conflict, the P5 of the UN can assert diplomatic pressure quickly on India and Pakistan, but can regional states be stopped so easily if they become economically more independent, like China (negating the method used in 1965 and 1971)? And will the UN, in light of criticisms over Bosnia, East Timor and Rwanda, continue to show the same unwillingness to get involved in 'internal' conflicts, however savage they may be?

Finally, there is the question of militant Islam and terrorism. Resentment of the occupation of Afghanistan is certainly keenly felt in Pakistan, and amongst hardliners in Afghanistan itself there is a growing desire for revenge against a 'puppet' or 'foreign' regime. Hamed Kharzai has struggled to extend his jurisdiction beyond Kabul, and the border with Pakistan is not cordoned. Limited operations by the UN Coalition and the Pakistan Army are unlikely to have much impression on the small bands of guerrilla fighters in the long term. The 'War on Terror' announced by President George W. Bush in 2001 may have the effect of persuading the South Asian states to share counter-terrorist intelligence and to work more closely with the international community, which will prove an effective way of neutralizing the networks of the extremists. However, whilst there may be more cooperation between India and Myanmar, the gulf between India and Pakistan, and to some extent Bangladesh, on such questions remains considerable. Furthermore, there will be a temptation by some South Asian governments to redefine political opponents, separatists and any form of resistance as a branch of global terrorism. A reliance on coercion is, in the long term, unlikely to defeat the relatively small numbers engaged in terror in South Asia.

Chapter 5

The Kashmir Dispute, 1947–2004

One of the most dramatic views in the world is that of the Karakoram and Hindu Kush mountains from the seat of a light aircraft. The sheer scale of the peaks is hard to comprehend. Plunging almost vertically down thousands of metres from the needle summits are vast glaciers and millions of tonnes of rock debris hewn from the mountainsides by the relentless ice. Yet, for decades, amidst this spectacular landscape, one could just make out the almost absurdly small crews of field guns, vomiting shells in an apparently pointless demonstration against nature. The Siachen Glacier at the heart of the state of Kashmir had the dubious distinction of being the highest battlefield in the world. In January 2004 long-awaited negotiations began to end a conflict that claimed thousands of lives. Most of the victims died not through conventional fighting, or the intermittent artillery exchanges across the ill-defined 'border', but through a bitter and interminable insurgency. As in so many insurgency conflicts in South Asia, most of the casualties were civilians. Asked about his home state, one Kashmiri simply said: 'This is hell.'

The Kashmir dispute rumbled on for so long that it appeared to be both an anachronism and an irrelevance to the rest of the world. The desultory shelling across the temporary 'line of control' between India and Pakistan seemed to achieve nothing, and the troops themselves faced greater dangers from the climate and the altitude than from their adversaries. Nevertheless, it is the fact that India and Pakistan are nuclear powers, which means the Kashmir dispute commands international attention. In Geneva in 1998, amidst an escalating crisis of nuclear testing, the United States Secretary of State, Madeleine Albright, appealed to the two sides:

> The whole world is asking India and Pakistan to stop, listen and think. Don't rush to embrace what the rest of the planet is trying to leave behind. Don't assume you are the only countries on earth that are immune to miscalculation. There is no point worth making; no message worth sending; no interest worth securing; that can possibly justify the risk.[1]

With several densely populated cities just three minutes from launch bases near Delhi or Rawalpindi, the devastation caused by a nuclear exchange is inconceivable. Reflecting on the vast arsenal of weapons, Sumit Ganguly commented: 'The costs would make Hiroshima look like a minor skirmish ... there is no point in surviving a nuclear war. In fact the survivors might actually envy the people who died.'[2] Even moderate estimates predict hundreds of thousands of deaths, millions of casualties from radiation and a vast area uninhabitable for generations.

The aggressive language from Delhi and Islamabad that accompanied episodic confrontations had just as much to do with impressing the domestic audience in each country as they were 'foreign policy' or 'border violation' issues. As a result, solutions to an apparently imminent nuclear exchange during the Kargil Conflict of 1999 were found in the domestic sphere as well as in international conferences. Appeals to the domestic interests of the two governments, and reminders to both sides of the disproportionate destruction that could be wrought for the sake of a relatively unimportant, albeit sensitive region, were enough to compel the protagonists to step back from the brink. Nevertheless, small-scale actions by Muslim Separatists groups more or less under the Pakistan government's control, and counter-insurgency operations by Indian security forces, continue to bedevil the state. Pakistan has conducted clandestine support for insurgents and sometimes fought in conventional operations. So many lives have been lost that both sides feel any settlement must reflect the scale of the national sacrifice. With each nation determined to prevent the other from claiming victory, the only solution may be that both sides believe they have suffered too much to continue the struggle. Indeed, the indecisive result, the sheer cost of the conflict and the change of international attitudes towards insurgencies and terrorism after 'September 11th', have encouraged India and Pakistan to seek some new dispensation.

THE PARTITION OF KASHMIR

The Kashmir dispute is partly a legacy of the historic partition of India and Pakistan in 1947, but it has also been distorted by more recent issues. India points to the 'Instrument of Accession' signed by the former Maharajah of Kashmir as both moral and physical evidence of its right to possess the whole state. On the other side, Pakistan's claim to the state is essentially twofold: the majority of the population of Kashmir are Muslim, and, fundamentally, Pakistan believes that its electoral majority must be honoured by India. As early as 1916, Mohammed Ali Jinnah, then a lawyer in the Muslim League, signed the Lucknow Pact with the Indian National Congress, and by the terms of the pact the League agreed to support Congress in return for recognition of separate Muslim electorates. Jinnah's subsequent actions seemed to reinforce the idea that Kashmir 'belonged' to the Muslims. He resigned from Congress in 1920 as a protest at the lack of recognition for Muslim interests and he continued to press for an independent state, despite British attempts to limit Muslim areas to 'autonomous' provinces.[3] Pakistan was an acronym for the new state, being made up of Punjab, Afghan, Kashmir, Sind and '-stan' (land). In 1940 Jinnah obtained the Muslim League's support for a separate Pakistan in the Lahore Resolution. Cooperation with the British during the Second World War, whilst the Indian National Congress pursued a campaign of civil disobedience, ensured that Muslim interests would be recognized and given some weight, even though it was clear that British power was on the wane.[4]

Significantly, though, it was the atmosphere after the war that was to sour Hindu-Muslim relations and create the Kashmir dispute. The dialogue between the League and Congress grew more antagonized in 1946, and Jinnah's posturing of strength in the so-called Direct Action Day on 16 August that year resulted in widespread sectarian rioting and the deaths of 4,000 people. Compromise looked increasingly unlikely as more died in the following weeks, and the prospect that Nehru might accept Jinnah's demands for separatism seemed impossible. In this situation, the British proposals for an interim non-British government, the Cabinet Mission Plan, were unable to gain any purchase on the two sides. Lord Louis Mountbatten, the last British Viceroy, accepted the inevitable: India's independence was brought forward to August 1947 and an independent Pakistan was accepted. The mounting crisis created by communal violence forced Mountbatten to concede that the Princely States, which included Kashmir, would be incorporated into one or other of the new countries. These rulers had been used to support the British Raj, but, in the interests of maintaining a united India, they were to be abandoned.[5] Their expectation was that they would be granted some degree of sovereignty, but Bengal and Punjab, which contained large numbers of both Hindus and Muslims as in Kashmir, had to be forced into one country or the other, or split up, and the leading parties saw no independent future for any of the Princely States.

The resulting partition of the Punjab created an important legacy for Kashmir. In an attempt to settle a boundary between the emerging nations, Sir Cyril Radcliffe was appointed to chair a panel of judges. Radcliffe tried to broker a line in the teeth of extravagant claims on both sides, and he had only seven weeks to complete the task. When the line was announced, thousands of Hindus tried to make their way into Indian Punjab, whilst a counter-flow of Muslims poured into Pakistan. In the world's greatest migration, perhaps in the region of six million on each side, the nadir of Hindu-Muslim relations was reached. Rioting, massacres and sustained fighting accounted for a total somewhere between 200,000 and 500,000 lives.[6] It was because of this tragedy that the Maharajah of Kashmir, Hari Singh, delayed the decision to join either India or Pakistan.

Hari Singh clearly hoped to avoid absorption into either India or Pakistan, and he had good grounds for believing it could be so. Kashmir had long been an independent hill state, with its own government. The British had annexed the territory at the close of the First Sikh War in 1846, but sold Kashmir and Jammu (the latter an amalgam of Ladakh, Baltistan and Gilgit) for £750,000 to Gulab Singh. Singh was a Dogra prince and former Governor of Jammu, who once had been a confederate of the Sikhs. He transferred his loyalties to the British for a generous reward. The British titled him the Maharajah of Kashmir, and thus ensured a loyal and grateful ruler on the border of British India.[7] Kashmiris furnished British India with soldiers known as Imperial Service Troops. This gave the Maharajah the appearance of independent status, although the troops were trained by British officers and formed part of the British Indian Army's order of battle.

Kashmir was more than just another Princely State to be absorbed into the provinces of an independent India. It lay astride the mountain system that separates the subcontinent of South Asia from the steppes of Central Asia. Ancient caravan routes traversed its valleys and defiles.[8] Yet, even more important was the state's strategic location. Although the British controlled the avenues into India through the mountain ranges of the North-West Frontier, such as the infamous Khyber Pass, there were passes through the mountains of the north that ran into India via Kashmir. British officers in India from the 1830s to the 1910s shared a concern that Russia, Britain's only real imperial rival in Asia, threatened India from the north. Whilst larger formations guarded the North-West Frontier, it was still thought necessary to garrison the northern provinces, such as Chitral, and, to cut costs, to foster close relations with the state of Kashmir. It was to be the 'guardian of the northern frontier, without the hostility, expense and added responsibilities which its annexation would involve'.[9] Kashmir, as a Princely State, was not just a pillar of the Raj: it was the northern bastion in the curtain wall of mountain defences for British India. For India and Pakistan, however, Kashmir was really a trial of national will and a question of territorial sovereignty.

In October 1947, with negotiations underway between Kashmiri Muslim leaders and Kashmir's Prime Minister, Sheikh Abdullah, a force of Pushtun Afridi tribesmen invaded Kashmir. Concerned that the Maharajah was about to hand over Kashmir to India, they proclaimed a *Jihad* and advanced on the capital, Srinagar. Hari Singh fled to Delhi, appealing directly to the new Indian government for military assistance. Mountbatten accepted Singh's plea provided that the Kashmiri people were offered a referendum to decide their future. Nehru, however, himself a Kashmiri Hindu, was personally involved from the outset and he flew troops to the state. (In contrast to British perceptions, Kashmir had no strategic significance for India, which, after all, dwarfed the small Pakistani forces. It was rather a question that, if India allowed Pakistan to seize a part of its territory, what implications did this have for other parts of the country, especially those that had a significant portion of Muslims?). The call for support by a Hindu ruler could not be ignored, however. There were plenty of Congress members still eager to prevent partition and unite India under their influence. Kashmir seemed to provide a test case for national resolve: it was an issue of identity, and India needed to assert itself over Pakistan. Pakistan responded to India's troop movements by despatching soldiers of its own. The decision seemed justified when Muslim soldiers of the crack mountain unit, the Gilgit Scouts, arrested the Kashmiri governor in Gilgit and demanded to be allowed to join Pakistan. Thus for Pakistan, Kashmir also became an issue of national identity and self-determination. As such, it was symbolic of the country's struggle for survival against its giant neighbour. Its name for the region, 'Azad [free] Kashmir', is thus viewed as a title loaded with both substance and moral significance.

With the conclusion of the fighting of 1948, the United Nations brokered a cease-fire in January the following year, and established the so-called Line of Control. It was agreed that India and Pakistan should each administer a part of Kashmir until a popular referendum could be held. Pakistan got the Gilgit Agency, Baltistan, and the western edge of the Vale of Kashmir, with a population of about three million, whilst India got the rest of Kashmir, Ladakh and Jammu, administering nine million. From 1950 the Indian government recognized Kashmir as a separate state with greater autonomy, but, in 1953, India removed the Prime Minister, Sheikh Abdullah, and shelved the issue of a referendum, apparently for good.

The relative strengths of the two armies and the interests of the superpowers were to play a crucial role in the development of the dispute. When the British Indian Army was divided up after independence, India had obtained the lion's share of its personnel and equipment. Pakistan lacked much of the administrative staff for a new state and suffered from its own initial disorganization. The Indians felt strongly that the Kashmir dispute gave them the chance to 'avenge the wrong' of partition. Jawarhalal Nehru stood against these popular sentiments, but he despatched army units to the border opposite Lahore when fighting broke out in Kashmir in 1947–8, in 1950 (against the background of communal massacres in the two Bengals) and again in 1951. Threatened by a much larger force, Pakistan looked to the United Nations Security Council for support, but also to its own resources. The Pakistan Army expanded, reinforced by the support of the CENTO (Central Treaty Organization) and SEATO (South-East Asian Treaty Organization) pacts and encouraged by John Foster Dulles, the United States Secretary of State, who saw some value in the stability that a balance of Indo-Pakistan forces would bring. As Pakistan shifted into the American orbit, and received weapons, India, whilst officially non-aligned, moved closer to the Soviet sphere. Thus Cold War geopolitics, as well as internal state building and national identity, shaped the dispute in its early stages.

THE POST-PARTITION CONFLICTS

The result of the buildup of Pakistan's strength was that it felt emboldened to test India over the disputed territory of Kashmir after India's disastrous performance in the India–China Border War of 1962. In 1964 Pakistan had concluded its own border negotiations with China and laid plans for the Karakoram Highway to link the two countries. In the same period, however, India expanded its own armed forces so that, by the early 1960s, it possessed an army five times the size of that of the late British Raj. Its weaponry consisted of Russian-built T55 tanks (later replaced by T-72s), BMP and BRDM armoured personnel carriers but also British-built Self-Propelled Artillery and Western hand-held anti-tank weapons like the Carl Gustav. Moreover, whilst the Indian Army had been defeated by the Chinese, this was only due to its lack of preparation for a conflict. Few of its units had been trained for high-altitude operations and it had to fight a war on two fronts, one in Ladakh-Aksai Chin and the other in the North-East Frontier Agency. Accepting American aid after the conflict, Nehru could rely on some American sympathy, which had hitherto remained exclusively with Pakistan. India's policy of non-alignment (whilst enjoying some Soviet support) enabled it to reap rewards from both East and West in the Cold War. The Pakistan Army was therefore guilty of a serious miscalculation in the fighting that developed.

The war of 1965 between India and Pakistan was triggered by a border infringement on the coastal Rann of Kutch in January, and serious skirmishes developed in the southern area three months later, although an agreement was concluded in June. By then, however, there had been several border incidents in Kashmir. On 5 August 1965 five Pakistanis were killed in a clash with Indian police. Four days later there was firing along different parts of the Line of Control. On 14 August a Pakistan Army battalion began attacks at Chhamb, and, on 16 August, the Indian Army captured two posts near Kargil. From 25 August the Indian Army sent forward three divisions, taking the Haji Pir Pass, and threatening Muzzafarabad on the Jhelum. After four days of this onslaught, the Pakistan Army launched its own full-scale attack on the Chhamb-Bhimbar line on 1 September, threatening communications between Jammu and Srinagar. The Indian Army therefore turned its attention to Lahore, and the Pakistani forces held the Indians with some difficulty outside the city. Unable to advance further, the Indians launched a second, well-supported attack towards Sialkot, apparently designed to tie up Pakistan's tank reserves, and an armoured battle developed. By the close of the fighting, Indian troops occupied positions just to the north-east of that city. The conflict then petered out as both sides exhausted their resources. Britain and the United States refused to supply further arms, and the Soviet Union, whilst maintaining its trade in weapons, also favoured peace in the region. On 23 September 1965 the United Nations imposed a cease-fire, and in January 1966 both sides returned to their pre-August positions after a conference chaired by the Soviet Prime Minister, Kosygin, at Tashkent. These events, particularly the containment of the war, demonstrate that international pressure was significant and effective. However, the conflict of 1965 escalated rapidly from a border dispute into a full-scale war. These were worrying precedents for the region.

Further fighting developed in Kashmir in 1971, during the third major outbreak between India and Pakistan, but there were no changes to the Line of Control. After 1984 the rival armies were entrenched on the Siachen Glacier (more than 6,000 metres high) north of the cease-fire line following the Indian Army's attempt to outflank Pakistan positions and prevent insurgents using the glacier as an entry point into Kashmir. This, the highest battlefield on earth, resulted in more casualties from high altitude and the cold than from operational activity. Soldiers described how, whilst patrolling one minute, individuals were lost in a crevasse in the next. Helicopters, essential for re-supply in the forward areas, had great difficulty in flying at high altitude, and weather conditions change very quickly. Moreover, the trajectory of artillery shells could not be accurately calculated because of the thin air. Despite recent negotiations between Islamabad and New Delhi, the area remains volatile and both sides maintain a high state of readiness.

THE CONTINUING CONFLICT

A diplomatic agreement was elusive because of different interpretations of previous understandings. By the terms of the Simla Agreement, drawn up on 2 July 1972, the Indian government claims that India and Pakistan have to settle the Kashmir dispute bilaterally, and not through international pressure from the United Nations. It points to the Instrument of Accession signed in October 1947 by Hari Singh as documentary evidence that a Union with India was accepted from the outset until Muslim troops invaded the state. Singh certainly agreed that India should have jurisdiction of defence, currency and foreign affairs. The Indian government also maintains that, since elections in the region have resulted in positive support for remaining in the union of India (that is, they have voted in Indian national elections, and therefore participated in the Indian state), no referendum on the future of Kashmir is needed. Since Muslims are in the majority in the region, and 60 per cent of the Indian sector alone, Pakistan argues that Kashmiris should be allowed to vote in a new referendum on their future. Both India and Pakistan, however, reject the so-called third option of Kashmiri independence. Indeed, at Simla both sides also agreed to respect the Line of Control and to resolve their differences 'by peaceful means', although there was no agreement on the nature or timing of a 'final settlement'.

Within Kashmir itself there are further complexities that sustain the struggle. In 1986 Indian Kashmir's ruling National Conference (NC) party, a group widely accused of corruption, forged a deal with the National Congress Party administration that threatened Kashmir's remaining autonomy. As a result, a new party, the Muslim United Front (MUF), attracted the support of a cross-section of Kashmiris, including Separatists, Kashmiri youth and the pro-Pakistan Jama'at-i Islami, an Islamist political organization. In Kashmir's elections in 1987, the Muslim United Front looked strong and they believed that election rigging was probably the factor that gave the National Conference party its victory. In the wake of the election, hundreds of MUF leaders and activists were arrested. Unsurprisingly, many of the younger MUF supporters switched their allegiances to the militant groups, which, until the election, had been declining in numbers and support. Some of the new recruits crossed over the Line of Control to Pakistan to obtain arms and training. Even though they were unable to unite over the issue of an independent Kashmir or accession to Pakistan, the militants nevertheless shared a common enemy in the National Conference-controlled state of Indian Kashmir. In 1988 and 1989 the groups began assassinating National Conference leaders and agitated for change using violent protests. Some groups also targeted Hindu civilians, forcing a steady, if small exodus of Hindus from Kashmir.

Religious conflict in Kashmir prevented a solution and fuelled the fighting, but it is really a question of where power lies that matters most to each side. From 1989, against a background of suppression of Muslim groups, insurgency against the Indian Army increased. Delhi repeatedly argued that Muslim Separatists were funded and armed by the Pakistan government, and whilst Islamabad admitted that it, indeed, offered 'moral support' to the Separatists cause, it denied actual physical support. The Jammu and Kashmir Liberation Front (JKLF), however, was certainly obtaining its arms from somewhere, as it carried out a series of bomb attacks on government offices, on buses, and against the homes of serving or former government personnel. The JKLF also organized an effective boycott of the national elections in November 1989, and in December, it kidnapped the daughter of the Home Minister, Mufti Mohammed Sayeed, releasing her when the government agreed to free five militants.

The JKLF was the largest pro-independence group, but its influence is thought to have waned in the past few years. In its place, new groups have emerged: Hizbul Mujahideen (HUM), Lashkar-e-Toyeba (LET) and Harkat-ul-Mujahideen. They were reluctant to stipulate in detail what they were fighting for, except that India should not govern Kashmir. The division of these groups was due to their different origins and composition. Lashkar-e-Toyeba, for example, was made up predominantly of non-Kashmiri fighters from Pakistan and conformed to a rigid form of Sunni Islam, but it has adopted the style of the Wahhabis. In contrast, Harkat-ul-Mujahideen was formed from a merger of two older factions and it is effectively an 'international brigade', made up of Afghans, Pakistanis and Arabs, not unlike the former Taliban of Afghanistan. Foreign elements first joined the insurgency in large numbers in 1994 and their numbers vary from 600 to 2,000. According to official Indian Army estimates, there are approximately 125,000 Pakistani troops and Muslim paramilitary groups in the Kashmir Valley. The Separatists groups resorted to random acts of terrorism, from shootings to kidnappings, punishment beatings and bombings. Yet it is the Kashmiris who suffer most and they have often been victimized by both sides.

In a sense there is an irony here. External influences are strong and no settlement for Kashmir will be achieved without input from outsiders, yet Kashmir has come to serve and even define national identity for Pakistan and India. The one province that divides them is also the one province they share a national cause about.

India's patience with those that call for independence or autonomy is limited. On 19 January 1990 the Indian government imposed direct control of Kashmir and this served as a prelude to a widespread crackdown on the militant groups. Demonstrators were fired on, and several suspected members of Separatists groups were summarily executed. As so often happens in these circumstances, the innocent are swept up with the guilty, and Human Rights Watch maintain a record of Indian Army excesses, alongside reports of murders and torture carried out by Separatists gangs.[10] The militants stepped up their retaliation after 1990: government officials and civil servants were kidnapped or murdered, whilst sabotage, bombing and arson were carried out against government installations. As the violence escalated, and murders increased, many Hindus wanted to get out. The Indian government agreed to assist in the evacuation of 100,000 Hindu Kashmiri 'Pandits'.

Although unrest in Kashmir kept the conflict alive, there were attempts to find a peaceful solution. In 1993 a united All-Party Hurriyat (Freedom) Conference emerged that campaigns peacefully for an end to India's presence in the state. The Hurriyat coalition contained 23 secessionist organizations, including trade unions and religious and political groups. Amongst the last are the political wings of some militant groups. Like the Separatists guerrillas, however, Hurriyat's influence in Kashmir is undermined by its lack of unity, and no decision about Kashmir's future after Indian rule can be settled. In addition, charges of corruption have marred its credibility as the organization to pull Kashmir out of the violence.[11] Nevertheless, the emergence of a single group demonstrates that religion is certainly not the only reason for the resistance to the Indian security forces. Ideological ambition and the desire amongst certain individuals to wield exclusive power in Kashmir keep the coalition divided, but also provides a strong focus for anti-Indian protest.

The increasing violence of the early 1990s convinced the Indian government of the need to return to a technique that the British had employed in the days of colonial rule to crush guerrilla forces: the recruitment of local auxiliary forces. Surrendered and captured militants were recruited, armed and trained by the Indian Army, although they remained outside the official command structure. They participated in patrols, operated with the knowledge of the army, and from time to time they were issued with specific orders from the Indian security forces. Despite official denials of their employment, liaison between the army and these paramilitaries was certainly close. However, the danger of employing paramilitary units is that they will exceed their instructions, operate outside the law and antagonize the civilian population, unless discipline is strict and officers, on attachment from regular service, instil an ethos of professional pride in them. This is where the Indian Army perhaps differs from the old British model of Imperial Service Troops.

In one Human Rights Watch report, Abdurashid Amin described how his brother, a former member of Hizbul Mujahideen, was beaten and killed. After a month of mistreatment in custody he was released, but he was rearrested just three days later. His brother found him tied to a tree:

> His body was riddled with bullets. The bone of his forehead protruded, one eye was out, all the fingers of his left hand were missing, and there was a bullet wound also in his left side. There were holes in his *pheran* [cape]. The army came shortly thereafter and took the body to the local police station where they filed a report claiming that Amin was a released militant who had been re-arrested to lead the army to an arms cache, and that he had done so. On returning to the camp, the report said, Amin tried to take one of those weapons and fire at the soldiers, upon which they killed him.[12]

Amin denied that his brother had known the whereabouts of any weapons. The circumstances of the man's death remain a mystery.

The nature of this one individual's death, a typical example, raises grave questions about the conduct and rigour of Indian security forces. The Kashmir State Police records show 3,197 complaints including 1,105 allegations of 'custodial deaths', 1,248 'innocent killings' and 512 'disappearances'. The police argue that many of the allegations are lies or exaggerations. In all, Amnesty International estimates that about 800 people, including children, are missing. Whilst the blame for the disappearances is laid on the Indian security forces, Amnesty are quick to point out that 'foreign-backed' Separatists are also responsible for human rights violations, including murder and intimidation. Furthermore, although the Indian auxiliaries were heavy-handed, and meted out some tough punishments, the Jammu and Kashmir Liberation Front declared a cease-fire in 1994, suggesting the government's forceful campaign was working.

In addition to the auxiliaries, the Indian Army raised the Rashtriya Rifles in 1993. This elite unit was trained specifically in counter-insurgency warfare in Kashmir and it has led operations in Doda, Rajouri and Punch. With the Central Reserve Police Force (CRPF) and the Border Security Force (BSF), the estimate of Indian security forces strength in 1999 was 400,000, and they are deployed both along the Line of Control and in the Kashmir Valley itself.[13]

Alongside India's strategy of counter-insurgency, however, there was an attempt to reintroduce democracy. In the parliamentary elections of May 1996 (the first elections since 1989), the vast majority voluntarily went to the polls, although once again there were accusations of vote rigging. The National Conference party formed the state government with Farooq Abdullah, the official accused of corruption in 1987, returned as Chief Minister. Despite this success, there was a widespread feeling of war weariness in Kashmir itself. Irfan Maqsood, a student, stated: 'If only we could turn back the clock. The fighting goes on and on, and for what? We belong to India, and India will never let us go.'[14] On both sides, the killing tended to foster even greater determination to avenge the deaths amongst families and Separatists. Abdul Majid Wani, an engineer whose son was killed whilst fighting the Indian security forces, proudly spoke of the martyrdom and repeated a graveyard epitaph: 'Do not shun the gun, my dear younger ones – the war for freedom is yet to be won.'

KARGIL AND THE NUCLEAR CONFRONTATION

The Foreign Ministers [of China, the Soviet Union, France, the United Kingdom and the United States] condemned the [nuclear] tests [of the 1990s], expressed their deep concern about the danger to peace and stability in the region, and pledged to cooperate closely in urgent efforts to prevent a nuclear and missile arms race in the Subcontinent, to bolster the non-proliferation regime, and to encourage reconciliation and peaceful resolution of differences between India and Pakistan.

This dramatic communiqué by the permanent five members of the United Nations Security Council on 4 June 1998 indicates just how dangerous relations between India and Pakistan had become. The UN Security Council agreed that they would prevent the export of raw materials, equipment and technology that could be used in the further development of a weapons programme, a move supported by 80 other nations, but there was also a commitment to initiating a process that would build confidence and trust between the two powers. The United States, like other countries, imposed sanctions on both India and Pakistan, until the testing was stopped, but the aim was not to ostracize either of them. In Madeleine Albright's words, 'we don't want to isolate these countries, or make them outcasts or pariahs. We must engage them.'[15]

Nuclear testing had caused relations between India and Pakistan to deteriorate sharply in 1998. In response to Chinese nuclear tests, India exploded five nuclear weapons at Pokhran in Rajasthan in the spring of 1998 – ostensibly to signal to the rest of the world that it could match China as an Asian superpower. The Pakistan government responded quickly, and test fired its new Ghauri intermediate range missile. Ghauri was the twelfth-century warrior who conquered part of India, so its title was politically tactless at the very least to Indians. India's leaders were quick to criticize the Pakistani authorities, but they could hardly claim the moral high ground, since they had begun the nuclear arms race with the detonation of South Asia's first nuclear weapon, the 'Smiling Buddha', in 1974. On 11 and 13 May 1998 Pakistan continued with further testing of the so-called Islamic Bomb in south-western Baluchistan. The testing attracted international criticism, crucially from the United States. Yet what made this situation unique was the eruption of more fighting in Kashmir – potentially the trigger for an escalation of the conflict. All along the Line of Control, shelling and shooting intensified and more than 100 civilians were killed.

If any observer had believed that the development of nuclear capabilities would cool both sides' willingness to fight over Kashmir after 1998, they were sadly mistaken. Although India and Pakistan argue that they regard nuclear weapons as a deterrent and a defensive weapon, the two countries lack intelligence systems to verify the movement or test firing of weapons. It would be very easy to misconstrue testing as actual preparations for war. If the other side then began to prepare for a conflict, it is easy to see how the Kashmir dispute has the potential to escalate into a nuclear crisis. Command and control, and other doctrinal issues surrounding the weapons, have yet to be formulated. The actions both governments would take in the event of a nuclear weapons accident are therefore difficult to predict. Nevertheless, the United States' economic sanctions in 1998 had an immediate effect, as did the pleas of the UN Security Council. Unfortunately, in the event of a nuclear confrontation, as opposed to nuclear testing, there would be very little time for diplomacy or sanctions to take effect. Reaching an agreement over Kashmir is therefore critically important as a first step in improving relations between India and Pakistan, and thus reducing the scope for misunderstanding.

In an effort to demonstrate India's commitment to peace, the Indian Prime Minister, Atal Behari Vajpayee, made a symbolic bus journey to the Pakistan border in February 1999 to reopen negotiations with Pakistan. He publicly embraced the Pakistani leader, Nawaz Sharif. The Lahore Declaration that resulted promised talks on Kashmir, and an agreement to alert each other to forthcoming nuclear tests. After such a warning, India test fired its new long-range Agni missile on 11 April 1999. Pakistan also alerted the Indian government to the test of its Gauri and medium-range Shaheen (Martyr) weapons on 14 and 15 April. The moves were heralded as a significant step forward at the time, but the testing went on: India detonated another long-range weapon on the 16 April. In fact, both sides quickly acquired a formidable stockpile. By 2002 India had about 60 operational nuclear weapons, and Pakistan had 30–40. In this climate of an arms race, the agreement on Kashmir seemed more pressing than ever, but, despite international pressure, both sides were too suspicious of each other to make negotiations a success.

In the summer of 1999 relations once again deteriorated. The Indian government pointed to a fresh wave of Pakistani and Kashmiri militants crossing the Line of Control and Pakistan regular forces in occupation of territory on the Indian side of the line. The Pakistan-backed militant forces were indeed re-equipped with AK47s and AK56 assault rifles, light machine guns, revolvers and land-mines. Night vision equipment and wireless communications were also provided, although the Pakistan government still denies that any 'direct' support was offered. It claimed its troop movements close to the Line of Control were designed to 'prevent' insurgents from crossing the border. If that were so, they were patently ineffective. In fact, the real Pakistan strategy was closely linked to its success with the Taliban in Afghanistan in 1996. Arming and equipping local fighters gave Islamabad the chance to exercise its influence beyond the borders. Guerrilla units infiltrated Indian Kashmir successfully and initiated a new round of fighting. If the Pakistan Army had decided to beef up the militants' means of resistance, however, the Separatists appear to have acted beyond Pakistan's expectations. Indeed, the Separatists' aim may have been to force Pakistan's hand, particularly if they detected that relations with India were improving after the Lahore Declaration.

Indian security forces, on the other hand, believed that the whole insurgency effort was part of a co-ordinated offensive organized by Pakistan. They believed that Pakistan's forces would seek to sever the Srinagar-Leh highway at Kargil, alter the status of the Line of Control and then 'internationalize' the dispute so as to open negotiations from a position of strength. It does seem likely that Pakistan felt emboldened by its new nuclear shield to raise the Kashmir issue. This was more than sabre-rattling or posturing. General Pervez Musharaff claimed that Pakistan would 'teach India a lesson' if it crossed the Line of Control.[16] Ominously, General V. P. Malik, the chief of India's army, was equally blunt about India's past restraint, stating: 'it may not be applicable in the next war.'

The Kargil Conflict of 1999 lasted two months, and, planned or not, it drew in the Pakistan regular army in an exchange of fire along the

Line of Control. In April 1999 it appears that elements of the (Pakistani) Special Service Group (SSG), the Chitral Scouts and Bajaur Scouts *were* moved closer to the Pakistan side of the Line of Control. The Indian Army later recovered identity discs from the dead that revealed their status as Pakistan regulars, even though they were dressed as local 'Mujahideen'. The Indian Army claimed that the majority of the personnel involved were from Pakistan's Northern Light Infantry (NLI), a force recruited from the northern provinces of Pakistan, that is, 'Azad' Kashmir and neighbouring Baltistan and Gilgit, but the troops involved were well armed. In addition to their semi-automatic weapons, they fought with rocket launchers, grenades and mortars. The state police chief commented: 'The new ones are better armed and better trained than we're used to. They're professionals, with good radios and heavy explosives.' Even if the Indian Army is mistaken on the nature of the forces involved, and they were, in fact, all militants, it is difficult to see how they acquired their weapons and training without the Pakistan Army's compliance. Ghulam Hussain Lone, a former anti-India militant, spoke of the way that Pakistan's Inter-Services Intelligence agency would provide him with money, guns and instructions: 'They told us what positions to hit – they gave us a list of people to be shot dead.' Lone, alias 'Papa Kishtwari', now works for the Indian security forces and claims that he follows a 'policy of extra-judicial killings', which is done to 'impress New Delhi'.[17] Reciprocating, the Lashkar-e-Toyeba took to massacring Hindu civilians in isolated villages in the hope of sparking communal violence, but random rocket attacks and opportunist political assassination were just as common.

When pressed, the Separatists units still deny any support from Pakistan. Hizbul Mujahideen officials privately admitted that they had sent *fidayeen* (martyr) squads across the border. Salim Wani, the leader of Tehrik-e Jihad, argued that the armament of his organization had changed in the course of the struggle: 'We started with firecrackers and petrol bombs [in 1996], but over time we started capturing armaments from the Indians and learned how to use their tactics and wear their uniforms.' Lashkar-e-Toyeba, however, an organization based inside Pakistan, openly espouses its propagandist and 'military' role. Abdullah

Muntazir, a spokesman for the organization, claimed that the 2,200 preaching centres in Pakistan were designed to generate public anger with India, broadcasting stories of atrocities by their security forces. Muntazir admitted that, having joined at eighteen, he was sent on a three-week training course in Afghanistan, where he learned how to use anti-aircraft guns, small arms and RPGS. In 'Azad' Kashmir, he continued his training into ambushes, raiding buildings and explosives.[18] Pakistan regulars of the x Corps certainly assisted in the build-up of the Separatists paramilitaries as they infiltrated across the border. In the fighting, it was Pakistan troops who soon bore the brunt of the fighting. The struggle quickly involved heavy artillery bombardments and air strikes in what appears to have been a deliberate strategy of widening an insurgent campaign.

Towards the end of the Kargil fighting, the Separatists were forced to withdraw (abandoning some 10 kilometres of captured territory), and, according to Indian Army sources, 464 militants and 725 Pakistan regular soldiers were killed. The cost to the Indian side was heavy: 474 officers and men were killed with a further 1,109 wounded. The conflict ended when the Clinton administration of the United States put diplomatic pressure on Pakistan, but the domestic repercussions of the Kargil war were enormous. As relations between Sharif and the Pakistan Army high command deteriorated, the civilian government tried to prevent Musharraff from returning to Pakistan in October that year by denying his plane permission to land. Musharaff had already planned the removal of the government for its failure in Kargil and a *coup d'état* left the general in charge of the whole country. India was concerned since it was widely believed Musharraff had, in fact, been behind the Kargil operations.

In response to a unilateral cease-fire by one of the militant groups in Kashmir, the Hizbul Mujahideen, in July 2000, and in order to get a peaceful solution to satisfy international opinion, India announced its own cease-fire against Separatists groups in November that year, but the violence continued. Hizbul Mujahideen represents about 1,000 of the 2,500 militant fighters thought to be in the state and predominantly they are made up of Kashmiris rather than the 'foreign' elements of other groups. Their demands were to end all human rights violations against their personnel, and that India should place itself in 'readiness to allow the Kashmiri people full political expression'.[19] Other Separatists groups that belonged to the United Jihad Council condemned Hizbul Mujahideen and they sacked its leader, Syed Saladuddin, as their chairman. There was no immediate effect, though, because the Indian Army continued its counter-insurgency patrols, even ambushing seven 'terrorists' on 26 July, but the tacit approval of Pakistan's military government changed the complexion of the offer.

In the hope of applying new diplomatic pressure on India, Pakistan's Foreign Ministry stated that it was up to Kashmiris to decide 'the manner in which their struggle should be waged'.[20] India responded. Vajpayee met the Separatists to open negotiations although he stated in advance that he could not 'change India's constitution', which was a strong signal that he regarded Kashmir as part of India and that there could be no question of changing its sovereignty. Moreover, many Indians now believed Pakistan had been behind the Hizbul Mujahideen cease-fire. They suspected an attempt to get Pakistan involved in negotiations so that the international community would have to recognize Musharraff as the legitimate ruler of his country, but that the negotiations themselves were not designed to succeed. On their side, the Pakistanis accused India of trying to 'divide and rule'. Khalid Mohammed of the Institute of Regional Studies in Islamabad thought India was trying to exclude Pakistan from a final settlement. He stated: 'India thought it could divide the militant camp – they were sadly mistaken.'[21] It is more likely, however, that India was trying to widen the base of those it could do business with, that is, the moderate groups. L. K. Advani, the Home Minister, argued: 'India will not deviate from its chosen course of talks with all those in Kashmir who eschew the path of terror and violence.'

Further attempts to get talks going between the Indian government and the Muslim parties foundered over Separatists' demands that Pakistan should be included in any dialogue. Delhi stated simply that Pakistan could not be represented whilst it continued to fund and support the Separatists militants, or, as they put it, 'support cross-border terrorism'. On 8 August 2000 Hizbul Mujahideen issued an ultimatum, two months ahead of schedule, and the peace process collapsed. Attacks on Indian Army camps resumed and a car bomb in Srinagar killed 9 and wounded 25 people. The sickening cycle of violence returned. In the winter of 2000, 400 civilians and 200 security personnel were killed.

The following spring there was a new attempt to restart the peace negotiations. Krishna Chandra Pant, the 69-year-old politician who had served in various senior government posts over 34 years and who had helped in the resolution of conflicts in the North-East, was tasked by the Delhi government to talk to Separatists groups and, crucially, to Pakistan. The initial reaction to Pant was hostile since the Indian government had announced that they expected all groups, including the Hurriyat, to participate in negotiations 'unconditionally'. Hurriyat wanted to send its delegates to Pakistan before it committed itself to the talks, but India denied them their passports since they accused the delegates of stirring up anti-India propaganda. This was not a fear without foundation. Syed Ali Shah Geelani, for example, was a notorious activist. Musharraff told *Asian Age*, an Indian newspaper, that he thought all talks between Delhi and the Separatists were futile unless Kashmir was dealt with directly by the two governments.[22] In this Pakistan perhaps had a point. It seemed that there was little chance of success without Pakistan's involvement. But the following month, India achieved a diplomatic triumph.

First, India declared an official end to its cease-fire on the Separatists who were still fighting, and simultaneously it invited Musharraff for talks on Kashmir in Delhi. At first sight, the policy seemed contradictory: did India want peace or war? Indeed, the invitation to Musharraff was a supreme irony. Although Musharraff was seen as the architect of the costly Kargil operations, he was now to be given the legitimacy he wanted as the ruler of Pakistan and he was about to get what he had long been calling for – direct talks between the two countries over Kashmir. Lashkar-e-Toyeba, which opposed all compromises, saw the Indian offer as a 'gimmick'.[23] Hurriyat accused the Indian security forces of using the proposed talks as a screen for more brutalities and claimed that thirteen people were killed whilst in custody in the week the announcement was made. The Indian government, however, made no secret of its determination to put pressure on the Separatists by means of military force anyway. Moreover, putting Musharraff on the spot with talks on Kashmir was probably designed to force him to condemn the violence of the Separatists and strain relations between Kashmiris and the Pakistan government. Furthermore, with Pakistan talking in Delhi, it was harder for the militants to refuse to do the same in Kashmir itself.

India and Pakistan continued to trade accusations at a summit in Agra in July 2001. Disagreements were fuelled by attacks inside India, including a bungled raid on the Indian Parliament that December in which fourteen were killed. When groups such as Jaish-e-Mohammad ('Army of Mohammed') emerged in Pakistan, under the leadership of the Islamic cleric Maulana Masood Azhar, the Indian government believed it could prove a direct link between Pakistan and the Separatists because Jaish-e-Mohammad calls on its followers to fight against Indian rule in Kashmir. In October another car bomb in Srinagar killed 38 outside the state assembly building, and although no group claimed responsibility, the new Jaish-e-Mohammed was suspected. Even though he was taken into custody in India, Masood Azhar was released from an Indian gaol in December 2001, in exchange for hostages taken on board a hijacked Indian airliner, which had landed in Taliban-held Afghanistan. Since the Taliban were pro-Pakistan, the prisoner release was widely seen as a humiliation in India. Both sides realized, however, that prisoner exchanges could not solve the conflict. New hopes were raised in January 2004 because of talks between Pakistan and India, and the Indian government's willingness to open a dialogue with the Hurriyat on devolution. Perhaps a whole cultural shift will be needed before either India or Pakistan accept that the Line of Control may, in the end, be the only viable border for Kashmir, or that Kashmir's independence may be the only way to solve the conflict.

EVALUATION OF THE KASHMIR DISPUTE

In the Kashmir operations, the deaths of around 24,000 people in the past two decades have mostly been caused by light weapons, such as the AK47, grenades and relatively small scale IEDs (improvised explosive devices). The fact that most casualties are not the result of air strikes or full-scale fighting does not mean that either side is pursuing the conflict in a half-hearted manner. Rather it reflects the nature of the struggle – a low-intensity guerrilla war complicated by a stand off between two heavily armed nation states. The annual estimate of ammunition expenditure on the Line of Control in 2000 was about 400,000 rounds per annum. Most of the firing was ritualistic: an announcement of the presence of each side, rather than an attempt to inflict any casualties. Even so, the signals were no less serious for all that. Most of the exchanges of fire took place in the relatively well-populated areas to the south of Muzaffarabad or Tithwal, where each side either provided cover or tried to neutralize infiltrators crossing the Line of Control. In a few places along the 700-kilometre border, Indian and Pakistani positions are no more than 100 metres apart. Elsewhere the lines are divided by valleys or by 5,000-metre peaks, but the environment can be as deadly as the gunfire. What makes this situation unique is that the cross-border tension is complicated by the violence going on inside Kashmir itself.

Farooq Abdullah, the National Conference Party leader, is widely seen as a 'Quisling' figure inside Kashmir, but his bid for more autonomy for Kashmir from the government in Delhi in July 2000 was designed to win him local support. He was determined to ensure that the Hurriyat party would not participate, because this would have ended in the destruction of his own movement. As it turned out Delhi rejected the demand. India has tried to make it impossible for insurrection to succeed and to prove to the local people that it is too costly to contemplate. To a large extent this explains the willingness to use tough tactics against the civilian population and Separatists suspects. Yet Delhi has a precedent already for offering some autonomy and cash aid in return for the establishment of its authority in Nagaland and Mizoram.

For Kashmiris, the absence of any progress has led to a stupor of war weariness. A common feeling prevails that Pakistan and India seem determined to 'fight to the last Kashmiri'. Muzafar Baig, a lawyer in the state, said: 'We want to stand up and say to them both "thank you for loving us but spare us the honour of being your battle-ground". Between 1 January 1990 and 15 July 1999 there had been 7,922 attacks with explosives, 9,393 random shooting incidents, 12,460 cross-border shootings/artillery exchanges, 3,553 abductions and 619 rocket attacks.

Currently, the Line of Control is monitored by the UN Military Observer Group in India and Pakistan (UNMOGIP) under the command of Major-General Hermann Loidolt of Austria. According to the UN, the UNMOGIP mission is 'to observe, to the extent possible, developments pertaining to the strict observance of the cease-fire of December 1971'. However, after the UN approval of operations in Afghanistan in 2001, and the American-led invasion of Iraq in 2003, Pakistan is angry that no action has been taken in Kashmir to settle the interests of the Muslim majority. India, on the other hand, sees Pakistan as a state that sponsors terrorism and precisely the sort of country that America ought to be dealing with in the name of its 'war on terror'. India and Pakistan, however, really share a desire to settle the border in Kashmir without 'international interference', which makes a settlement without recourse to arms unlikely. Yet, popular federalist tendencies in both countries threaten the interests of Delhi and Islamabad. Kashmir groups had begun to discuss the possibility of independence from India and Pakistan, and similar regionalist demands inside India and Pakistan may develop a momentum of their own. Both India and Pakistan have rejected Kashmiri independence as an option, and, given that this is one of the few areas both countries can agree on, neither side is likely to change this policy line unilaterally.

The Kashmir dispute developed from rival nationalist claims at a time when India and Pakistan were asserting their national identity. Suspicion, an escalation in the arms race between the two powers, and the legacy of casualties from each of the three conflicts, in 1947–8, 1965 and 1971 (as well as the more serious border skirmishes), make a solution to the conflict elusive. The legacies of conflict are also powerful and symbolic: both sides claim sovereignty over Kashmir either on the basis of the instrument of accession or the majority population. To both, it is an issue of national self-determination and resistance to an aggressor. Foreign pressure has not always proved effective. In recent years, General Colin Powell and President Bill Clinton visited the two countries and urged an end to the Kashmir dispute. India has tried to persuade the United States that former Taliban from Afghanistan could be operating in Kashmir. The USA, however, wanted the support and cooperation of Pakistan to deal with Afghanistan. They are conscious that Musharraff is someone they can deal with, and an Islamic extremist alternative would not serve their regional interests. In Pakistan itself there has been disquiet with Musharraff's cooperation with America, especially amongst Islamists. More moderate voices, however, call for the return of democracy.

The military presence in Kashmir, like the testing of nuclear weapons, has maintained a strong sense of patriotism and religious symbolism at home. The Kashmir Dispute provided the governments with a *cause célèbre* of national consciousness and that can be important for governments eager to win approval. Yet, paradoxically, in periods of peace there has been indifference or even hostility to the aggressive policies of the governments towards Kashmir in both India and Pakistan. For example, in India, each *military* phase of the Kashmir dispute has led to a wave of support for the government of the day. The BJP party was less popular in 2002 and there was strong pressure on Vajpayee to go along with the hardliners and send troops or aircraft across the Line of Control to neutralize Separatists training camps (in the same way the USA dealt with the Taliban), but Vajpayee managed to avoid the solutions put forward by the more belligerent members of the Indian Army with the support of moderate civilians like Jaswant Singh (the Foreign Minister).

Islamist groups in Pakistan have been more enthusiastic about Musharaff when they are reminded of 'Azad Kashmir', but the majority of Pakistanis are less enamoured with the interminable conflict in the north. Since the Pakistan government appeared to support action against 'fellow Muslim states', the Kashmir issue has proved to be an important rallying cry, and crucially keeps the Islamist militants broadly in line with the military government. That is not to say the government is entirely cynical: it is rational enough to know that the threat of force from India, the chance that Separatists might go too far in their campaign of violence, and the need for American support (especially financial aid) severely limits what Pakistan can actually do about the 'lost province'. Indeed, the voters in Pakistan and India are more interested in fundamental economic matters that affect the trajectories of their future.[24]

Both sides believe the issue to be a serious one of national identity and international credibility, and there is a fierce determination to defend their national interests. Nevertheless, until the presence of substantial armed forces is scaled down and replaced by responsible civil policing, the 'militarization' of the Kashmir dispute will continue to obstruct a diplomatic and political settlement, and thus generate further conflict. In 2004 tentative negotiations in this regard looked promising, but the future is uncertain, and predicting it in such a volatile environment is treacherous. India, may have to accept some cooperation with Pakistan eventually to resolve the conflict, but that requires Pakistan to abandon the militants too. The alternatives are too tragic to contemplate. Either the misery will go on in much the same form as the present, or the willingness to fight – and the well-stocked nuclear arsenals – could produce perhaps the most terrifying catastrophe of world history.

Chapter 6

The India–China Conflict of 1962

On a bitterly cold October morning, as the first grey light lit the horizon, the 400 men of the 9th Punjab Regiment tried to stir themselves to action. Spread along a 12 kilometre front, the troops had been supplied only with great difficulty from airdrops several kilometres in the rear. Now, occupying shallow shell scrapes (no tools were available to dig any deeper), they pulled their overcoats around them a little tighter and peered into the half light. There had been great uncertainty about their chances of survival, for just a couple of days earlier a platoon-sized detachment of their regiment had been sent across the Namka Chu River to the 5,000-foot-metre high Thag La Ridge to the north, but, before their eyes, it had been attacked by a battalion of Chinese troops and almost wiped out. Fourteen had been killed or captured and a further eleven wounded. There were rumours that high command had ordered another advance, but every soldier could see that the Chinese had dug themselves in thoroughly with revetted bunkers and clear fields of fire. The best they could hope for was a political solution, but there was no sign of that. What these Indian soldiers did not know was that the Chinese had used the cover of darkness to outflank and infiltrate the Punjabis thinly spread positions.

Within days of the battle at the Thag La Ridge the Indian Army had been driven out of the North-East Frontier Province and every formation had been destroyed. In the plains, there was something approaching panic as evacuation of towns and villages in the path of the Chinese offensive got underway. Hundreds of kilometres to the west, the Chinese had also overwhelmed Indian forces, although there were intact brigades waiting for them in and around the town of Leh in Ladakh. Nevertheless, this was a comprehensive defeat for India, one that was to have major repercussions not just in India but also across the world. Perhaps more than anything else, and for the first time since independence, it shattered the illusion that India was the rising power in Asia. Indeed, it raised doubts about the whole 'independent' status of India altogether.

On independence in 1947 it seemed that India was eager to preserve the continuity of the British Raj with respect to its northern borders. In 1949 an uprising in Sikkim led to an intervention by Indian troops that turned into a permanent occupation. Bhutan was given a new treaty but told that India would exercise control over its foreign affairs. In 1950 Nepal was given Indian military assistance and left with the strong impression that Delhi intended to control its destiny too. The only anomaly was Tibet. In the middle of 1949 Tibet had declared itself independent and expelled the Chinese embassy. Fearful of the new Communist regime, the Tibetans requested arms and ammunition from India. India obliged and sent military advisors as well, a move the Chinese condemned as 'imperialist designs for the annexation of Tibet'.[1] Despite this assistance, the Tibetans expected the Indians to return the territory they claimed, including Ladakh, Sikkim and the Darjeeling District (known to Tibetans as Dorji Ling), which had been ceded in 1835. Moreover, to the Chinese, including the nationalists, the borders that India occupied were British 'imperialist' ones that needed to be renegotiated.

What India had not yet realized, but the war of 1962 would make evident, was that its relationship with China had changed fundamentally. During the nineteenth century the British had held the upper hand over China, inflicting a number of humiliating defeats and imposing territorial changes or treaty obligations on Beijing. But in 1949 the Chinese Communist government was keen to give notice that, with Britain gone, India had no right to intervene in Chinese affairs. Warning that its troops were on their way to reassert control of

Tibet, Beijing informed Delhi that this was a domestic matter in which the Tibetans were to be 'liberated'.[2] India condemned the 'invasion' but was still eager to win Chinese friendship and so it reiterated its desire to support Communist China's application to be recognized by the United Nations, hoping, in fact, that Chinese control would be little more than the age-old suzerainty it had claimed under the emperors. Both sides viewed the diplomatic overtures of the other with suspicion, however, a feeling that was not dispelled by Indian diplomacy in Bhutan or Chinese negotiations with Nepal. These fears of influence or expansion were to distort future relations between the two countries.

The Chinese occupation of Tibet in 1950 brought to an end the buffer state policy exercised by the British and it was met with considerable protest in India amongst the educated elite. Nehru, who was eager to win over the Chinese, was accused of weak acquiescence. The Deputy Prime Minister, Vallabhbhai Patel, suggested the Indian Army should be redeployed to meet this new threat, but Nehru would not be deterred and he continued to support China at the UN. Nevertheless, he extended his authority over the border area by setting up the North-East Frontier Agency (NEFA) and making clear and unambiguous claims to a border along the Macmahon Line, a demarcation decided by the British from 1914 but not recognized by the Communist Chinese as legitimate. Yet it was what was happening on the ground that was even more significant. Indian border posts were set up in the Tawang Tract, an area adjacent to Bhutan, in February 1951 and the Tibetans, who protested, were ignored.[3] In fact, Delhi directed its negotiations to Lhasa and not to Beijing, but the absence of any reaction persuaded the Indian government that China was not interested in local border issues. If so, it was to be a dangerously complacent attitude: China was occupied by the more pressing issue of the American presence on the Yalu River and the Korean War, but it was not uninterested in any of its frontiers. India should also have heeded another lesson from the border area. Tribesmen on the Subansiri River welcomed a 70-strong Indian patrol of the Assam Rifles, and then massacred every one of them. Eager to avoid the sort of reprisals that had led to a long-running conflict with the people of Nagaland, Delhi contented itself with a show of force.

The fundamental problem with the Indian position regarding the frontiers was that it refused to negotiate any changes to what it had inherited from the British era. Like many post-colonial states, it was eager to assert its right to its inheritance, even though the British frontiers bore little resemblance to the pre-colonial epoch. When Chou Enlai, the Prime Minister of China, suggested to K. M. Pannikkar, the Indian Ambassador, in September 1951 that the Tibetan frontier should be 'stabilized as soon as possible', the Indian position was simply that the borders could not be negotiated.[4] Since the Chinese did not react, Nehru assumed that this course of action was the right one.

There is little doubt that Nehru bears a great deal of the responsibility for the descent into conflict in this period. Although he had the bearing of a statesman, there was a misplaced belief that, having delivered independence, somehow Nehru's word could not be questioned. When he spoke in the Lok Sabha, he was able to hold court without interruption. During heated debates, his voice was able to still the arguing factions almost as if he were the Speaker of the House. He was virtually unchallenged in Cabinet, although it has to be said that Cabinet ministers often seemed to act without reference to each other anyway.[5] Nehru, who was both Prime Minister and holder of the portfolio of External Affairs, was also the President of the Congress Party and chairman of the Planning Commission and the Atomic Energy Commission. Like a latter-day Mughal emperor he was the figure to which all India's problems, and they were manifold, were brought. Nehru was simply too busy to examine the details of many cases.[6] Unfortunately the standards of service in India's foreign service were low; poor training and low *esprit de corps* tended to breed sycophancy. Given Nehru's reputation and status, his will was all. Fortunately, Nehru was eager to befriend the power he thought would partner India's domination of Asia. He had not been treated well by Mao in his view, and he disliked the dogmatism of Communism, but he saw the great potential of an entente with China.[7]

In 1954 India concluded an agreement over Tibet, recognizing it as Chinese territory. There seemed to be a cause for considerable optimism about the future. Indeed, the agreement became famous for the statement of the Panchsheel, or 'Five Principles': mutual respect for each other's territorial integrity and sovereignty; mutual non-aggression; mutual non-interference in each other's internal affairs; equality and mutual benefit; and peaceful coexistence. Yet, even while Indians enthusiastically chanted 'Hindi Chini bhai bhai', Nehru had already decided to push Indian check-points up along the Macmahon Line to present the Chinese with a *fait accompli*.[8] This policy had already worked in Tawang Tract, so he saw no reason to doubt its success a second time. But what made this policy so dangerous was that Nehru believed the border was 'not open to discussion'.[9] Moreover, he was about to apply the same reasoning to the western portion of the border with Tibet, even though it had never been firmly settled.

The Aksai Chin is a high mountain plateau that was an ancient Silk Route thoroughfare between Tibet and Xinjiang province. The British regarded this bleak and barely inhabited area as a useful buffer between their Indian empire and the Russian dominions to the north and west. Although one survey had placed the plateau within British India, all the others had placed it outside its jurisdiction. Indeed, surveys of the area had never been completed owing to its remoteness and inaccessibility. The most advanced Indian post after 1947 was Chusul in Ladakh, outside the Aksai Chin, but Nehru firmly believed that it was Indian territory and ordered army patrols into the area. In the central and southern parts, patrols did indeed go forward, but the entire northern sector, a vast area, was beyond the resources of the army. Tibetans were eager to take advantage of the meagre grazing on both sides of the passes that entered the Aksai Chin from the south, but the winter months drove back border guards and farmers alike. Each spring was marked by a race to secure the passes and complaints were made on both sides that trespassing was taking place across the borders.

What changed the situation was the construction of a road. Since their operations in 1950, the Chinese had used the Aksai Chin to transfer troops into western Tibet, which was a far easier route than trying to reach it from the east or north, given the vast mountain ranges that ran across the region. Using 3,000 civilian labourers as well as additional troops, the Chinese laid the road over 1,200 kilometres of high-altitude mountain desert in just nineteen months, completing the project in March 1956. The Indian government, however, only learned about the road construction in September 1957, when Chinese newspapers reported the triumph: since it was regarded as Chinese territory by Beijing, they had not bothered to tell New Delhi about it at all. Indeed, Delhi was hardly in a position to complain – it was at that moment engaged in road building in Tawang Tract, even though China still did not recognize India's claim to it. Hoping to confirm that a Chinese road now existed in Aksai Chin, the Indian government ordered that army patrols be sent on a reconnaissance. Since it was almost winter when the orders arrived, the two small detachments did not set off until July 1958. The first penetrated into the Aksai Chin, but the other disappeared.

The Indian government laid its formal complaint about the Chinese road crossing 'part of the Ladakh region of India' on 18 October 1958 and enquired after the missing patrol: the Chinese responded with a counter-complaint about Indian Army patrols penetrating Chinese territory, and they curtly informed the government of India that the missing army patrol had been deported.[10] Despite the presentation of maps to support the Indian claims, the Chinese insisted that the Aksai Chin was their territory and they suggested that whilst small revisions might be made in detail, the boundary alignment was clear. The reaction in India was to harden their own position. In a letter to Chou Enlai in December 1958, Nehru wrote: 'There can be no question of these large parts of India [which the Chinese believed were theirs] being anything but India and there is no dispute about them.'[11] Since there could be no dispute about India's borders, there could no room for negotiating them either.

Chou Enlai's response was to suggest that, whilst accepting the status quo for the time being, there would be mileage in meeting to discuss the borders at some future date since the existing ones, which were imperialist in origin, did not reflect the interests of the two nations. Nehru and the Indian Cabinet were furious. Under the umbrella of Panchsheel, it seemed as if the Chinese were seizing parts of the borderland by stealth. Building a road, claiming jurisdiction over Aksai Chin, and then asking for the status quo to be respected appeared perfidious. Coming at the same time as deadlock in a Chinese–Burma border settlement, Nehru was fearful that the Chinese were set on a policy of territorial expansion. Already stung by accusations of 'appeasement' after he had accepted the Chinese occupation of Tibet, Nehru was therefore determined to show that independent India was capable of defending its national interests robustly.

The optimism of the Panchsheel was finally shattered by the outbreak of a rebellion in Tibet. Beginning in the north-east in 1956, the unrest had spread into central and southern Tibet by 1958, and thousands of refugees were pouring over the borders of India and Nepal to escape the fighting. The Dalai Lama, having declared Tibetan independence, abandoned Lhasa and fled to India via the Tawang Tract. In India there were demonstrations outside the Chinese Embassy, but Nehru had to admit that this was an 'internal' matter for China. Nevertheless, he privately confessed that Kalimpong on the Indo-Tibetan border had become a 'nest of spies': what he meant was that Tibetan Khampa rebels had set up a base there and they were receiving help from the CIA.[12] To rub salt into Chinese wounds, the Dalai Lama chose Kalimpong to make an appeal for intervention to the United Nations. In Beijing it was widely held that the rebellion had really been engineered from Kalimpong, a view reinforced by the fact that far from simply offering asylum, the Indians were helping the Dalai Lama to propagate his message to the world through Indian embassies and media organs.[13] At the Chinese National People's Congress, India was condemned for aiding the rebels, 'walking in the footsteps of the British imperialists', and 'harbouring expansionist ambitions towards Tibet'. The government, however, tried to reconcile India: it had no wish to become embroiled in a dispute over the long southern border when it was at that moment involved in a dispute with Taiwan as well as a rebellion in Tibet.

Thus the relations between China and India had deteriorated significantly, but two clashes between border guards converted a political dispute into a military confrontation. For months, Indian and Chinese border posts had closed up and become adjacent east of the Tawang Tract in the NEFA. Indian troops had been told to resist trespassers by force and, perhaps accidentally, border guards had exchanged fire in the so-called Longju Incident of 25 August 1958.[14] The Indian press believed the Chinese had deliberately started the shooting to lower the morale of Indian troops and impress the tribesmen of the frontier with their military superiority. Even the Praja Socialist Party called for a firm response to face the challenge to India's 'manhood and personality'.[15] Just two months later, on 21 October, there was a second and more serious clash between border guards. Whatever the true cause of the incident, the Indian press condemned the Chinese for their 'massacre' of Indian soldiers.[16] It was only now that the Indian people were informed about the 'secret' construction of the Chinese road across the Aksai Chin, which inflamed and incensed them all the more. Indeed, the whole tone of Indian political opinion was transformed from hostility to outright bellicosity.

According to Nirad Chaudhuri, Nehru's greatest flaw was his willingness to change his principled stand on any issue under the pressure of public criticism.[17] It was for this reason perhaps that, having approached the Chinese with a firm but friendly attitude, he now addressed the Lok Sabha in less ambiguous terms. He accused China of 'bullying', talked of standing up to Beijing 'on equal terms', and argued that this was now a question of India's asserting itself as an independent state.[18] The nationalist spirit thus ignited, he would not find it easy to contain the blaze that followed. To Chou Enlai he dropped all reference to 'debatable' borders. He claimed that the Aksai Chin was Indian and the Macmahon Line too. What Chou did not appreciate was that every attempt Nehru made to play down the seriousness of the issue was greeted with accusations of betrayal and appeasement. To demands for rearmament and a military offensive, Nehru replied that the army was perfectly capable of defending Indian soil. He would live to regret such optimism.

The Indian reaction to the Chinese 'occupation' of Aksai Chin can only be understood with reference to a heightened sense of nationalism. For many, the remote Aksai Chin was as much a part of India as the Punjab, and it would be unthinkable for Indians to accept a Chinese invasion and then settle for 'negotiation' concerning the details of the new boundaries.[19] Few stopped to question the legality of the Indian claim, which was, at best, doubtful. Chou Enlai did his best to defuse the situation. He suggested that all military forces should be withdrawn 20 kilometres from the original border and suggested a summit to discuss the issue. Nehru knew that a crisis would develop if he did not meet the Chinese, but he found it hard to resist popular pressure to reject a summit. He compromised, and pleased no one. He agreed to a summit but made it clear that the borders could not be negotiated [20] He could only agree to 'talks', to persuade the Chinese to accept the Indian viewpoint. Against a background of détente between the USA and USSR, Nehru convinced himself that both superpowers would support India. Indeed he believed, like many Indians, that their non-aligned stance had actually brought about the détente in the first place. Indians believed that their country was a beacon of peace in a world shackled by nuclear weapons and Cold War confrontation. Such was the goodwill towards India internationally, Nehru reasoned, that his policy could not fail to attract universal backing.

The failure of negotiations meant that Nehru had to take some action to resolve the situation. He would not begin a war and endanger India's reputation for peaceful international relations, so he accepted a suggestion to send Indian Army patrols into the Aksai Chin to maintain a presence there. This would fulfil several purposes. First, if there was to be a negotiated mutual withdrawal, India could insist that the Chinese pull back out of the Aksai Chin. Second, Indian troops could prevent further advances. Third, it would give the impression to an international audience that this was Indian territory. Finally, if the patrols were attacked, India could claim the moral high ground, underscoring Nehru's faith in the Gandhian principle of Satyagraha. Nehru believed that a Chinese attack was simply inconceivable: the Chinese would not launch an unprovoked offensive against a country with such high international standing and such a strong reputation for pacifism. This military option would also be more acceptable to the hawks of Indian politics. Any military confrontation would simply mean the Chinese could be thrown out of Indian territory as a 'police action'.[21]

THE FORWARD POLICY

The instrument of Nehru's policy was the much-neglected Indian Army. After the Second World War it was inevitable that the British

Indian Army would be drastically cut, and the partition in 1947 had meant that a portion of the armed forces was transferred to Pakistan, but the pacific policy of the government reduced the total to 280,000. Nehru calculated that, in the international climate of 1947, no one power would ever be permitted to control India as the British had done, and, despite the brief fighting over Kashmir and outbreaks of communal violence in the period 1948–51, the army could be reduced. The persistence of the conflict over Kashmir, however, meant that further planned cuts did not materialize. Indeed, the army had increased to 350,000 by 1953, and it was divided into seven divisions (six infantry and one armoured). These formations were deployed facing the areas of greatest threat: three divisions were stationed in Kashmir, and one in the hills of Nagaland to deal with the insurgency there. A strike force of two divisions was placed at Jhansi ready to move against Lahore if necessary. The border issue, however, meant that the 4th Division was redeployed to the NEFA (covering Sikkim, the border with Bhutan, Nagaland, the Macmahon Line and East Pakistan) and a new 17th Division was raised to replace it.

Despite this apparent strength, the Indian Army was a shadow of its old wartime self. It was so short of equipment that there was insufficient for the existing divisions let alone the new 17th. There were acute shortages in boots, radios, batteries and even weapons: it needed a further 60,000 rifles, 700 anti-tank guns, 200 two-inch mortars, 5,000 radio sets and a further 20,000 trucks just for existing formations. Two regiments of tanks were not operational because of a shortage of spares. To requests for more equipment, Nehru replied that the government could not afford the import of foreign arms and the forces would have to make do. In fact, civil–military relations were strained for a number of reasons. Krishna Menon, the Defence Minister, was a short-tempered man who, according to Neville Maxwell, 'veered between angry impatience and remorseful cordiality . . . he was open in his contempt for those he regarded as fools, and given to an intellectual superiority which inclined him to judge most people as fools at one time or another'.[22] He dismissed the appeals of General Thimayya, Chief of the Army Staff (equivalent of commander-in-chief) and belittled senior officers generally. Yet what really damaged the morale of the army was the appointment of the ambitious and highly political General Kaul to the post of Chief of the General Staff.

Kaul was an unusual figure who put great store on personal prestige and action. Trained at Sandhurst, he transferred from the Rajputana Rifles to the Army Service Corps and served at Kohima during the Second World War. This move from a fighting arm to a supporting branch of the army made it more difficult for him to obtain the highest rank later, and led to accusations that he had shirked a real combat role. He would try desperately, even recklessly, to make up for this deficiency later in his career. In the 1940s, like many Indian officers, he was troubled by the dilemma of serving the British – 'remaining true to his salt' – and serving his country as it approached independence. Although he did not join the pro-Japanese nationalist INA, he certainly sympathized with them and stole documents to help in their defence after the war. The man he passed them to was Jawarhalal Nehru, which initiated a friendship that Kaul was to cultivate in the years to come. This cordiality with the political elite earned the disapproval of older soldiers and senior officers. Major-General Sam Manekshaw, who represented the traditional approach to soldiering, was especially critical of Kaul and the ring of 'K-boys' who supported him. Manekshaw, who had been decorated for his bravery during the bitter fighting in Burma during the war, had recognized that the ethos the British had imparted to the Indian Army had nothing to do with imperialism: it was the means by which professionalism, political impartiality and integrity were maintained. Kaul used this traditionalism against Manekshaw, and it was clear to the rest of the army that, to progress in one's career, one had to keep quiet and fall into line with 'K's policies.[23]

It was Kaul's responsibility to implement the political will of his masters and push forward the patrols that would mark India's claim to the northern borders. The problems facing the Indian Army in this task were immense. In the NEFA there were no east–west roads that could assist in the patrolling of the frontier. Deep ravines cut down from the Tibetan plateau, and their steep sides were festooned with dense forests and jungle undergrowth. The border could be reached only by narrow trails on foot, and consequently deployment was slow. In January 1960 it had been possible only to get one company of infantry to the Bomdi

La, 80 kilometres short of the Macmahon Line. By August that year, there was only one battalion in the Tawang Tract and a further two battalions in the NEFA (penny packeted along the border), but supplying them was proving a Herculean task. In the west, there were just two battalions of Jammu and Kashmir Militia, no regular troops and no supporting arms. As in the east, there were no roads and all movement was by foot, with supplies airlifted or brought in on mules. There were two airstrips at Leh and Chusul. To match the Chinese presence in Aksai Chin (which was estimated at one regiment – the equivalent of an Indian Brigade – and supporting armour and artillery), military intelligence believed they would need five infantry brigades along with their heavy guns and tanks. Although the politicians wanted a rapid deployment of these forces, only one battalion, the 1/8th Gorkhas had reached Ladakh by mid-1961. The army unit commanders were also keen to avoid patrols being sent forward until they could offer these men proper support in terms of logistics, heavy weapons and reinforcements.

The Chinese were fully aware of the sluggish build up of Indian forces and they wasted no time in constructing feeder roads across the Aksai Chin to support their border guards. Although the Indian troops had to pick their way up the steep and tangled terrain of the Himalayas, the Chinese soldiers were already well acclimatized and could move more easily across the plateau. It was relatively straightforward for them to bring units closer to the border to choke off any Indian attempts to cross the frontier, and the forces at their disposal in 1961 were estimated at divisional strength. Delhi, however, interpreted this new deployment as evidence that the Chinese were preparing for another advance into Ladakh.

Amid rising civil unrest in India the border issue had the potential to unite the country. With language demonstrations in southern India, militant Sikh demands for a separate state, guerrilla warfare in Nagaland and communal violence in pockets across the country, there was clear evidence that a 'foreign threat' could bring India back together. In 1961 there had been renewed interest in anti-colonialism and a focus on the future of the Portuguese colony of Goa. Although a violent demonstration had been fired on in 1955, the government began to claim that the Portuguese were mistreating freedom fighters, harbouring NATO weaponry and even protecting Pakistani insurgents. As an Indian division was poised on the border, Goa residents were astonished to hear fabricated accounts of a virtual civil war in the colony on All-India Radio. When Nehru hesitated to bring this colonial enclave to an end by force, it was General Kaul who urged him on.[24] There was no resistance and so the Indian government could claim that the whole affair had been a 'police action' and that its troops had been highly efficient. The seizure of Goa had several implications. Internationally, India's reputation for peace was irrevocably damaged, although it was hard to appreciate this in India itself, where the move was highly popular. It gave the government false expectations about the performance of the army and an inflated opinion of what India was capable of. An undefended Portuguese colony was one thing, but taking on the Chinese Army quite another. It was on the border that the most tragic legacy of Goa was to emerge: the deployment of troops to substantiate a territorial claim without negotiation.

Whilst Kaul and his political allies congratulated themselves over Goa, the commanders in the western sector of the frontier were warning that it was becoming impossible to supply the detachments already deployed in Ladakh and they might have to be withdrawn. In the Indian press, announcements that new Chinese border posts had been set up was exaggerated into fresh acquisitions of territory, and consequently there were ever more belligerent calls for military action. The government urged the army to 'go forward' and establish posts that would 'dominate' the existing Chinese ones.[25] Thus the civilians were entirely out of touch with the realities of the military situation. For 114 Brigade, the three battalions available were expected to cover over 3,000 kilometres of front, and patrol 160 kilometres forward from their bases into territory controlled by the People's Liberation Army of China. Even though they had to airlift almost all their stores, including water, and even though they were outnumbered five to one, they were still expected to set up posts overlooking or even behind Chinese lines. They possessed no heavy weapons beyond a platoon of medium machine guns and they were all armed with the .303 rifle, whilst the Chinese had artillery, heavy mortars, heavy machine guns and their troops were armed with semi-automatic shoulder arms.

When the Chinese surrounded a Gorkha post in the Galwan Valley and threatened to remove it, the little patrol was told to stick it out. For Indians, it seemed to epitomize the whole struggle: a brave band representing the claim to lost territory and defiantly refusing to submit to force.[26] However gallant it may have seemed at home, for the Gorkha soldiers it was a deadly game of bluff. Infrequently supplied and then cut off altogether, they were subjected to endless propaganda messages from loudspeakers, whilst Chinese troops made threatening moves within 100 metres of their sangars. A patrol sent to relieve them was turned back by the Chinese. They made it clear that any future attempt would be fired on.[27]

Although the West tended to see the dispute in the ideological terms of democratic India against the Communist Chinese, Britain had doubts about the border claim itself. Nevertheless, given its own recent clash with Chinese forces in Korea, its support was firm. The Non-Aligned countries were less enthusiastic. For some time there was disquiet with India's assumption that it was the natural leader of the NAM, and many African and Asian states listened to the Chinese arguments sympathetically.

On the ground the situation was becoming ever more precarious. Ranging fire was brought to bear around the Indian positions in the Ladakh area. The Chinese moved their own positions closer to Indian drop zones and some were so close that supplies destined for Indian troops landed in Chinese trenches. In September a Chinese foot patrol had been fired on and several were killed and wounded. It must have been clear that the political motive of pushing forward patrols and establishing a presence was in danger of becoming a full-scale conflict. General Daulet Singh detected the danger and pleaded to be allowed to withdraw his advanced posts and consolidate in stronger defensive positions. He called for reinforcements of four brigades with all their supporting arms and services. General Kaul overruled him, stating that, after a few rounds, the Chinese would run away. Indeed, Kaul firmly believed that the Chinese would not attack the Indian positions and he frequently reassured Nehru on this point. Few dared to criticize Kaul, such was the position he occupied, and those who did were soon silenced.

In the NEFA the situation was no better. The supply shortage was just as critical with the added problem that bad weather and low cloud cover limited the number of airdrops. It is estimated that as much as 30 per cent of all the drops were lost in jungle thickets and ravines, or destroyed because of faulty parachutes. The supply chain that inched its way on the ground was hampered by heavy rains and snow. There were few bridges, and porters had to balance huge loads whilst negotiating slippery, moss-covered boulders and pick their way down into and then up from the deep ravines. Insufficiently acclimatized, the troops had to carry huge loads of rations to sustain themselves. Lieutenant-General Umrao Singh tried in vain to alert the General Staff to the problems he faced, but Kaul was unsympathetic.

In fact, the whole situation on the eastern border was about to deteriorate because of the Indian attitude to the Thag La Ridge, the highest feature in Tawang Tract.[28] Unable actually to survive on the ridge itself, Indian troops had set up posts in the valley to the north. So, in fact, the Indians had not only pushed beyond the Macmahon Line, for practical reasons they now had forces some way inside territory that even they recognized as Chinese. It was at this point that the Indian government and the General Staff decided on the forced eviction of the Chinese from 'Indian' territory, starting with the Thag La area. Operation Leghorn, as it was known, was a complete change from the prevailing 'forward policy' of pushing Indian patrols and outposts to the limit of Indian claims. Perhaps it was not surprising that this new aggressive approach was championed most strongly by General Kaul.

Brigadier John S. Dalvi, the commander of 7 Brigade, was incredulous that such an order could have been given. His men had no winter equipment and were expected to hold a high-altitude summit with winter just weeks away. Each soldier had a blanket and just 50 rounds of ammunition. Other than light entrenching tools, there was nothing in the way of defence stores, and the frozen or rocky ground made the construction of any positions rather academic. The Chinese, who now occupied the Thag La Ridge, outnumbered the Indians and were more easily supplied by roads from inside Tibet. Any advance, everyone could see, would entail crossing the fast-flowing Namka Chu River and crossing a long stretch of open rising ground under the fire of Chinese guns.

Moreover, the nearest supporting units were several kilometres in the rear. The 1st Sikhs were on the edge of the Tawang Tract but they, like the 1/9th Gorkhas coming on behind them, were dressed in summer uniforms and also had no winter equipment. They too had no heavy weapons and limited supplies of ammunition. Still Kaul urged the local commanders to make greater efforts. The brigade commander, Dalvi, was ordered forward to the Namka Chu itself in the bizarre belief that his presence at the front would spur the troops to greater urgency.

The illusion that the General Staff and politicians surrounded themselves with was compounded by the reports of B. N. Malik, the Director of the Intelligence Branch. Malik, like Kaul, convinced himself that the Chinese would not attack the Indian units on the border, despite the build up of Chinese forces.[29] It was as if those around Nehru were so eager to please their leader that they dare not bring any news that did not tally with the political line. What made this attitude so criminal was the fact that the army commanders on the frontiers were reporting just how weak their forces were. General Niranjan Prasad, the divisional commander of 4th Division, calculated that the only way his men could dislodge the Chinese would be to make a flank march, but this would require the airlift of 580 tonnes of supplies, guns and ammunition.[30] Faced with mounting criticism of inaction from the press and politicians in Delhi, Kaul took the unusual step of placing himself in command of the NEFA. Nehru was pleased, for he could rely on this 'man of action' to get things moving. On arrival at the front he dismissed all the advice offered by the existing staff officers and demanded that all units make an immediate advance even if supplies had not arrived.

The Chinese were now well protected with stone and timber bunkers with interlocking fields of fire and any assault without artillery or air support was unlikely to succeed. Kaul contented himself with long radio despatches to his superiors back in Delhi outlining the problems but reassuring them at the same time that the Chinese would not attack. He then ordered the Gorkhas and 2nd Rajputs out of their defensive position on the Tsangdhar Ridge and down into the valley of the Namka Chu, where there was no cover and the troops occupied a forward slope. He decided to send an entire battalion across the river to occupy the Yumtso La, but Dalvi and his battalion commanders were dumbstruck: the Chinese had already shown that they were prepared to prevent a crossing of the river and the dispatch of a third of the force simply invited retaliation. Kaul was forced to compromise and accept the deployment of a fighting patrol of platoon strength to the intermediate position called Tseng Jong. When they succeeded in establishing themselves Kaul believed he was vindicated, but the next day, at 4.05 a.m., the Chinese bombarded the platoon with heavy mortars. Minutes later a whole battalion of Chinese infantry began their assault. The Punjabis sold their lives dearly, but the survivors were forced to flee back to the Namka Chu.[31] Kaul left the scene immediately, suddenly aware that the Namka Chu position was hopeless. He recommended a withdrawal but no orders were issued: he argued that he would first have to seek government approval, even though the military decision was obvious.

It was clear to the Chinese officers that the Indians meant to resume their advance at some stage. The Indian troops had not constructed well-prepared defences and their deployment along the river suggested they were poised to go forward. They had left bridges across the river intact, and the main feature that offered a good defensive position, the Tsangdhar Ridge, was only thinly held. To remain on the defensive themselves, reacting only to Indian thrusts, made no sense, especially since it might only encourage Tibetan guerrillas in the rear. Thus they made preparations for the one event Kaul believed they would not dare to attempt: a pre-emptive strike.

THE CHINESE OFFENSIVE, OCTOBER 1962

In the early hours of the morning of 20 October, the Chinese infantry crossed the low waters of the Namka Chu and their preliminary bombardment blasted the Indian positions. Each position was overrun, sometimes after being attacked from two sides in a classic envelopment. At the Tsangdhar Ridge, the vastly outnumbered defenders were wiped out. The advance was so rapid that communications were lost within hours and Dalvi's brigade headquarters was evacuated under fire. In the Ladakh area, at the other end of the frontier, a simultaneous attack neutralized one small Indian position after another. The terrible logic of the penny packet strategy, where some posts were held by groups no more than 20 or 30 strong, was unfolding. Although the Chinese testified to the courage of the isolated, the result was inevitable. The small post at Galwan, cut off for so long, was simply annihilated. The Chinese rolled up through the whole area, the stuttering of machine guns echoing through the mountain flanks. Each ominous silence that followed marked the demise of another Indian platoon.

The reaction to the news in India was shock, but all wanted to rally behind Nehru and express a strong sense of patriotism. Menon, long the target of his political opponents, was sacked in favour of Y. B. Chavan.[32] More venom was reserved for Chinese inhabitants in India and several were attacked. Many Chinese 'suspects' were interned. There were demonstrations; recruitment into the armed forces increased dramatically; and sandbags and trenches appeared in the capital. The government announced the formation of rifle clubs, a Home Guard and Cadet Corps. It also made it clear that there would have to be economic sacrifices. There were fanciful comparisons drawn between Nehru and Churchill as the press surpassed itself with jingoism. Yet the precautions were absurd and the whole atmosphere in India was unreal. Fortunately Nehru realized that to send bombers across the border would only invite the destruction of Indian cities in reprisals. Consequently, the frontier war was still a distant issue.

Nevertheless, the matter was taken seriously enough by the United States and other Western powers. The Americans made an immediate offer of military aid, which Nehru, usually the opponent of such an idea, readily accepted. The Non-Aligned countries were more muted.[37] The Arab states did not offer their support and the Africans were non-committal. Kwame Nkrumah used the opportunity to criticize the British, but his Communist credentials were well known. Moscow was pacific. Criticizing 'reactionaries' in India for the conflict, it cancelled its promise of MIG fighters, although Krushchev had another agenda at that moment: the first freighters carrying nuclear weapons had just docked in Cuba and the world would soon be gripped by the prospect of a war between the Soviet Union and the United States.

The Indians tried to rally their defences in the Tawang Tract at the Se La pass, a strong position but one that was difficult to supply. In addition, they envisaged the establishment of three lines in depth. The first, or outpost line, was to fall back as soon as contact was made with Chinese forces, since its role was merely to indicate where the main Chinese thrusts were coming from. The second line would delay the Chinese by fighting from defensive positions or in ambushes. The third line would be the main defensive line, which had the advantage of being nearer its sources of supply on the plains, and would extend the Chinese lines of communication along narrow corridors of difficult terrain. What was needed was time to consolidate these lines, but the return of General Kaul was to change the situation once again.

At Walong, the Chinese had made swift advances on 20 October, but they had been checked by the determined resistance of the 6th Kumaon regiment on the 24th. Brigadier M. S. Pathania believed that, with an additional battalion to augment the existing three under his command, he might be able to counter-attack the Chinese. Kaul seized on the opportunity, and encouraged the attack, but Pathania was not informed on the most recent intelligence on Chinese strengths and not given any additional troops. The 6th Kumaon, which had been in action almost continuously, made a night assault on Chinese positions on a hill at Walong for six hours. Although they gained a foothold, by daybreak they were simply too exhausted to go on. A renewed assault by fresh troops at this stage might just have tipped the balance, but a Chinese counter-attack cleared the survivors from the hill and pursued the Indians so vigorously that they penetrated the main defence line. Several Indian units fought until destroyed and gunners fired until their ammunition ran out, but the Chinese poured through the gap. Kaul's failure to await reserves had resulted in disaster.

In the western sector, the last pockets of resistance were being picked off by the Chinese. The Gorkhas at Pangong Lake fought with fanatical resistance, but they were wiped out and nearby Demchok soon fell to the Chinese. General Daulet Singh, the General Officer commanding the area, no longer waited for instructions from Delhi. He extracted as many men as he could from Kashmir, without weakening the defences facing Pakistan, and concentrated around Leh in Ladakh. By

November he had acquired two brigades, and, gathering what was left of the isolated units, he impressed on his subordinates that ground would only be held if it was tactically significant. In an attempt to stem the main Chinese thrust, Singh placed the 13th Kumaon regiment in the hills to the east of the Spangur Gap. After a reconnaissance, the Chinese shelled the Indians hastily prepared sangars and then sent in waves of infantrymen. The first attacks were actually beaten off, so a fresh bombardment of rockets, shells and mortars was used whilst the infantry enveloped and then finally overran the position. In five hours of fighting the Spangur Gap was open, but the cost to both sides had been heavy. In one company of the 13th Kumaon, there were only three survivors. The Chinese advance halted on the limit of their claim line.

THE COLLAPSE OF THE EASTERN SECTOR

The main defence line south of the Tawang Tract was 100 kilometres long. It stretched from the Se La position, through Dirang Dzong to Bondi La, and the last of these was the strongest. Nevertheless, the troops were shaken by their defeats; they were still insufficiently supplied or supported and there were some weaknesses to their positions. The most obvious weakness was the Bailey Trail, an old path that was dismissed as impractical for large bodies of men but which outflanked the Se La position and emerged at Dirang Dzong. On 15 November the outpost line at the head of the trail was wiped out and it was decided to send six companies at intervals up the trail to plug the gap. This decision fatally weakened the main position at Bondi La from which they were drawn, but Brigadier Gurbax Singh was reassured that reinforcements were already on their way. Nevertheless, the companies of the 5th Guards that had been sent up the Bailey Trail were soon in difficulties. Overwhelmed by sheer weight of numbers, they tried to fight their way back down to Bondi La. In the gathering darkness cohesion was lost and the survivors were scattered into the jungle. At a stroke, the Chinese had unlocked the flank of the Indian line.

The next to fall was Se La. A screen force in front of Se La was able to beat off five separate Chinese attacks and extricate itself. The main position was strongly held by five battalions under the command of Brigadier Hoshiar Singh. Yet despite this strength, General Pathania could see that the Chinese were enveloping him from the east. His instinct was to abandon Se La and consolidate all his strength at Bondi La, but it was not easy to effect an orderly withdrawal of so many men in the face of the enemy. Nevertheless, he requested permission to make a start, only to be told that General Kaul, his senior officer, was unavailable to sanction it. The troops were preparing to pull back when news arrived that a 200-strong fighting patrol had been utterly anni-hilated. Precisely at the moment when one battalion was moving out of its trenches, the Chinese advance began. Holding their fire until they were on top of the position, the Chinese caught the Se La defenders by surprise. In the darkness, a bitter close-quarter battle ensued, but it was chaotic. Singh tried to extract what was left of the brigade, but, packed on the only trail from the position, his men were shelled and machine-gunned. At Dirang Dzong, which had not been prepared for defence, the Chinese also achieved surprise. Resistance collapsed and even the few tanks available were abandoned. Small parties attempted to escape and some offered sporadic resistance, but the rout was so rapid that Corps headquarters did not even know that the position had fallen.

The following morning, Gurbax Singh was ordered to send rein-forcements to Dirang Dzong, even though his own relief force had not arrived. Sending two companies of the remaining six, the Bondi La position was now fatally weakened. Just ten minutes after the men had set off, the Chinese shelled the position and caught them in the open. It was now a simple matter of overrunning the position. Once again, the Indian troops displayed considerable courage in a hopeless situa-tion. Kaul ordered that a new stand be made at Rupa, but the Chinese enveloped the position on three sides at midnight on 20 November. The collapse of the sector was complete and the survivors were harried out of the hills and onto the plains.

With no formations left to resist the Chinese, India seemed to be on the verge of a total defeat. The Assamese believed that the Indians were about to abandon them. Tezpur was evacuated in pandemonium. There was panic in Delhi. Nehru announced the disaster without any Churchillian rhetoric in the Lok Sabha, and, for once, he was unable to silence the bombardment of criticism levelled at him and his government. Not even the press could hide the scale of the disaster to appease the patriotic sentiments of the people. Desperate now to defend the heart of India, Nehru called upon the Americans to make air strikes against any Chinese units on Indian soil. The aircraft carrier they sent never launched its bombers, but a fleet of c130 transport aircraft did arrive along with a military mission. Had the bombers been able to reach their targets, the outcome of this conflict might have been quite different, but to almost universal surprise the Chinese announced a unilateral cease-fire.

What was even more stunning was the Chinese announcement that they would withdraw to their original claim lines. This was a double humiliation for India. Not only had it been defeated, it now had to accept the magnanimity of the Chinese offer. Nehru stalled for time: he asked for clarification. He hoped to retain international support without actually rejecting the Chinese cease-fire, so he restated India's mantra that it could not negotiate away its sovereign territory. Chou Enlai insisted that the Indians would not be allowed to take up their 'forward policy' positions, so the matter was not settled. The Chinese troops carried out their withdrawal, returning captured equipment and the prisoners they had taken. But they manned the line they claimed and the Indian Army kept a respectful distance.

ANALYSIS OF THE REPERCUSSIONS OF THE CONFLICT

There is no doubt that India's defeat in the border war of 1962 seriously damaged the prestige of the country, but also of its Prime Minister. Nehru did not resign, his own party would not have allowed it, but his moral authority was gone. Commentators noticed that he aged visibly and, just two years after the conflict, he died. In the Lok Sabha he had lost that commanding presence. His attempts to have the border issue referred to the International Court at The Hague, for example, were shouted down. Kaul disappeared from his entourage too. He had been dismissed even before the Chinese cease-fire announcement, replaced by Lieutenant-General J. N. Chaudhuri. An inquiry was conducted, but it was denied any chance to make comment on political leaders and could not name any individual for blame. The army, however, got a blank cheque to rectify its appalling shortages with a budget of 8,161,000,000 rupees in 1963, doubling the previous annual allowance. Six new infantry divisions were raised, all of them kitted out for mountain warfare and supplied with American and British equipment. Civilian interference in military matters was reduced, but Malik's Intelligence Branch bugged and spied on the senior officers in fear of a *coup d'état*. It revealed how little Malik understood about the ethos of integrity and service that prevailed amongst India's officer corps.

Domestically, the fervour of the war effort petered out soon after the Chinese cease-fire and with it any semblance of heightened national unity. The Communist Party of India split between the Maoist and the Soviet interpretation of Marxism under the strain of the conflict, but other political alignments were unaffected. Much was made of the strength of the Chinese in Indian appraisals of the conflict, along with their stealth, and there was a good appreciation of the difficulties posed by the terrain and the climate, but few were prepared to acknowledge their own errors. The only morsel of comfort was the blatant fabrication by the Chinese propagandists to the effect that their 'border guards' had been attacked on 20 October and their response had been one of self-defence. It was obvious to everyone that it was the regular army, the PLA, and not a border militia that had launched such a sustained offensive.[33]

The Indian defeat was due to four crucial factors. One, there was over-confidence in India's military power. Two, deployment was hampered by the terrain and the weather, and insufficient attention had been paid to logistics. Three, training levels in mountain warfare were low and equipment inadequate for the theatre of operations. Finally, the strategy of 'penny-packeting' detachments was militarily unsound, and served only a flawed political agenda.

The damage to India's international status was the most significant outcome of the conflict. There was no doubt from the attitude of the Non-Aligned countries that India had forfeited its assumed leadership of the movement. There was criticism of its association with the West and it was evident that India was weaker, militarily and economically, than its previous posturing had suggested. Indeed, despite India's wounded cries of betrayal against the NAM members, its praise for Western support showed just how weak India really was. Over three years, India was dependent on the influx of American and British equipment and weapons (France also offered support, but insisted that India should pay for it). Roger Hilsman, a member of the American military mission, noted that it must have been difficult for Nehru to 'greet Americans over the ruins of his long-pursued policy of neutralism'. In the final analysis, however, the border war was a damaging episode for India, and Nehru must shoulder at least some of the responsibility for it. But worst of all, it convinced Pakistan's high command that India could be defeated decisively. Just three years later, they seized their opportunity.

Chapter 7

The India–Pakistan Wars of 1965 and 1971, and the Bangladesh War of Independence

The advantage of a regional study is that it permits an analysis of two conflicts that are often seen as distinct, but which were, in fact, intimately connected. The India-Pakistan War 1965 was a prelude to the larger conflict of 1971, which, although often subtitled the Bangladesh War of Independence, was contested as determinedly on the western frontiers of India and Pakistan as it was in Gangetic delta of the former East Pakistan. The second war was especially significant for Pakistan since it cut the country in half, an event that was to have immense psychological and strategic implications. The wars deepened the divide between India and Pakistan, persuaded India to move closer to the Soviet Union diplomatically, and antagonized relations between the United States and South Asia. What was striking was how important international pressure could be in controlling the military aspirations of the protagonists. Both India and Pakistan based their strategic objectives on the anticipated speed of foreign intervention, and the 'good offices' of the United States, Soviet Union and United Nations were instrumental in ending the fighting. Unfortunately, the good relations established in 1971 between India and an independent Bangladesh were not to last, although they were not so embittered as the negotiations between Bangladesh and Pakistan, particularly over lingering accusations of genocide and the question of 'Bihari' refugees. Most significant of all perhaps was the Simla Accord. Ostensibly designed to end the conflict between India and Pakistan, it failed to bring any lasting peace to Kashmir. Given the precedent for escalation by both sides in these two wars, and the failure of the Kargil operations of 1999, the legacy of this period is significant.

THE WAR OF 1965

Soon after the conclusion of the India–China border war, India and Pakistan had begun negotiations on the future of Kashmir. However, the five-month talks (27 December 1962–May 1963) made little progress. Zulfikar Ali Bhutto, Pakistan's Foreign Minister, became convinced that Pakistan had the potential to become South Asia's leading power. When Nehru died in May 1964, Bhutto regarded his successor, Lal Bahadur Shastri, as a weak individual who might be overawed by a show of force. Furthermore, Bhutto believed that the Indian Army, recently defeated by China, would be demoralized and less able to offer resistance. There was also a sectarian agenda. Between 1962 and 1964 there had been serious disturbances by Hindus against Muslims in East Pakistan that had sparked retaliatory communal violence in West Bengal and Bihar. In Kashmir, Bhutto was convinced that the people had become alienated by the Indian government and would welcome an attempt at liberation. Crucially the Pakistanis calculated that the international community, which had shown little interest in India in 1962 or in the Kashmir negotiations, would turn a blind eye to Pakistan's military pressure, particularly if operations were short and decisive, or even clandestine in nature.

During planning for its military campaign the outbreak of fighting in the Rann of Kutch resulted in minor military successes and a somewhat long-winded international reaction (Despite a cease-fire on 30 June 1965, after 170 sittings the minor adjustments to the India–Pakistan border in Kutch were not finally settled until 1968.) This seemed only to confirm Bhutto's assumptions. Consequently, more ambitious operations in Kashmir were set in motion. Thousands of tribal militiamen, recruited from Azad Kashmir and grouped as *lashkars*, were to infiltrate the Indian portion of the province. Their mission was to disrupt communications networks, attack military installations, and command and control centres. Airports, river crossings and strategic road links were to be captured. In addition, the local Kashmiris were to be enlisted to force the Indian security forces to withdraw through demonstrations. The plan was that, if further military assistance were required, regular troops of the Pakistan Army would cross the border in support of the 'revolutionary government' being established in Srinagar. With this in mind, Pakistan raised extra troops and reinforced its irregular forces to *circa* 100,000 men.[1]

Whilst officially denying any involvement, Pakistan launched its irregulars across the border in Operation Gibraltar on 5 August 1965. It soon became apparent, however, that the Kashmiri population had no intention of 'rising' in support of paramilitaries, especially when the Indian security forces showed no sign of weakening. The first 5,000 infiltrators met some determined resistance. Captured paramilitaries confessed to being trained by the Pakistan Army for at least six months prior to the operation and several admitted to being officers in the Pakistan regular army on secondment.[2] General Nimmo, the UN chief military observer, confirmed that the guerrillas were Pakistan-trained. There were about eight forces in total, each one subdivided into six groups of 'Mujahideen' numbering 110 men each. Despite their clandestine nature, by the end of the month it was clear that their tactics were not working. Bhutto therefore decided to move Pakistan regular forces in support of the Kashmir 'insurgency'.

The aim of the offensive, code-named Operation Grand Slam, was to cut off the Indian forces in Jammu and Kashmir from reinforcements and supplies in the south by striking at Chhamb. It was based on the assumption that India would be reluctant to expand the conflict, and, if taken by surprise, Shastri might simply capitulate. Pakistan's forces did indeed achieve an element of surprise, but as their tanks and mechanized infantry advanced towards Chhamb and Jaurian, Indian troops quickly recovered. Shastri unleashed the IAF (Indian Air Force), not just to disrupt the armoured thrust, but also to strike targets inside Pakistan. An armoured counter-stroke was authorized in the direction of Sialkot and Lahore, the capital of Punjab.

The fighting was short but intense with heavy casualties on both sides. Indeed, both sides lost almost 30 per cent of their armour in the

22 days of combat: 12,500 Indians became casualties, 2,700 of them killed and a further 1,500 taken prisoner or missing; Pakistan lost 3,000 killed, 2,000 prisoners and missing and *circa* 9,000 wounded. In the air, India's ageing aircraft (Gnats, Hunters, Mysteres, Vampires, Canberras, Packets, Dakotas and Austers) performed badly with estimated losses of 59 planes. Pakistan, with more modern F104s, F86s and Sabres, lost 43. The fighting was not confined exclusively to the west, however. The IAF managed to bomb Chittagong in East Pakistan whilst the Pakistan Air Force strafed air defences and air bases in West Bengal and Assam. It should be noted that both sides dispute the statistics on losses and exaggerated claims were made to 'prove' military victory in what was actually an indecisive conflict.

India's strategic aims were modest – it aimed to deny the Pakistan Army victory, although it ended up in possession of 720 square miles of Pakistani territory for the loss of just 220 of its own. Despite later accusations that India intended to overrun Pakistan and 'undo partition', or, at the very least, capture crucial Pakistani cities like Lahore, the military objective was to relieve Akhnoor, defeat the thrust against Chhamb and apply pressure by crossing the border in the direction of Lahore. The operations were marked by caution, especially since it was known that Lahore was well defended and that street fighting would be costly. From a strategic point of view, India had managed to deny Islamabad its objectives. Having suffered heavy losses, it was clear that further fighting would not produce the required political outcome in Kashmir. The fact is that Shastri had not shied from escalating the conflict and the morale of the Indian Army had not collapsed. However, with China threatening 'retaliatory action' on the northern border for 'over 56 border violations' in support of Pakistan, Delhi was just as eager to close the conflict.[3]

The United States was in an unenviable position. As the supplier of much of Pakistan's military equipment, including radar, armour, surveillance and communications systems, the Americans were criticized by Delhi for not cutting off its aid immediately. On the other hand, America was accused of not supporting its ally Pakistan vigorously enough when India retaliated in the Punjab. In fact, the United States was disappointed that its offers of support in the wake of the border war with China had not produced better relations with India and it still regarded Pakistan as its primary ally. Nevertheless, Dean Rusk, the Secretary of State, advised Chester Bowles, the US Ambassador in New Delhi, to take an even-handed approach and to rely on UN mediation. The UN Secretary-General, U Thant, had already been shuttling between the capitals with marginal success when the Soviet Union offered to broker a peace settlement at Tashkent. The Americans were delighted since they would not have to handle the delicate negotiations themselves, and, with a cease-fire holding by November, the Tashkent conference went ahead with Indian and Pakistani approval in January 1966. The Soviets were not acting without a degree of self-interest, however. The Tashkent conference was seen as the first step to improving relations with a number of states across the region so as to acquire energy resources and even warm-water port facilities on the Indian Ocean. Even though Shastri died during the talks, India got the best deal. Initially Pakistan tried to argue for the liberation of Kashmir on the basis of self-determination, a diplomatic solution to its failure to gain its military objectives, but India really achieved more by insisting on, and achieving, a restoration of the *status quo ante bellum*.[4]

After the Tashkent Conference, Bhutto tried to blame the defeat and 'surrender' negotiations on President Ayub Khan. Demonstrations, the most strident by war widows, added an emotional dimension to the protests, and rioting broke out in several major cities. There was widespread anger because the Pakistani people had anticipated victory, but the failure of the war of 1965 seemed to epitomize the failings of Pakistan's political leadership. By the middle of the following year, Bhutto had resigned from the government and gone into opposition. In 1967, following an assassination attempt on Ayub, Bhutto was arrested, sparking more nation-wide disturbances. The situation became so critical that Ayub stepped down and was replaced by the Chief of the Army Staff, General Yahya Khan. Yahya Khan's agenda was essentially to suppress the calls for democracy in West Pakistan, but increasingly in East Pakistan too.

The existence of a single bifurcated state, known as East and West Pakistan, was a post-colonial anomaly. Emerging from the Muslim League's struggle for independence from the British, it was defined only on the basis of what it opposed, namely that Muslims should not belong to a Hindu-dominated India. Beyond religion and the legacy of struggling for freedom, the two halves of Pakistan had little in common. In fact, the creation of Pakistan was a contradiction that can be explained only by the ambitions of the Muslim League and their rivalry with the Indian National Congress. The sole way of creating a separate state from India had been to define a national identity on the basis of religion – Pakistan was to be based on 'Pan-Islamic ideals' – but it was soon clear that the architects of the new nation state were eager to assert a secular constitution. If Pakistan was to be a secular country, there seemed little justification for its secession from India; being a 'Muslim state' was therefore a means to another power-political end. Jinnah had been eager to see strong deliberate leadership and resented the rabble-rousing tactics he saw in the Indian National Congress. In Ziring's words he wanted to 'wean the illiterate masses from the religious obscurantism so illustrated by the subcontinent's caste-ridden society'.[5] He endured the strongest criticisms from the Deobandi school of Islam and the *ulema* clerical elite led by Maulana Abul Kalam Azad, in his desire to create a moderate nation state that left millions of Muslims in Nehru's India.[6] That the Muslims of Pakistan did not constitute one homogenous nationality became apparent when East Bengal broke away from Pakistan: it demonstrated that national unity based only on religious conceptions of the state, however moderate, could not prevent disintegration.

East Bengal was a predominantly rice and jute-growing region suddenly cut off from the major cities of India that had served as the conduit for its produce and the supplier of its industrial needs. The 40 million small farmers and their families were amongst the poorest in the subcontinent, and they were separated from their new administrative headquarters by almost 2,000 kilometres of Indian territory. Moreover, the province was surrounded on three sides by this potentially hostile country, and the headwaters of the major rivers that fed its agricultural lands were also in India's hands. The presence of the giant neighbour, its weak strategic position, and the outbreak of fighting between India and West Pakistan in 1948 over the fate of Kashmir, which also had a majority population of Muslims, left East Pakistan in a vulnerable position. The situation, however, made Jinnah, and then Liaquat, his successor, even more determined to centralize the new country. Jinnah had demanded that Urdu, a language alien to all but 3 per cent of the population of East Pakistan, be imposed as the official state tongue. The justification for this was that Urdu was derived from Persian and therefore was more 'Islamic', whilst Bangla, a Sanskrit language, was effectively 'Hindu'. Critics argued that Urdu was simply the language of the political elite in the Punjab and the language issue would make it more difficult for provincial personnel to serve in government and therefore diffuse their powers. A series of strikes failed to change the government's mind, but the decision to fire on a crowd of demonstrators on 21 February 1952 was a turning point.

Several students and bystanders were killed in the shootings, which led to widespread anger and the formation of a determined United Front pressure group. Still commemorated as Eukushey February, or Martyrs' Day, it marked the beginning of a Bangladeshi nationalist mass organization. The Awami League, an opposition party led by Maulana Bhashani, had already been established in June 1949, but the events in Dacca radicalized the movement. A youth wing emerged and it rejected the more moderate approach of the former Muslim League members, calling for the nationalization of industry and the abolition of the *Zemindari* (landlord) system of land ownership that had been introduced by the British. The inequalities of state aid fuelled the anger of the activists. Although East Pakistan generated 3,969 million of the exports between 1952 and 1957, compared to West Pakistan's 3,440 million rupees, East Bengal only received 40 million rupees in development expenditure whilst West Pakistan received 80 million rupees (the lion's share of which went to Punjab). By 1967 the disparity had worsened. Whilst East Bengal was producing a trade surplus over the 20 years since independence of 5.7 billion rupees, West Pakistan had generated a deficit of 18 billion rupees. Up to 1961, East Bengal had received just 76 million rupees in aid, whilst West Pakistan had 1010 million rupees. When West Pakistan concentrated on the Indus Basin Accord with India for the management of water resources, and neglected the much-needed flood relief schemes of East Pakistan, including the Farraka Dam barrage project, there was dismay in East Bengal.

The United Front, consisting of the Awami League, Krishak Sramik Party and the Ganatantric Dal, issued a 21-point agenda for the elections of March 1954 and won 227 out of the 236 'Muslim' seats, whilst the ruling Muslim League gained only 10 out of the 309 available. It was a profound shock to the leadership of West Pakistan and prompted the Governor-General to dismiss the Constituent Assembly and proclaim a State of Emergency. Iskander Mirza's presidency tried to use dialogue to create a sense of national unity, but when no solutions were found, martial law was reimposed on 7 October 1958. Political parties were banned, forcing the Awami League underground. General Ayub Khan offered no new solutions to Bengalis except a still-born notion of 'Basic Democracy'. Whilst offering the franchise to an equal number of approved voters in both East and West Pakistan, there was a great deal of condescension about the Bengalis. When martial law was lifted, vocal critics of West Pakistan fell foul of the law. The leader of the Awami League, Sheikh Mujibur Rahman, was arrested and released several times between 1965 and 1970 before being accused of high treason in the Agartala Conspiracy Trial. The agitation for secession he had set in motion escalated when he was taken into custody. Attempts to restart negotiations with the Round Table Conference failed and it fell to General Yayha Khan, Ayub Khan's successor, to produce a permanent solution.

Other than Yahya Khan's unwillingness to share power with East Pakistan, three issues sparked the conflict of 1971: the question of Pakistan's security, the natural disaster of 1970 and the flagrant refusal to accept the election results of that year. After the war of 1965, Pakistan's defence expenditure rose from 19 per cent of its revenue ($473 million) to 32 per cent by 1971. Whilst the size of its armed forces remained at a steady 350,000, it increased the number of MBTs (Main Battle Tanks) to 850 with the bulk of its equipment coming from China and the USSR. The rearmament of Pakistan encouraged India to increase its own forces, and the IAF had 745 aircraft compared to Pakistan's 447, and a million men under arms.[7] What alarmed Bengalis was that the bulk of the armed forces were deployed in West Pakistan. In the 1965 war, the IAF had operated with virtual impunity across East Bengal's skies, and there was a strong sense of vulnerability. What stuck in their throats was having to pay for West Pakistan's security.

In November 1970 the feeling of being neglected was exacerbated by West Pakistan's handling of a natural disaster. The cyclone that swept in from the Bay of Bengal killed in the region of 150,000 to 200,000 people and left approximately two million people homeless. A flood of refugees poured into India, which placed enormous stress on the infrastructure of West Bengal and Calcutta. Despite the costs to India, Delhi offered immediate aid in the shape of medicines, foodstuffs, tents, hospital facilities, medical personnel and helicopters to East Bengal, as did many other countries at the time. Although it was obvious that India's aid would reach the stricken areas first, Yahya Khan turned down Delhi's offer, claiming that it had enough support from the international community already. The humanitarian crisis quickly assumed a political character. The delay to the elections in East Pakistan was seized upon as evidence that Yahya Khan intended to abolish democracy in the province, whilst the government claimed that disturbances made the election impossible until law and order had been restored. In India, there was growing concern about the congestion, pollution and communal antagonism the refugees were causing, and anxiety about how Naxalites, a Maoist terror group from northern Bengal, were exploiting the unrest to further their own cause.[8] In fact, the refugee crisis was about to get a lot worse.

It was the election of December 1970 that brought matters to a head. The Awami League won 160 out of the 162 seats allotted to East Pakistan and they were the largest single party in the national elections. It was a massive endorsement of Mujibur Rahman's policy of seeking autonomy for East Bengal. Bhutto, whose Pakistan People's Party had acquired just 88 seats, refused to accept Awami victory. Declaring that the PPP was 'not prepared to occupy Opposition benches', Bhutto demanded that any constitutional changes must only take place in consultation with the parties of West Pakistan, but he also accused the Awami League of being a pro-Hindu organization that was not only in receipt of Indian funds but was also trying to subvert the Islamic identity of Pakistan. Bhutto argued that he and his party could not attend the National Assembly until his demands were met. Talks between the parties broke down, as Bhutto had intended, and Mujibur upped the ante on 7 March 1971 by declaring that his party would now struggle for independence.

The declaration was the signal for Yahya to initiate a military crackdown, code-named Operation Searchlight. In the opening phase, East Bengal regiments were disarmed and police headquarters were surrounded. Pakistani troops were flown in and the Pakistan Navy unloaded heavy equipment and more men in just two weeks. By the end of the month, Yahya had amassed forces 70,000 strong in East Pakistan. The second phase was the unleashing of the troops. It is believed the ISI may have provoked violent demonstrations to justify the imposition of martial law, but full-scale attacks began on 25 March. All the troops at the headquarters of the East Pakistan Rifles were wiped out. Troops fired into Dacca University, and hundreds of students were killed. Troops set fire to the shanty towns on the city's outskirts, and shot down demonstrators. There were accusations of torture, murder and rape. All the major urban centres were shelled and the loss of civilian life was considerable: accurate figures have never been calculated, but the Bangladeshis often use the term 'genocide' to describe this period.

The Awami League lost their political leader Mujibur Rahman early on: he was captured by Pakistani troops, but a pre-recorded broadcast declared independence. East Bengal military personnel fought back as best they could, assisted by enraged civilians, but the youth wing of the Awami League gradually emerged as a leading resistance force under the title of Mukti Bahini.[9] Charismatic leaders, such as Sheikh Fazlul Haq Moni, Kader 'Tiger' Siddiqui, Tofail Ahmed, Abdul Razak and Abdul Kuddus Makhon, gathered followers who were to become the nucleus of a guerrilla army. An interim government and a radio station were set up in exile in India, but there was little they could do for the 10 million refugees who trekked out of the country to escape the Pakistan Army.[10] That burden fell to India, which was spending some $200 million a month on feeding the refugees, a figure that does not include the generous support of individual citizens in West Bengal. India appealed to the United Nations, insisting that this was no longer a matter for Pakistan alone.

The American senators Frank Church and Edward Kennedy reminded Richard Nixon that American military support for Pakistan was intended to be a shield against Communism, not a tool for the suppression of the people, but Nixon was already committed to using Yahya as an intermediary in secret talks with China, Pakistan's ally. Consequently, the United States did not feel it could take steps against West Pakistan, especially since India had just moved into the Soviet sphere by signing its treaty of friendship. India, by contrast, was already involved. It supplied weapons, equipment and training camps for the Mukti Bahini and some Indian intellectuals advocated direct involvement. K. Subrahmanyam, the Director of the Institute of Defence Studies, was especially outspoken and called for an attack on West Pakistan.

Indira Gandhi was considering military intervention but heeded the advice of Swaran Singh, the Foreign Minister, and General S.H.F.J. 'Sam' Manekshaw, the Chief of the Army Staff, not to rush into action. Manekshaw argued that the army was not in a position to fight and would require months of preparation.[11] In addition, the monsoon would make any operations in East Bengal extremely difficult. Gandhi agreed to a delay, but urged that the time be used to ready the armed forces in case diplomatic efforts failed. Her aim was to see the creation of an independent, moderate Bangladesh, which was free of Maoist militants, and an end to the refugee burden.[12] To do this, she looked for international support, and increased assistance to the Mukti Bahini.

THE INSURGENCY AND THE EVOLVING STRATEGIES

Although the Pakistan Army had taken control of the towns and cities by May 1971, it was unable to capitalize on its success without a political solution. As the year went on, the troops were attacked by an increasingly well-organized resistance. The response was to take a tougher line on the insurgents and their political supporters. Activists, intellectuals and former government staff were rounded up and some were executed. Two paramilitary forces were created: the Razakars and the Al-Badrs, many of whom were recruited, in the hope of safeguarding their interests in the future, from migrants of Bihar and Uttar Pradesh. The enlistment of these forces was to leave a bitter legacy of ethnic antagonism after the war. In international circles, there was deepening concern about the conduct of the security forces, which reacted robustly to raids, ambushes, bombings and assassinations.[13] Although there was a noticeable decline in the morale of the troops, it was clear that the Mukti Bahini alone could not eject the Pakistan Army from East Bengal.

Dixit, a former Indian Cabinet official, justified Indian intervention on the grounds that the United Nations had failed to resolve the issue. He pointed to the widespread sympathy for Bangladeshis in world public opinion, which contrasted with the inaction by governments in the West and in the Non-Aligned Movement.[14] There can be no doubt, however, that national interests were also at stake for India: the destabilization of Pakistan was a cause for concern so soon after the war of 1965. Intervention was made easier by the clashes between Mukti Bahini and Pakistan forces close to the border. Indian artillery supported the resistance, and the Pakistan Army retaliated. A series of enclaves was seized by India along the border leading to further fighting, but neither side officially acknowledged that a state of war yet existed.

In East Bengal, the strategy of Pakistan's Lieutenant-General A.A.K. Niazi was based on the need to fulfil two distinct tasks. First, he had to struggle to maintain internal security against a rising tide of insurgency. Second, he was tasked with manning a frontier defence so as to prevent cross-border raiding by the Mukti Bahini, or a potential attack by the Indian armed forces. He faced a number of problems, however, that made the fulfilment of these objectives somewhat quixotic. Numerically superior Indian forces threatened on the three landwards sides of East Bengal, whilst the Indian navy could prevent any support from the seaward side. Air defences were inadequate and the single squadron of the PAF (Pakistan Air Force) was unlikely to survive against the fourteen squadrons of the IAF for more than a few days. The guerrilla action of the Mukti Bahini made the movement, re-supply and security of ground forces difficult. They also denied Pakistan formations intelligence and exhausted the troops.[15] Brigadier Khan of 14 Division remarked that his men suffered from 'terrible fatigue and sleeplessness'. Furthermore, the monsoon made deployment difficult especially since the province's infrastructure was very weak and several swollen rivers could be crossed only by ferry or the two railway bridges – the Hardinge Bridge across the Ganges (Padma) and the Ashunganj

Bridge across the Meghna.

Nevertheless, Niazi's greatest problem was the shortage of manpower for the tasks he had been given. He commanded just three regular infantry divisions and two of them lacked sufficient artillery, signals equipment and transport. There was one armoured regiment, 29th Cavalry, made up of outdated American M-24 Chaffees and Russian PT-76s. In an effort to convince Indian intelligence that there were more formations in theatre, a number of 'ghost' divisions were created that were brigade strength at best. The ruse failed and merely added to the confusion in command and control that dogged Pakistani forces in the conflict. Niazi believed his primary objective was the suppression of the Mukti Bahini and his meagre forces were deployed accordingly, although Dacca was practically undefended. Describing his approach as a 'forward posture of defence', he wanted to 'seal' the entire frontier, but allowed for screen forces to fall back to 'strong-points' in the unlikely event of a major Indian attack. Beyond this, the idea of an offensive by India was not really considered, and Niazi even forwarded a plan to Army Headquarters for offensive operations against India, in the hope of receiving more men. It was perhaps unsurprising then that Major-General Rahim Khan believed that 'the defeat in East Pakistan was inevitable.'[16]

The Indian strategy was to launch an overwhelming assault on East Pakistan so as to occupy as much territory as possible and to destroy the bulk of the enemy forces there before the international community had a chance to intervene.[17] Three corps under the command of Lieutenant-General Jagjit Singh Aurora were allocated to the task, and each one was allotted a specific zone dictated by the configuration of the river systems: II Corps were to take the south-west; XXXIII the north-west and IV corps the east. The Indian navy were ordered to prevent a withdrawal of the Pakistani forces into Burma, and the light carrier INS *Vikrant* would launch air strikes into the interior in support of the IAF air offensive. The only concern was the possible intervention of China, so a portion of Eastern Command was deployed in defence of the border. One of the reasons that Manekshaw delayed the campaign until late in the year was so that snows closed the passes to prevent Chinese intervention.

The Mukti Bahini was also involved in the planning of the offensive. Its role was to fight in a guerrilla fashion, gathering intelligence and disrupting Pakistani forces in the rear, but, supported by Indian units, some Mukti Bahini also had a conventional role. Each group was assigned a 'sector' and brigade-sized units called 'forces' (namely Zulu, Kilo and Sierra) were organized. In total there were some 100,000 fighters to augment the Indian armed forces. In early December, guerrilla attacks had reached a new level of intensity and the Pakistani troops in East Bengal were in danger of losing control of the situation.

Pakistan, however, would defend East Bengal by attacking in the West. Having already exchanged fire with Indian Army units that had taken enclaves on the border, Yahya Khan gave orders for air strikes to be launched from West Pakistan into India on 3 December 1971 as a prelude to an offensive. In a lightening campaign, he hoped to threaten Kashmir and the Indian Punjab to buy time for American and perhaps Chinese intervention. The speed of the attack was essential given equipment shortages and the fact that its 365,000 men were outnumbered by India's 833,000 strong army. In this way, the internal unrest and insurgency of East Bengal escalated into a major war between India and Pakistan.

THE WAR IN THE EAST

When news of the air strikes on air bases in Jammu, Kashmir and Rajasthan, and on cities in western India, was received, one of Indira Gandhi's advisors remarked: 'The fool has done exactly what one expected.'[18] The Indian armed forces immediately swung into action, bearing down on East Bengal with overwhelming force. Unlike Pakistan, India intended to limit operations in the western theatre by taking a defensive stance (albeit with opportunities for counter-offensive action), in order to concentrate on defeating the Pakistani forces in the east.

In the south-west of East Bengal, Pakistan's 9th Infantry Division was completely outnumbered. It had already lost most of the MBTs of its sole armoured squadron in fighting for the enclave at Garibpur on the border on 21 November, but it was able to offer some stiff resistance to the Indian battalions as they tried to advance on Jessore, the principal town. After two days the Pakistanis broke and fell back towards Khulna in confusion. To the north, on a second axis, the Indian 4th 'Red Eagles' Division managed to neutralize and bypass Pakistani forces on the border. The division, however, was drawn into the pursuit of Pakistani troops and was diverted from its primary objective, namely the capture of the strategically important Hardinge Bridge.[19]

In the north-west there were fewer river obstacles and both sides deployed the bulk of their mechanized formations to the area. Pakistan's 16th Division was widely dispersed, which not only made command and control difficult, but destroyed the cohesion of the formation. India's XXXIII Corps, however, was not without its own difficulties. It could not call on its 6th and 20th Mountain Divisions or 71st Mountain Brigade because of the need to guard the Chinese frontier. This meant a reliance on one axis of advance from the west by 20th Division, but this formation was held up by the determined defence of the border village of Hilli by Pakistan's 4th Frontier Force. The fighting lasted from 24 November to 11 December, until Lieutenant-General Thapan used 340th Brigade to outflank the border defences to the north.[20] Despite sporadic resistance in a few small pockets (mainly the urban centres), Pakistan's 16th Division was broken by the manoeuvre and the front collapsed.

In the north and east, Indian units had first to break through Pakistani forces that held the border, and resistance was again tough. Once the defence line had been pierced, however, there was no question of Niazi being able to fall back on his projected 'strongpoints'. Instead, it was just a question of Indian forces racing towards Dacca to bring the war to an end. At Kamalpur, the 31st Baloch Regiment held out for three weeks until its supplies of ammunition and food were exhausted, seriously delaying the Indian advance. At Ashuganj, the Pakistani 27th Brigade managed to hold up India's IV Corps, and destroyed the vital bridge. General Sagat Singh, however, used his initiative to launch an improvised crossing of the Meghna using helicopters and a motley collection of river vessels so as to push on to the capital. In a similar vein, India's 23rd Division made a second improvised crossing at Daudkandi. The brigade commander likened his final advance on Dacca to a 'Mughal army of yore . . . we marched northwards helped and surrounded by civilians'.[21] Moreover, Mukti Bahini attacks, and an airborne drop, seriously disrupted Pakistani resistance. The only disappointments were logistical problems. Indian troops were simply unable to supply their forward units because of the country's poor infrastructure, and, as senior Indian officers admitted, had the Pakistanis been able to contest the river crossings, the outcome of their offensive might have been quite different.[22] Indeed one problem that sprang up in the sector was the temporary isolation of the 4/5th Gorkhas who had been heli-lifted to the outskirts of Sylhet. Astride the main axis to Dacca, the Gorkhas found themselves counter-attacked before 'Echo Sector', a Mukti Bahini formation, could assist them. Nevertheless, three separate Indian units converged on Sylhet and the Gorkhas were relieved. Pakistani resistance was thus quickly neutralized.

The final drama of the eastern sector was around Chittagong. India's Special Frontier Force, assisted by Mizo tribesmen, managed to cut off any chances of Pakistani units retreating to Burma by blowing bridges and tying down regular units. In fact, no such withdrawal had been contemplated and only a handful of helicopters fled across the frontier. A somewhat unnecessary Indian amphibious landing was attempted at Cox's Bazar but failed, although it had no influence on the outcome of the campaign. On 16 December Bangladesh was liberated when Niazi, who had previously stated that he would 'fight to the last man', signed the instrument of surrender.[23]

Niazi had misled the army headquarters in Pakistan by a series of optimistic reports during the fighting, but he complained that he had not been kept informed of operational decisions in the west. Several senior officers, including the Commander-in-Chief of the Pakistan navy, only learned of the attacks of 3 December from the newspapers.[24] The breakdown of communications continued down to a tactical level. Hastily formed militias and paramilitaries in East Pakistan were isolated and deprived of command and control by guerrilla and IAF action. Some Pakistani units fought well, despite the odds, but their deployment and the nature of the terrain told against them. Given their numbers, at best all they could have been expected to achieve was a delaying action.

The character of the war in the west was quite different. In the north, the mountainous province of Kashmir, with narrow valleys hemmed in by exposed or thickly forested slopes, made movement difficult. The high altitude of the most northerly section proved as exhausting and dangerous of the conflict. In the south, the Great Thar Desert presented its own problems. A sparse infrastructure, shortages of water, minimal manpower and vast distances hindered both sides, although the fighting here was decided as much by airpower as ground forces. In the centre, large formations slogged it out on a plain dissected by watercourses and fortified villages and towns, suffering high casualties for relatively little gain.

The plan for the Pakistani forces was to probe the Indian Army in the Chhamb area in order to draw in their reserves. A main thrust would then be launched by II Corps, hooking northwards towards Ludhiana from the border. Other 'off-balancing' attacks would be made along the border so as to conceal the main thrust, although a probe in the south went so disastrously wrong that the whole concept of operations, centring on II Corps attack, had to be abandoned. In fact, communication problems were exacerbated by the fact that the Pakistan Army was also embedded in the national administration. Command decisions were sometimes delayed because officers were enmeshed in other duties. The Indian armed forces enjoyed a more efficient chain of command and their aim was to maintain the defence of the border whilst making two offensives into Pakistani territory. One was to be made into the Shakargarh Salient to disrupt any northward thrust towards Jammu. The second was to be made across the desert to secure the 'green belt' of the banks of the Indus near Hyderabad. In the event, neither of these operations succeeded in their entirety.

In the far north, relatively small sub-units were engaged, a situation imposed by the terrain and the logistical difficulties it presented. A hastily raised force called the Nubra Guards supplemented the existing Ladakh Scouts and made a series of attacks on Pakistani posts at high altitude at night suffering almost no loss. The weather, however, seriously hampered 121st Independent Infantry Brigade further south at

Kargil. Pushing against the Karakoram Scouts, five battalions managed to take 110 square kilometres but did not secure their final objective: the confluence of the Shingo and Indus rivers. Driving winds and snow caused 517 casualties through frostbite, far more than the 55 killed and 195 wounded by enemy action. Pakistani losses were similar. South of the Zanskar range, around Tangdhar and Uri, the mountainsides are covered in thick woodland. Here, the atrocious weather and widely dispersed deployments meant that the fighting was sporadic and focused on the capture of small tactical features. By contrast, the Pakistani 12th Division around Punch was more concentrated and managed to use the forested terrain to infiltrate two battalions (9th and 16th Azad Kashmir) across the border prior to a two-brigade assault. Indian surveillance, however, had detected a build up before the outbreak of 3 December and so the infiltration battalions were stopped, contained and thrown back. Accurate, well-co-ordinated and sustained artillery fire was instrumental in the action and the heavy casualties inflicted forced the Pakistani 12th Division to abandon the offensive.

In contrast to the successes in the mountains, the main Indian offensive on the Shakargarh Salient, launched on the 5 December 1971, quickly ground to a halt. India's 54th Division took two weeks to nego-tiate its way cautiously through the frontier minefields, gaining just 13 kilometres in the process. It was then subjected to repeated counter-attacks by Pakistan's 8th Independent Armoured Brigade. Both sides suffered heavy casualties in just two days of fighting. The Indian advance was stalled but the Pakistani forces made no progress in driv-ing back their adversaries either. Just to the north, near Chhamb, the initial Pakistani attack on the night of 3 December had caught India's 10th Division unprepared. After three days of intense fighting, the Indians withdrew behind the River Manwar Tawi, losing two batteries of guns to infiltrating infantry. To the south-east of the river, however, the Indian 26th Division drove several kilometres into the 'Chicken's Neck' Salient in just two days, although it got no further forward by the time the war ended.

The largest concentration of forces lay on the border between Lahore and Amritsar and yet curiously there was little action here by either side. The reason for this was that Pakistani divisions were only supposed to advance once the attack by II Corps to the south had begun, and this attack never came. The Indians, by contrast, intended to remain on the defensive in this sector. At Ferozepur, the larger formations were kept in reserve and the only success was achieved by Pakistan's 106th Brigade, which managed to overwhelm the defences of Hussainiwala. At Fazalka, the Pakistan Army also managed to seize a small enclave, but the II Corps planned assault, under its code-name of Operation Changez Khan, meant that no other forces were committed to follow up their success.

Way to the south, Pakistan's 18th Division was given the ambitious task of protecting a long border opposite India's Jaisalmer, whilst launching an almost unplanned attack. In their path lay the Indian 12th Division which was planning to attack, but which was taken by surprise on 3 December. Although the Pakistani brigades lacked training, equipment, logistical support and, most importantly, air cover, they managed to reach Longenwala. At this point India's 23rd Punjab Regiment put up determined resistance, and an air attack by just four Hunter aircraft of the IAF caused chaos on the long transport columns. Three days later, having lost most of their armour, the Pakistani brigades were in retreat. Such was the confusion that 33rd Division, which had been earmarked for the great II Corps push, was redeployed to cover the gap. Consequently, it was this setback, in a location of no strategic significance, that caused the main Pakistani offensive to be first postponed and then cancelled. The decision caused enormous controversy in the Pakistan armed forces, with some sources citing leadership errors and others arguing that inadequate air cover from PAF was the cause.[25] In another sense, it may just have been a reaction to the success of the Indian Army and the uncertainty of knowing where the bulk of the Indian forces would be committed. With reserves being shorn to fill gaps, the consequences of II Corps attack failing might well have left the country open to an irresistible counter-offensive. Something of that nature could be detected in the operations at Longenwala, but also further south. In the Barmer sector, India's 11th Division, whilst delayed by logistical problems, stormed through the desert to reach the railway junction of Naya Chor. Here it was halted by a combination of an extended line of communication, PAF air attacks and the stubborn resistance of two Pakistan Army brigades. Had this failed, the Indian Army might well have advanced right to the Indus as it had planned.

Naval and air operations caused some disruption to the forces on land, but did not have a decisive effect. The PAF air strikes on 3 December failed to achieve as much damage as hoped, but only 30 sorties were launched instead of the 400 that would have been needed (based on its 250 combat aircraft) to neutralize the IAF and their air defences. The IAF, for their part, started with retaliatory air strikes on PAF bases, but switched to close air support for ground units as the main attacks got underway.[26] This meant that most losses occurred as a result of anti-aircraft fire, rather than air-to-air combat. The Indian navy's air arm was also primarily engaged in striking ground targets, and missiles were launched against Karachi, oil installations and Pakistani shipping. The navy's main task was blockading the Pakistan fleet in its harbours and in this it was successful, losing only the frigate INS *Khukri* to a Pakistan submarine attack. Pakistan's naval losses were heavier: the submarine *Ghazi* exploded whilst laying mines, and a destroyer and ten small gunboats were sunk.

The Indian strategy of winning the war in the east meant that the fall of Dacca brought the conflict to an end. From 20.00 hours on 17 December, India announced that its cease-fire would also apply to the western theatre. In fact, India was eager to end the conflict before there was any foreign intervention. Already the United States had despatched a carrier fleet to the Bay of Bengal to demonstrate its desire to protect Pakistan from being overrun, and to send a signal to China that it was willing to support their mutual partner. The fleet's movements, however, were widely seen in India as irresponsible 'nuclear gunboat diplomacy' and an unwelcome threat in the hour of victory.[27] Coming within weeks of the Indian Treaty of Friendship with the Soviet Union, the affair marked a nadir in Indo-American relations. Ironically, many Pakistanis were convinced that America was insincere in its support, having failed to defend the country when it was under Indian attack.

Despite some desultory fighting in Kashmir, the Simla Accord, which ended the war, enabled Pakistan to recover most of the territory it had lost during the fighting, except, of course, Bangladesh. Pakistan was also able to get back its 93,000 prisoners of war, although some prisoner exchanges were not completed until 1974. Pakistan was able to prevent any changes to its stance on Kashmir, since the Line of Control established by the United Nations became an almost permanent division of the state. Internally, however, the war of 1971 had serious repercussions. There was universal disappointment in the outcome of the fighting, but, at the same time, an almost universal feeling that India intended to overrun West Pakistan as it had done in the east. There was considerable resentment that India had armed the Mukti Bahini and therefore the determination to fight for Kashmir was even more intense. Islamists argued that Bengalis were not really 'Muslim' at all and that Pakistan was better off without these 'Hindu' elements.[28] In domestic politics, Bhutto managed to shift the blame for the defeat and became the Chief Martial Law Administrator in 1972.[29] But there was no hiding the fact that its economy was damaged, its army was close to collapse, the concept of a united Muslim nation was discredited, its influence over Kashmir was weakened and its chief rival, India, was triumphant.

Strategically, despite the loss of resources, Pakistan's security situation had actually improved, particularly since India's relationship with Bangladesh deteriorated in the late 1970s. The myth, however, that the Pakistan Army had not been defeated, just betrayed, could not conceal the fact that the army had failed in a number of respects. It had no clear political objectives beyond repression and this policy had merely fostered an armed resistance movement. Whilst that movement could not dislodge the Pakistan Army on its own, there was little chance of the insurgency being defeated when the population was so alienated. India's backing for the Mukti Bahini, and then its armed intervention, had not been fully appreciated and consequently strategic planning was weak. Communications, command and control were also poor, and the army found that it was unable to fight a war in two theatres whilst also trying to run the civil administration.

The legacy of the war was that the Kashmir dispute was not resolved and India's hopes for a more quiescent neighbour to the north-west were not realized. Pakistan continued to be accused of a genocidal policy in Bangladesh, although Musharaf's apologies in 2002 went some way to calming the critics. There is still no progress on the fate of the 'Biharis', those who fought on the Pakistan side, still living in refugee camps in Bangladesh thirty years after the conflict ended. Thus the results of the war have been fossilized to some extent in these two phenomena: the Line of Control and the question of refugees. Ironically, the lesson that the Pakistan Army learned, that the mistreatment of civilians generates insurgency, seemed to have been lost on the Indian security forces in Kashmir. Since 1971 it has been Pakistan that has fuelled the conflict there by supplying the guerrillas. Unlike the war in Bangladesh, there will be no flying columns sweeping towards Srinagar to 'liberate' the people. Unfortunately, there is a risk that an internal dispute could rapidly escalate into an inter-state conflict, just as it did in 1971.

Chapter 8

Afghanistan:
The Soviet Occupation, 1979–89

On the pine-forested slopes above the Kunar River, and accessible only by mountain tracks, stands the settlement of Kerala. Just 20 kilometres to the east is the Pakistan border. The 5,000 inhabitants of Kerala were Pushtuns, and the border, an artificial creation of the late nineteenth century which had divided them from their ethnic brothers, meant little to them. Remote from the affairs of the Afghan state, the Pushtuns had little sympathy for the 'kafirs', or unbelievers, who had recently seized power in Kabul. They had flatly refused to support the new Communist government and freely supplied the resistance fighters – the Mujahideen. On 20 April 1979 a motorized unit of Communist Afghan troops and military police came to Kerala: the atmosphere was ominous. Khalil Ullah, a teacher, noted: 'They knew very well we had been secretly giving the Mujahideen food, ammunition, shelter and money.'[1] Nevertheless, no one had foreseen what was about to happen next.

Summoning all the menfolk to a *jirga* (meeting), the troops and their Soviet advisors tried to get the men to shout Communist slogans. They replied defiantly: 'Allah o'Akbar!' Ordering them to kneel, the troops lined up behind. Some of the men began to pray. Seconds later they were all machine-gunned, the staccato bursts echoing through the hills and valleys. A bulldozer immediately buried them, including those that were still moving. The troops then moved through the settlement, dragging the remaining men from the mosque and the houses – and despatching them in short order. In total, 1,170 unarmed men were murdered. The stunned survivors, who had been out in the fields at the time, and the women and children, stumbled over the border into Pakistan a day or so later.

The massacre at Kerala was one of the first to be reported to the Western media, but it was not an isolated case. Across Afghanistan during the bloody years of occupation, scores of civilians were bombed, killed in cross-fires, tortured and executed. Estimates of the total figures vary, but even a conservative assessment would reach several hundred thousand. Noor Ahmed Khalidi believes that the numbers killed in the war between 1978 and 1989, the year the Soviets withdrew, was 876,825.[2] A further 1.5 million were, according to the World Health Organization, permanently disabled. The numbers suffering from psychological trauma have never been calculated. At the height of the conflict, some six million people were refugees outside the country, but internal displacement was also common. The damage to the infrastructure was catastrophic. Bridges, roads, schools, hospitals and thousands of other buildings were wrecked. Critically, the irrigation channels, on which the staple wheat crop is dependent, were often destroyed in the fighting. These statistics suggest a war of great intensity, but it was one fought without decisive engagements. Rather it was one of escalating violence and bitterness, as much a civil war as an interstate conflict between Afghans and the Soviet Union; it was also a war in which the Afghan state, a precarious edifice, was destructured, layer by layer, until authority collapsed completely. It was for this reason that the war did not end in 1989, and a new period of 'Keralas' unfolded.

Although the Soviet invasion of Afghanistan produced a penumbra of books and articles, it is only since the opening of the Soviet archives, after the collapse of the USSR, that a full history of the war can now be written. These new sources have, in many cases, reinforced assumptions in the West about the conflict, but new interpretations are also possible. The Soviet invasion was not, as right-leaning observers at the time believed, the inevitable march of Marxist-Leninist expansionism into the Middle East. The sources instead suggest decision-makers of the Soviet regime, devoid of checks and balances, making a series of

—

miscalculations and blundering into a military occupation. That occupation rapidly degenerated into a civil war, and a failure to resolve the conflict caused a radical reassessment of how the Soviet Union conducted not only its foreign policy, but its domestic affairs too. The USSR's decision makers displayed a stunning ignorance of the complexities of Afghan politics. Despite decades of peace and the existence of a state, Afghanistan is, to borrow Metternich's phrase, more of a 'geographical expression'. It is made up of ethnic groups, clans and networks (*qawm*) that are more or less porous. The majority are Sunni Muslim, but there are significant minorities of Shias, such as the Hazaras and those near the Iranian border, as well as Hindus, Sikhs and Jews. Even amongst the Sunnis there are differences in religious observance, and tribal traditions. Local village mullahs, who sometimes exercise a degree of 'political' authority in Pushtun areas, have long held ideas at variance with the intelligentsia of Islam. Moreover, decision making is equally complex at a local level. In some areas, tribal notables or village *maliks* hold sway, but the democratic *jirga* or *shura* (council) is just as often the respected authority. Within this milieu, loyalties to family and clan overlap, and prominent individuals can be lobbied or persuaded. As far as its international borders are concerned, these were imposed by external powers throughout the nineteenth century and there are significant numbers of Afghans who share affinities with the Baluchis and Pushtuns of Pakistan, or the Tajiks, Uzbeks, Turkmen and Kyrgyz of the Central Asian republics. This fragmented society was held together by a state structure that was frequently authoritarian, but its political elite commanded little loyalty.

It was as a result of declining state revenue and rising costs that Mohammed Daoud, the Prime Minister, was replaced by a movement called 'New Democracy' in 1963. Almost immediately, corruption and nepotism stalled chances of reform and a famine sealed the fate of the new government. The monarchy was overthrown in a coup in 1973 by Daoud, but, in an attempt to legitimize his actions, he referred to the coup as *inquilab* (revolution). This had the effect of removing the one symbol of unity the country had enjoyed, namely the king, Zahir Shah, and giving licence to Daoud, and whoever wanted to succeed him, to use state violence to secure power. Daoud enlisted the support of the

Communist group known as *Parcham* ('Banner', the name of its news-paper), which immediately caught the attention of the Soviet Union. The Soviets had already had an uneasy relationship with Afghanistan. Despite attempts to establish a pro-Soviet presence, the Afghans had remained fiercely determined to maintain their independence whilst accepting Russian arms and support. In 1955, claiming to support the Non-Aligned Movement, Krushchev visited Kabul to offer arms and economic aid. His real intention had been to match the support the United States was offering Pakistan so as to secure the southern flank of the Soviet Union. The result was that the first military loan of $32.4 million was made in 1956 and this grew to $1.25 billion by 1979.[3] In addition, there were 2,000 Soviet personnel in the country. The change of attitude by the Afghans stemmed from their clash with Pakistan in 1949. A tribal uprising in the North-West Frontier Province of Pakistan had been supported by Pushtuns on the Afghan side of the border. Air raids across the international border incensed the Afghans and they declared themselves in support of an independent 'Pushtunistan'. Pakistan responded by cutting supplies of petroleum and Kabul was forced to look across its northern border to the USSR, exchanging fruits and natural gas in return for oil and financial aid. But that aid was really the beginning of a new dependence. Moreover, the close connection with the Soviet Union encouraged an ideological penetration that would further complicate Afghan politics.

A division in the Afghan Communist movement would dog the Soviet era and contribute significantly to the failure of the occupation. Parcham was one faction led by Babrak Karmal, a Kabuli whose followers were also drawn from the capital. The rival group was the Khalq (Masses) under Nur Mohammed Taraki (until 1979) and Hafizullah Amin, and their men were largely Pushtuns. In theory both factions were united in the Hezb-e Demokratik-e Khalq-e Afghanistan or PDPA (People's Democractic Party of Afghanistan), but Daoud had allied himself with Parcham, emphasizing a split.

The crisis that led directly to the Soviet intervention occurred in 1978 following the so-called Saur Revolution. The chain of events began with a visit by Leonid Brezhnev, the Soviet General Secretary, in 1977. When Brezhnev demanded that NATO advisors be removed from

Afghanistan, Daoud, who was essentially a nationalist anxious about growing Soviet influence, refused. It has never been established if Brezhnev decided to remove Daoud, but the murder of a Parcham ideologue mobilized the PDPA, and, when Daoud tried to have the Parcham leaders arrested, they carried out a coup, the so-called revolution of Saur (the zodiac symbol of Taurus) on 27 April 1978.[4] The presidential palace was stormed by armoured units supported by MIG 21 fighters and Su7 bombers. Daoud and his allies were massacred. A wave of arrests followed, particularly of nationalists and middle-class Kabulis. Executions were carried out at Pul-e Charki prison in Kabul on a large scale. The prison commandant remarked: 'A million Afghans are all that should remain alive. We need a million Khalqis. The others we don't need, we will get rid of them.'[5]

The radicalism of the Khalqi faction, the unwillingness to compromise, and inexperience in government immediately began to undermine the new administration. It became more and more common to rule by decree and to use coercion rather than establish any consensus. Demands for land reform caused disbelief in rural areas and a radical restructuring of gender relations outraged conservative religious sensibilities. Maley comments that the PDPA was essentially a 'movement of rage' whose aim was simply to destroy the old order. But their arbitrary government, intolerance and even brutal massacres fuelled resistance. When Khalqis and their Soviet advisors were attacked by gunmen at Herat on 17 March 1979, to cries of 'Allah o'Akbar!', Moscow grew concerned that pan-Islamic unrest might spread into the southern republics of the Soviet Union. There were discussions about intervention but two factors deterred them: international opinion and the prospect of having to fight the Afghans rather than liberate them. Nevertheless, there was already a precedent for successful armed intervention in Eastern Europe in Hungary and Czechoslovakia. In the end, it was events in Afghanistan that finally persuaded Moscow it had to act.

Hafizullah Amin became Prime Minister in March 1979 and immediately stepped up the programme of state terror to establish control. Secret police brutalities increased and Giradet estimates that some 20,000 were killed in purges or state executions.[6] Attempts to resist led to furious repression. Columns of vehicles simply opened fire indiscriminately on villages suspected of harbouring any fighters. When rebels tried to seize the Bala Hissar fortress in Kabul in August, the secret police were forewarned and they massacred the insurgents. The breakdown of order in Afghanistan, the focus of international attention on the Iranian revolution, and the growing anxiety of Moscow leaders on the deployment of medium-range nuclear missiles around the Soviet Union (which might include Afghanistan if it left the Soviet orbit), persuaded the Politburo that the time had come to intervene.[7]

THE SOVIET INVASION

In late December 1979 Soviet units landed at Afghan air bases as the spearhead for a land invasion from Termez by 360th Motor Rifle Division. On 27 December Amin, who had fled to the outskirts of Kabul, was assassinated by Department 8 of the KGB, and soon after Radio Kabul announced that he had been overthrown. As far as the Soviet armed forces were concerned, this was a short-term measure. They aimed to stabilize the country and deployed accordingly. Following the European model, 40th Army (as the army in Afghanistan was known) secured the main corridors of communication and urban centres. Expecting to see the establishment of a new pro-Soviet regime in Kabul, they made little attempt to expand their control of the countryside: indeed, with only 85,000 men, they would not have been able to do so. The new leader, Karmal, was also expected to comply with the occupation and make arrangements for the improvement of the Afghan Army, the forging of unity in the PDPA, to strengthen the relationship between the state and 'the masses', and to develop the country economically.

The main problem for the Soviet Army was the lack of experience in counter-insurgency warfare. Essentially its strategic and tactical doctrines were centred on conventional warfare and owed much to the lessons of the Second World War. The occupation started from the basic assumption that, without Amin in power, Communist control backed by the presence of the Soviet armed forces would be accepted. In fact, the very existence of foreign troops negated the legitimacy of the

Karmal regime as far as the Afghan people were concerned. Moreover, the Soviet armed forces represented yet another tool of coercion for a party that had already exhibited a ruthless disregard to the interests of the population. To make matters worse, the Soviets did not embark on a hearts and minds campaign so the success of their initial *coup de main* was squandered. Indeed, the Soviet troops had little love for their new posting. Known for its harsh discipline and endemic bullying, the Soviet Army's mistreatment of civilians was almost inevitable, particularly when many Slavs harboured racist beliefs about the Afghans (although it should be noted that Central Asian personnel were far more sympathetic to the local people). When attacked by Mujahideen in their civilian clothes, it was easy for them to assume that all the Afghan people were in league with the resistance. Low morale, high levels of sickness and increasing acceptance of reprisals increased the divide between occupiers and occupied in the years that followed.

The Soviet tactics for dealing with insurgents were singularly ineffective. There was a tendency to measure success in ground taken, and the initial operations consisted of sweeps to 'control' areas. Far from filtering out the resistance fighters, whole areas were effectively cleared, only for Mujahideen to reoccupy them once the Soviets had withdrawn. The levels of destruction inflicted antagonized local people and these methods really just exposed troops to sniping, especially if air support, armour and heavy weapons were not available. In fact, armour was limited by the terrain. Tanks were often consigned to convoy protection, although armoured personnel carriers were used effectively as mobile fire bases to support infantry assaults. The greatest asset was Soviet air power. Helicopters could be used to deploy troops, to transport combat supplies and even retrieve damaged vehicles (which the Afghans were often able to cannibalize to use against the Soviets). The Hind gunship was especially feared by the Mujahideen and was far more useful than the fixed-wing strike aircraft, which could only attack identified targets. The main problem, ironically given the size of the Soviet armed forces, was a shortage of manpower and equipment of this nature. At any point, approximately 35 per cent of Soviet forces were engaged in 'guard duties' of crucial roads, posts and urban centres, limiting their flexibility.

The most effective units in the Soviet campaign were the 'special forces' of Spetznaz and GRU (Military Intelligence). Their culture of devolved command and versatility was copied later in the campaign by other units and they made up 20 per cent of all the forces in theatre by 1989. Eight Spetznaz battalions operated along the Pakistan border, but sometimes the bombing of an area prior to their deployment merely alerted Mujahideen to their presence. Small detachments were wiped out in some cases, but they were able to mount rapid air assault operations and to carry out close reconnaissance work. There were never able to close the Pakistan border fully as ordered, but this was really a waste of their resources. Although unpalatable to current thinking in the West, the defeat of guerrilla forces is really dependent not on territorial acquisitions, but on the 'body count'. The total annihilation of some guerrilla cells, and the steady capture of others, soon demoralizes the remainder. This, in conjunction with the segregation, protection and patient cultivation of good relations with the civilian population, is the hallmark of successful British counter-revolutionary warfare operations since 1945. Instead of winning the support of the civilians, however, the Soviets continued to alienate them by a scorched earth policy. The deployment of mines may have been used to deny access in remote areas, but it also had the consequence of killing hundreds of civilians too.

Nevertheless, the least effective aspects of Soviet tactics were in intelligence and their use of the Afghan armed forces. Whilst four SIGINT units were deployed around Afghanistan, two of these were concerned with external monitoring and the other two were really only able to pick up a limited amount of signals traffic. The main reasons for this were the 'low-tech' approach of the Mujahideen to communications and the mountainous nature of the terrain. HUMINT was really dependent on the information acquired by KHAD (the Afghan Communist secret police) and its KGB supporters. The Afghan army, however, was the weak link in the whole chain. Treated with disdain by the Soviets, some Afghan troops killed their officers or Russian advisors and defected. Others turned into informers for the resistance. The number of volunteers was maintained only through pay and even then 'ghost pay-rolling' was a common scam.

By contrast, the morale and motivation of the Mujahideen were high. Resistance was able to spread and evolve due to the policies adopted by the regime and their Soviet allies, and fighters shared a common desire to protect their country from outsiders and foreign influences. Islam became a unifying badge of association against the atheists in power in Kabul and the Soviet Union. Religion offered the fighters a higher authority and the mobilizing cause of *Jihad*.[8] The idea of Jihad, or struggle, appealed to Afghans at a collective and personal level. In an offensive conflict, the *Fard Kafiya* was an obligation to serve, whilst in a defensive war, the individual is compelled to protect under the *Fard 'Ayn*. Neither of these concepts, in fact, meant that all Muslims in Afghanistan would take up arms against an invader. There are, as in all societies, many reasons why men enlist to fight and collaboration is often just as common as resistance in episodes of imperial occupation. The defence of Islam, however, gave the resistance a moral dimension and encouraged a sense of self-sacrifice.

The emphasis on Islam had further consequences. It encouraged other Muslims, including political elites in Pakistan and Saudi Arabia, to participate in the conflict. In Afghanistan itself, village mullahs were given new prominence, although this was perhaps only a reflection of a stronger sense of community heightened by an external threat. The loss of family or clan members was, in fact, just as effective at mobilizing the survivors, and those who had lost all their property saw little option but to fight. For the young men displaced into the refugee camps, there was little to do but wage war, especially if it offered the chance to improve one's social standing, and more pacific roles, such as farming, were simply denied them. This militarization of the new generation offered little hope for the future reconstruction of the country.

Despite the unifying effect of religion, however, the resistance remained hopelessly fragmented.[9] There were parties, clan networks, so-called Islamist groups and military bands held together by 'warlords'. Of the Islamists, there were several prominent leaders such as Gailani, Mojadiddi, Muhammedi, Khalis, Hekmatyar (who enjoyed the patronage of Pakistan), Rabbani and Sayyat (who was favoured by the Saudis). Yet the Shia clerics added a rival layer of Muslim resistance under the titles of Behesti, Mazari, Akbari and Mohseni. Nevertheless, even the

Shia were divided. Disputes over the relative influence of the Iranian revolution led to the equivalent of a civil war in the Hazara region until 1990, when Iran urged unity under the new Hezb-e Wahdat organization. The warlords were more than just military leaders, but, in keeping with Afghan tradition, virtual institutions in themselves. The most well known were Mawlawi Haqqai, Ismail Khan of Herat and Ahmad Shah Massoud, the Tajik leader of the Panjshir Valley. Urban resistance movements had little contact with rural movements until quite late in the campaign, and the greater density of secret police made operations far more difficult. In Kabul, in February 1980, 800 demonstrators were killed in a crackdown. Periodic arrests often ended in torture and execution. Nevertheless, the situation was never straightforward. University students, who were often engaged in anti-regime activities, also provided the largest number of informers.[10]

EXTERNAL INFLUENCES

Resistance to the Soviet occupation of Afghanistan was sustained by external powers, including Pakistan and the United States. Pakistan acted as the conduit through which American supplies passed into the hands of the Mujahideen, but Islamabad played a more influential and independent role than any other country. Pakistan became a base from which resistance fighters could mount operations, protect civilians and recruit new personnel. Pakistan's reasons for permitting this situation were complex and rooted deep in the country's history. Essentially, before 1978 Pakistan felt that Afghanistan was in India's orbit. Kabul had blocked Pakistan's request to join the United Nations and there was a concern that, in the event of conflict with India over Kashmir, the Afghans might try to 'liberate' Pushtunistan – their name for the North-West Frontier Province. It was a case of a 'war on two fronts'.

Therefore, after 1979, Pakistan was eager to support any groups that might become more favourably disposed towards Islamabad, including Hekmatyar's Hezb and later the Taliban. General Zia ul-Haq, who had seized power in 1977, was willing to exploit the language of radical Islam to garner support for his regime, so it was no surprise that he seemed to have something in common with the Muslim fighters in Afghanistan. Moreover, in an attempt to win over conservative opinion at home, Zia made much of his support for the Mujahireen, those that had made a religious flight in emulation of the Hajira, in the refugee camps. The camps were not the exclusive sphere of influence of Pakistanis, however. Radical groups, administrators and resistance fighters all battled with each other for the support of the people. Nevertheless, Zia was also exercising *realpolitik*. The USSR was effectively an ally of India and the close proximity of Soviet troops was of little comfort to Pakistan. Given the United States' antagonism against Iran and the USSR, Zia knew that Pakistan offered the only alternative route for the support of anti-Soviet fighters and Zia got, as he anticipated, American aid to the tune of $3.2 billion over six years.[11]

Pakistan's actual assistance to the Mujahideen was channelled through the ISI (Inter Services Intelligence) of the Pakistan Army. To avoid detection by the USSR, funds, arms and supplies were handled exclusively by the ISI's Afghan Bureau without any checks. This autonomy grew, perhaps unsurprisingly given that the regime was a military one anyway, but along with it came an erosion of the army's secular values. Islamist views gained currency as a way of justifying decisions that could not then be questioned. There had already been a precedent for this under Zulfiqar Ali Bhutto, when he had used the rhetoric of radical Islam to win over the Pushtuns of the North-West Frontier Province. The consequence of all this was that Pakistan favoured Gulbuddin Hekmatyar as their protégé in Afghanistan. Hekmatyar, in fact, commanded little loyalty amongst the Pushtuns, even in Paktia, and his effect on Soviet forces was minimal, but what impressed ISI was his ruthlessness. In addition, Hekmatyar carefully stockpiled his weaponry, insisted on the exclusion of Afghan rivals from the refugee camps and concentrated on cultivating his allies in Pakistan. The irony was that Hekmatyar, an anti-American Islamist, was the main recipient of arms, equipment and supplies shipped via ISI from the United States.

The United Nations condemned the invasion of 1979 in Resolution ES6/2, but the veto power of the USSR, a permanent member of the Security Council, meant that no action was taken.[12] Although there was a general willingness to negotiate a withdrawal (a decision that was dependent on the occupying power), the Soviet occupation revealed a fundamental flaw in the United Nations ethos which it has still not resolved. In dealing with a 'government', it actually gave the Soviet puppet regime of Karmal a degree of legitimacy whilst denying the resistance groups any representation at all. This reluctance to deal with 'rebel groups' continues to bedevil the UN in its attempts at conflict resolution.

The Western powers were angry about the invasion and concerned lest the USSR make a further bid for influence in the Middle Eastern oil states. Relations between the East and West deteriorated and talks on Strategic Arms Limitation (SALT II) failed. The United States boycotted the Moscow Olympics, enforced a grain embargo and made available $2 billion of aid to the Afghans. President Reagan's decision, however, to make available the 'state of the art' Stinger surface-to-air missiles to the Mujahideen caused some consternation in the United States because it was so clearly an American weapon system. The missiles had some effect in redressing the imbalance of air power that the Soviets had enjoyed, but there were never enough of them to clear the skies of Soviet aircraft. In addition to the missiles and existing weaponry, special forces teams were also despatched, although it seems it was envisaged that they would perform only a training role in Pakistan.[13]

Saudi Arabia's General Intelligence Service also made available large sums of funding for the Mujahideen, largely in an attempt to contain radical Shias in Iran by supporting the establishment of a pro-Saudi Sunni regime at Kabul.[14] Some Saudis of the radical Wahhabi sect, however, including Osama Bin Laden, made their way to Afghanistan as volunteers. Pan-Islamists, such as the Palestinian Dr Abdullah Azzam, also joined the resistance and fostered the sense that the Muslim world was under attack from all sides. This creed has been the single most important outcome of the war, because it has contributed directly to the development of global Islamist terrorism.

The most intense fighting took place in the central and eastern regions of Afghanistan, perhaps because these were the easiest to reach from Pakistan and the sources of its supplies, arms and ammunition. In 1980 there were major operations in Kunar in March and June, the latter precipitated by the ambush of a Motor Rifle Battalion south of Kabul. The following year the Kabul-Jellalabad road was secured after operations in Sarobi, but, in 1982, Bagram air base was attacked and 23 aircraft destroyed. In Paktia, in 1984, the besieged garrison of Jaji was relieved and for the next two years there were major actions along the border, culminating in the capture of a Mujahideen base at Zawar in April 1986. Despite these apparent successes, the withdrawal of Soviet forces allowed the resistance to reoccupy each area, and the border with Pakistan was never sealed, even in the depths of winter when many high passes were closed by snow.

In northern Afghanistan, the resistance found it difficult to mount attacks across the rolling open terrain of the region. Abdul Qadar, who called himself Zabiullah, claimed to command 20,000 fighters, and he made a reputation for himself for attacks on Mazar-i-Sharif. He was subsequently killed by a land-mine in December 1984. In western Afghanistan there had been major clashes in 1981, and in 1982, in common with other regions, the Soviets resorted to bombing selected areas to 'depopulate' them. In June 1985 the Mujahideen launched an attack on an air base, destroying 20 aircraft. Attempts to retaliate failed and the regime's forces found themselves striking into thin air.

Perhaps the most successful resistance was that mounted by Ahmad Shah Massoud in the Panjshir Valley. Located along the strategic corridor that linked the USSR with Kabul, including the vulnerable Salang tunnel, the Soviets launched no fewer than nine major operations in the Panjshir region. Massoud worked hard to gain the confidence of the civilian population, warning them of forthcoming attacks and assisting in their evacuation to side valleys. Nevertheless, in 1984, after an especially hard winter, Massoud agreed to a cease-fire. Whilst the regime regarded the arrangement as a victory,

Massoud simply used the time to build up his forces and made a break-out to the north so that he could continue fighting later.

Meanwhile the regime continued to falter. Not only did Karmal command no support, even the PDPA remained bitterly divided between its Khalqi and Parchami factions.[15] Worse still, the KHAD secret police, led by Dr Najibullah, was often at loggerheads with the Sarandoy (Interior Ministry) under Sayid Mohammed Gulabzoi, which hampered the efficiency of its internal security work. Khedamat-i Attalatt-e Dawlatti (KHAD), which had originally been set up as AGSA in 1980, and then retitled KAM, was designed to defeat 'internal enemies' of the regime by counter-intelligence, surveillance (including the party, the government and intellectuals), counter-insurgency and operations across the border into Pakistan. Bombs detonated in Peshawar in 1985–6 have been blamed on KHAD, as was the kidnapping of an Australian aid worker and his wife at Quetta, and a vast number of atrocities across Afghanistan itself. Najibullah was a Parcham Kabuli who encouraged atrocities to terrorize the population. His ruthlessness caught the eye of the KGB and he was nicknamed 'the bull' because of his behaviour. Yet, ironically, his methods contributed to the collapse of the order he was trying to assert, and the Taliban, making use of his techniques, later executed him in 1992. Certainly the KHAD atrocities are amongst the darkest in the history of war. Farida Ahmadi, a Kabuli medical student who was arrested for distributing anti-Soviet bulletins, claimed that she was brutally interrogated by six women guards. She was beaten, electrocuted and witnessed the dismemberment of other prisoners. One, she stated, had had her eyes gouged out by a male guard, a point to which she was prepared to testify to human rights hearings in Paris, Geneva and the United States.[16] Mrs Nassery, a female high school teacher, also saw victims of torture. She claimed that a pile of hands, feet and breasts that had been cut off were piled in the corner of her cell.[17] Prisons were frequently used to conceal the murder of opponents and suspects. Most arrests were made in the middle of the night by armed squads. Reasons for the arrests were rarely given to relatives. Yet, despite the atmosphere of terror, even some KHAD agents were working for the resistance and passed on information. Such a system had little chance of success.

To give the regime more legitimacy, Karmal issued a new constitution under the heading 'Fundamental Principles' in April 1980. It avoided reference to the normal rhetoric of revolutionary socialism and instead espoused the values of Islam. A Loya Jirga was convened, but its bribed members were shepherded away from contact with the people and an attempt to resurrect the notion of a foreign enemy by calling for a war of liberation in Pushtunistan attracted little interest. The fact was that the Mujahideen had already expropriated the symbolism of Islam and the regime was still too closely connected to the Soviet Union to gather more supporters. As evidence of Karmal's failure, the Minister of Tribal Affairs was murdered, and the National Fatherland Front, a new brand name for the PDPA, flopped miserably.

Changes in the USSR broke the impasse in Afghan politics. Against a background of worsening East–West relations in the early 1980s, Mikhail Gorbachev was appointed as Party General Secretary. From the outset he was determined to change the Soviet Union, to break *zastoi* (stagnation) with a new spirit of *glasnost* (candour). Gorbachev regarded Afghanistan as a 'bleeding wound', and he had Karmal retired on 'health grounds'. Unfortunately this led to the appointment of Najibullah and the worsening of the situation.

Najibullah's new strategy was the creation of militias that would take on the defence of crucial roads and urban fringes.[18] In return, they were paid subsidies and given greater autonomy in how they controlled their own areas. In this way, Najibullah unwittingly contributed to the destructuring of the Afghan state: a precedent had now been set for the independent action of militia leaders.[19] For the Soviet forces, however, operations in eastern and southern Afghanistan did not diminish. The emphasis was no longer on 'driving off' the population, but the control of towns and communications. In August 1986 there were sweeps into Logar and in May 1987 a major operation was launched to relieve Jaji in Paktia. On 28 November 1987 the largest operation of the campaign, Operation Majistral, was begun to relieve the town of Khost. It involved 10,000 Soviet and 8,000 regime personnel and took a month to complete, but all their positions were abandoned by January 1988. At Kandahar, missile attacks by the resistance were the most effective way of disrupting Soviet air power in an otherwise open landscape. In July 1987 a SAM brought down a military aircraft as it landed at Kandahar airport, but otherwise attacks on the city achieved very little. The fact that fighting erupted between Mujahideen and the Esmatullah Muslim militia added a new bitterness to the war. This conflict was to continue after the Soviet withdrawal.

The greatest psychological blow to the regime came on 17 June 1988 when Qalat, astride the Kabul–Kandahar highway, was captured briefly by the Mujahideen. After four days the town was retaken, but it was a clear indication that even urban centres were not safe. Kabul too was increasingly vulnerable. On 26 August 1986 the Kargha ammunition dump was attacked and there was serious fighting in the Paghman suburbs to clear them of insurgents. A car bomb killed 27 people on 9 October 1987 and the following April a large truck bomb killed six more. A series of rocket attacks into the capital was designed to undermine the people's confidence in the regime and its security, but the cost in civilian lives mounted accordingly. In Herat in the west, there had been episodes of street fighting in 1986 and 1987, but the defection of Major-General Fazal Ahmad Samadi was a serious development for the regime. In the north, fighting continued in the Panjshir Valley, but Massoud managed to attract some of the other rebel leaders to support a united Shura-i nazar-e Shomali (Supervisory Council of the North), which co-ordinated attacks on the regime.[20] It was the fall of Kunduz in August 1988, however, that caught the headlines. Najibullah blamed the fall of the town on treachery, but there was no disguising how serious it was to lose a major settlement on the strategic Kabul–Termez route.[21] It was also poignant that the resistance soon lost the confidence of the people of Kunduz because of their mistreatment of the inhabitants.

Najibullah made no attempt to reunite the PDPA, still split along the Parcham–Khalq fault line, and he had no success in attracting any more support for the regime. Coercion was his only option, and, as the former chief of KHAD, he exercised this authority more thoroughly than Karmal. Moscow urged the adoption of a policy of 'national reconciliation' and this manifest itself as another new constitution in November 1987.[22] Although it permitted private enterprise and the practice of Islam, it offered little of any substance. Opposition members were invited to join the administration, but only in subordinate roles. Moreover, the offer of a 'cease-fire' of six months, subject to the continuing right to deliver decisive blows, failed to impress either the resistance or members of the PDPA, who saw the offer as 'surrender'. Arrests continued and freedom of speech was still not tolerated. Even though Najibullah survived as leader until 1992, he did so only through buying his support, and the verdict must be that 'national reconciliation' was mere window dressing.

The Soviet decision to withdraw was taken in November 1986, although no announcement was made until early 1988. Gorbachev, according to Soviet records, was the main mover, but there seems to have been little dispute from other members of the Politburo.[23] Gorbachev seemed to have hoped for a wider social base of support for Najibullah, which could only really be achieved without an overt Soviet presence. In this respect, the staged withdrawal did not mean an end to Soviet influence. Sarah Mendelsohn believes that Gorbachev may have been trying to build a consensus for internal reforms within the Soviet Union, using the issue of Afghanistan as a platform.[24] Maley disagrees, suggesting that it was 'tactical learning', that is, a realization that the USSR was being beaten in the field, that led to the decision to pull out.[25]

In fact, negotiations had been going on for some time under the auspices of the United Nations. Javier Perez de Cuellar, the Secretary-General's Personal Representative, had orchestrated shuttle talks between Islamabad and Kabul between 1982 and 1984. Iurii Andopov had little interest in accepting UN interference, but fortunately the diplomacy continued, and, between 1984 and 1988 there were proximity talks that led to the establishment of the Geneva Accords.[26] The Accords allowed the USSR to clothe its withdrawal in the language of diplomacy, gave the Najibullah regime a degree of legitimacy, and offered President Zia the chance to ensure that no threat emerged from the Kabuli government against Pakistan. However, there was no provision for the Mujahideen and no reference to the form of government Afghanistan should adopt. The UNGOMAP (United Nations 'Good Offices' Mission to Afghanistan and Pakistan) peace-keeping troops were too few in number to exercise any control and did little more than observe the Soviet withdrawal. The UNOCA, the office for the co-ordination of aid, was simply unable to assist the refugees, who were deterred from returning by continuing conflict. The civil war prevented reconstruction and exasperated donors. As it was, estimates for the cost of mine clearance alone were far too low anyway. The USSR's decision to leave $1 million worth of military equipment for Najibullah's regime fuelled American suspicions about their motives, so the United States decided that its support for the resistance would continue.

Najibullah, conscious that his administration was vulnerable, visited Gorbachev and, in vain, urged radical solutions, including a joint offensive against Pakistan. On the other side, the UN Representative, Diego Cordovez, was no more successful in arranging a cease-fire or in bringing Najibullah's regime to an end. There were simply too many rival groups, and no consensus.[27] The Afghan state was now little more than a coercive tool in hands that no one trusted. Pakistan too was left dissatisfied. Zia was killed in an air crash in August 1988 and so was unable to influence the post-occupation Afghanistan. Despite meetings between Soviet officials and two Mujahideen leaders (Abdul Rahman of Jaimat-e Islami, and Ghairat Bakeer of Hezb-e Islami) in November 1988, there was no progress at building a post-war government. The following year, Pakistan hosted the first meeting of an Interim Government at Rawalpindi, but Saudi and Pakistan intelligence services tried hard to influence the outcome by backing their own factions. With bitter divisions between Sunnis and Shias, and only a third of the Afghan groups represented anyway, in Maley's view the event verged on farce.[28] Pakistan had not achieved the kind of stability on its western border it desired, although it could at least claim to have helped to force the Soviet Union back across the Oxus.

Soviet troops were authorized to use considerable force to 'break clean' from the guerrillas and they used it. It seemed to epitomize the whole campaign: the wielding of violence for no political gain. In fact, the occupation had cost the USSR 60 million roubles, and 13,833 Soviet soldiers had been killed or died of wounds. A further 49,985 were wounded. Added to this was a core of embittered veterans, many of them traumatized. What they left behind was a country in ruins, a state with no chance for reconciliation, no funds and with precious little legitimacy. For the Afghan factions, battlefield victory seemed to be the only way to assert their authority. The Afghan state had finally been exploded and the nation resembled a scattered field of broken shards incapable of reconstruction.

The Soviet occupation of Afghanistan had been a disaster. The crucial problem had not been the lack of numbers deployed, nor even flaws with Soviet tactics and troops, although these cannot be discounted. It was the fundamental misjudgement of what the conflict had been about. The invasion of 1979 was based on false assumptions about how the Soviet Union would be received. It was designed to bolster a Communist regime, but the presence of the Soviet Union's forces merely removed the remaining legitimacy of an already unpopular ideology. Furthermore, the occupation failed to win the hearts and minds of the Afghan people – indeed, Soviet and regime forces alienated the population with inappropriate tactics. The secret police acted with great brutality until the state became little more than an organ of terror. Divided by factions and personal rivalries, even the regime's political elite failed to provide the basic leadership to manage the country effectively. Some critics, like Galeotti, have likened the conflict to America's experience of Vietnam, but Maley argues that, since the United States did not break up in light of the fall of Saigon, the Soviet Union's 'Vietnam' in Afghanistan was far worse.[29] Given the legacy of the war for both sides, it is hard to disagree with this verdict.

Chapter 9
Afghanistan:
The Civil War, 1989–2001

For a decade after the Soviet withdrawal, Afghanistan was fought over by factions eager to assert regional or national control. Overshadowed by other international events, such as the collapse of the Soviet Union and the Gulf War of 1991, at the time few realized the implications that the emergence of the Pakistani-backed Taliban would have for the rest of the world. The fiefdom of Mullah Mohammed Omar, the Taliban leader, set itself the mission of becoming a beacon for the rest of the Muslim world by establishing a 'pure' Islamic society. This radicalism attracted foreign extremists, including Osama bin Laden and others who saw Afghanistan as a base of operations for international terrorism. A series of outrages, culminating in the attack on the Pentagon and World Trade Center's 'Twin Towers' in New York on 11 September 2001, caused a world coalition offensive led by the United States. Within weeks, the Taliban were routed and the United Front established in Kabul. For an impoverished and war-weary people, the painful process of rebuilding a country, including the creation of a state apparatus under UN supervision, could begin. Nevertheless, significant obstacles remain and it is estimated that reconstruction will take at least ten years.[1]

It was perhaps surprising that Najibullah, a puppet of the USSR, survived in power for four years after the Soviet withdrawal. In fact, the Soviet Union continued to supply him, suggesting that maintaining their influence – whilst saving the lives of their troops – was the strategy behind their departure in 1989. Air freight sustained Kabul with essential supplies; the regime received $300 million a month in financial aid; and military equipment poured in, including R17 'Scud' missiles. The Scud was particularly feared by the resistance. It evaded stinger SAMs, and travelled at the speed of sound; it could therefore hit targets without any warning. Najibullah also took the precaution of printing more money, which he could use to buy the allegiance of local militias and their commanders.

He concentrated particularly on the militias that were drawn from the ethnic minorities of Afghanistan, such as Nadiri's Ismaili Shiites and Dostam's Uzbek 'Jawzjani' militia. The brutalities inflicted by these forces meant that there was little chance they could defect to the resistance, but, like all mercenary organizations, their loyalty depended on the continuation of the cash flow. In fact, Dostam had no feelings of loyalty towards Najibullah at all. He established an autonomous region in the north, linking up with the Central Asian republics as they struggled free of the Soviet Union, and ruling as an independent potentate from his 'capital' at Mazar-i-Sharif. Najibullah tried to cloak the obvious disintegration of his power by retitling the party: PDPA was dropped in favour of Hezb-e Watan (Party of the Nation). He tried to foster a sense of nationalism by criticizing the foreign interference of Saudi Arabia and Pakistan, but he also tried to invoke Islam as legitimacy for his rule, arguing that only practising Muslims could serve in the 'new' government. In fact, places to non-PDPA members were limited, and when Khalqis criticized his move in December 1989, he had 100 leading members of the faction arrested.

Evidence of just how narrow Najibullah's base of support had become was manifest in the coup attempt of March 1990. Lieutenant-General Shahnawaz Tenai, the Afghan Army Chief of Staff, tried to seize Kabul and open a route for Hekmatyar's men from the east. The attempt failed, enabling Najibullah to effect a new purge of the party. It has been suggested that the KGB may have been behind the coup.[2] Certainly there was growing criticism in the Soviet Union of Najibullah, but whatever the truth of their involvement, Najibullah claimed that foreign intervention was to be resisted. The change in attitude in the Soviet Union was nevertheless significant since, without its backing, Najibullah's regime was doomed.

Although Najibullah was deeply unpopular, the resistance itself was bitterly divided and unable to unite against him. Without the common cause of defeating foreign Soviet forces, factionalism prevented concerted action. Moreover, guerrilla forces, whilst wearing down Soviet conventional units, were less suited to all-out attacks on prepared defences. This was exemplified by the attack on Jellalabad in the summer of 1989. The Mujahideen made poorly co-ordinated assaults, lacked good communications and were repulsed by well-prepared defenders. They failed to prevent supply convoys coming in from the west and were demoralized by Scud missile strikes. When Arab extremists massacred prisoners, the number of regime defections declined rapidly: the troops decided it was safer to fight it out. After four months of fighting, the resistance gave up and Jellalabad was still secure. The adverse effect on the morale of the resistance was considerable, and there was a suspicion, which Bradsher believes has substance, that Pakistan had tried to promote the offensive as a first step in getting their protégé Hekmatyar into power in Kabul, without consulting other resistance groups. Yousaf and Adkin, however, reject the idea that it was Pakistan's guiding hand that caused the failure, arguing that the Mujahideen were simply incapable of defeating the regime at Jellalabad.[3] Whatever the truth of the case, it proved that the success of the guerrilla resistance was by no means inevitable.

Hekmatyar was certainly proactive in trying to gain power. One of his men, Syed Jamal, murdered 30 of Massoud's leaders in the so-called Farkhar Massacre in a clear attempt to neutralize a rival faction. At the same time, he withdrew from the Interim Government in exile in Pakistan, claiming it needed to be elected if it was to be legitimate: an ironic claim for someone aiming for exclusive power in Kabul. The murder of the Interim Government's Defence Minister was widely rumoured to have been Hekmatyar's work too, although it was never proven. When the resistance captured Khost in March 1991, Pakistan was quick to claim it was Hekmatyar's faction that had been responsible, even though it wasn't, in order to attract Afghan popular support. However, these moves seemed more and more desperate. When a military leaders' *shura* met in Pakistan in 1991, there was a new determination to cooperate against the regime, and the United States agreed to support this military effort by supplying the factions directly rather than through Pakistan's ISI as in the past. This removed Pakistan's ability to fund Hekmatyar from external means, and prompted Hekmatyar to try new stratagems, including the offer to work with Najibullah if he was given a prominent place in the government.

In fact the Bush administration of United States, angered by criticism of its war with Iraq by Hekmatyar and other Islamist factions in Pakistan, had been working more closely with Gorbachev in the hope that the Russian leader could be persuaded to end financial support for Najibullah. There was not, as some have suggested, a deliberate policy of 'abandoning the Mujahideen', but rather a shift in priorities.[4] The Middle East was far higher on the Bush administration's agenda, and arrangements for a political settlement in Afghanistan were rightly left in the hands of the United Nations. Javier Perez de Cuellar, and his successor, Dr Boutros Boutros-Ghali, followed a consistent line in appealing for a broad-based, representative assembly convened after a period of consultation. Some of the resistance leaders, however, simply refused to accept any process, and even the moderate Massoud believed there could be no peace in Afghanistan until Najibullah stepped down. Najibullah was one of the few to accept the UN plan, but only to sustain his position in power. Nevertheless, as Gorbachev faced new opposition from hardliners in a coup in Moscow, then from Boris Yeltsin, the United States finally managed to cut off Najibullah's financial lifeline. The USSR ceased to exist in January 1992, and it seemed it was only a matter of time before Najibullah was deposed by force.

Najibullah's regime began to unravel when he started to replace personnel from other ethnic groups in his administration with Pushtuns. General Momen, a Tajik who had already secretly been working with Dostam, defected, and, with Dostam's help, took Mazar on 18 February 1992. Najibullah knew it was all over and resigned, enabling the UN to step forward with a new plan for the establishment of an interim government. Former members of the regime, however, began to break off in favour of resistance factions for reasons of self-interest. They did so on the basis of religious conviction, ethnicity and opportunism. Parchamis tended to gravitate towards Tajik groups; the Khalqis, being largely Pushtuns, moved towards Hekmatyar, who also represented a radical version of Islamism. Massoud tended to attract moderate Muslims. Crucially, the armed forces were also divided up as commanders swung behind different factions. Pakistan hedged its bets. Whilst the ISI still supported Hekmatyar, it cautiously welcomed the UN plan in the hope of securing a pro-Pakistani authority in Kabul one way or the other. The Interim Government, however, represented by Rabbani and Mojadiddi, rejected the UN proposals and called for the immediate establishment of an Islamic government. Dostam was not prepared to wait for negotiations either. He flew 1,000 men into Kabul's Khwaja Rawash airport on 15 April 1992. forcing Najibullah to flee to the UN headquarters for safety.[5] Massoud and Hekmatyar also moved their own forces to the outskirts of the city.

By late April 1992 resistance groups had begun to negotiate on the formation of a national government excluding, rather poignantly, Hekmatyar. In response, and perhaps emboldened by Pakistan's support in the past, Hekmatyar smuggled fighters into the capital, only to be ejected by Massoud's own men who claimed to be acting in defence of the Interim Government. That month a 51-person delegation had signed the Peshawar Accord, which agreed that Mojadiddi should serve as President for two months after which Rabbani would take over for a further four months. Having set up this authority, a Council of Supreme Popular Settlement would convene to organize elections 18 months later. Hekmatyar, still excluded, greeted the arrival of Rabbani in office with a rocket attack on the capital, killing many civilians. Although Rabbani was thus openly at war with the Hezb-e faction, he tried to compromise by offering Hekmatyar the post of Prime Minister in March 1993. No arrangements were made for the disarmament of his faction, though, and it was difficult to see how the two rivals could ever have worked together. By mid-April Hekmatyar had resumed his rocket attacks on Kabul in an effort to dislodge Massoud's men who supported Rabbani. It was clear from this episode that force, rather than compromise, was still the option most favoured by the various factions. It should be noted, however, that Rabbani's offer was really the result of pressure from Saudi and Pakistani officials.[6] With the army split, the Rabbani government was totally dependent on the cooperation of armed militias. Dostam, though, was angry at being marginalized and his support ebbed away. The Afghan state, such as it was, simply lacked the means to enforce its will and effect a permanent settlement.

Kabul thus became the focus of an intense power struggle. Still the only symbol of a nation state, Hekmatyar tried to erode any faith in Rabbani's authority by firing indiscriminately into the city. Kabul itself was divided up between the key factions. Massoud's Shura-i-Nazar controlled the north, Sayyaf's Ittehad-e Islami (Saudi-backed Sunnis) patrolled the Paghman suburbs, Dostam's Jumbesh-e Meli Islami (National Islamic Movement) concentrated on the Bala Hissar in the centre, whilst on the western outskirts stood Abdul Ali Mazari's Hezb-e Wahdat Shias. On 2 June 1992 Ittehad and Wahdat forces clashed and Massoud moved to try and disarm Wahdat that winter in order to maintain order. Wahdat responded by denouncing the Supreme Popular Council and then, waiting for Massoud's men to be engaged with another Hekmatyar attack, launched their own assault from the west of the city. On 11 February 1993 Nazar and Ittehad fighters joined forces to counter-attack Wahdat, and Dostam joined them, forming the nucleus of what became the United Front. Skirmishes continued, but a massive rocket attack by Hekmatyar in January 1994 failed to suppress Massoud's men, and the following month he fled to Iran.

Between 1992 and 1995 conservative estimates suggest some 9,800 were killed and a staggering 56,100 wounded. There were also massacres of Sikhs and Hindus accused of being pro-Najibullah. The worst atrocity was the Afshar massacre of 11 February 1993 in which large numbers of Hazaras were butchered, although it is still unclear which faction perpetrated it. Assassinations, rape and looting were widespread.[7] Yet despite the intensity of the fighting and the complex-ities of the shifting alliances, Kabul experienced a brief period of peace in 1995. This was largely because Nazar and Ittehad established a short-lived hegemony over the city in 1994, and the Taliban, which had swept in from the south, had failed to enter the city. Wahdat had briefly allied with the Taliban, allowing them to take over their forward positions, but the Wahdat faction had split and some had attacked the Sunni Taliban. When the Nazar-Ittehad forces counter-attacked, they drove the Taliban and Wahdatis out of the city altogether. The Taliban responded to their defeat by executing Mazari. Dostam, who had tired of the internecine warfare of the capital, withdrew north to administer his personal 'khanate' or realm at Mazar.

Outside the capital, regional commanders and local factions clashed with each other in a bid for supremacy. 'Taxing', a euphemism for expropriating any material wealth from the people, proved vital to buy loyalties and assert a sort of baronial legitimacy to rule. Kandahar was especially divided. Jellalabad was governed by Haji Abdul Qadir, who maintained relations with both Rabbani and Hekmatyar, tolerated the opium growers, who provided him with revenue, and allowed Arab extremists, including Osama bin Laden, to establish a presence in the area. Herat was the base of Ismail Khan. With a monopoly of military power in the west, Ismail Khan also enjoyed cordial relations with the Iranians, although he was cautious lest they try to assert their influence. The Taliban later claimed that they had restored peace and order in all these regions, but it has to be said that, other than Kandahar, there was no 'disorder' in any of them.

If there was an absence of fighting outside the capital, it was not necessarily evidence that Rabbani's government was accepted. Factions seemed as remote from each other as ever and the UN's proposals for a cease-fire – and the initiation of negotiations – were ignored. The UN envoy, Mahmoud Mestiri, even went so far as to suggest that Rabbani should be removed in mid-1994, a view that served only to encourage the Taliban and Hekmatyar to further resistance. Moderates maintained a neutrality, preferring to see who came out on top, but each of the factions tended to identify with their own ethnic group, including Massoud's Shura-i-Nazar, which ostensibly supported the Rabbani administration. In May 1996 Rabbani again offered Hekmatyar the post of Prime Minister in an attempt to bring the factions together. Hekmatyar was delighted because his power had been on the wane since the arrival of the Taliban, but Kabulis were alarmed when the new premier began to enforce a strict code of conduct, especially on women. The Taliban reacted to Hekmatyar's appointment by shelling the capital again and launching rockets into the centre. Hekmatyar therefore demanded that Massoud's men redeploy to cover Hekmatyar's bases and lines, a decision that only served to weaken the city's defences because the fighters available were too thinly spread to hold every position. Hekmatyar's acceptance of the premiership did not go unnoticed in Pakistan either. The Pakistan army was convinced that Hekmatyar could no longer deliver what they wanted: a compliant, pro-Pakistan authority in Kabul. ISI swung its full weight behind the Taliban and supported its assault on the capital in September 1996. A last-minute resurgence of interest from Iran served only to deter the United States from supporting Rabbani, and the Soviet Union was now preoccupied with its own domestic issues. Deprived of external support, Rabbani was unable to stem the Taliban tide on his own. Jellalabad fell on 11–12 September and, to avoid a siege, Massoud pulled his men out of Kabul on the 26th. The Taliban entered the city in triumph the next day.

THE TALIBAN

There are two versions of how the Taliban came into existence in the mid-1990s. William Maley believes that Pakistan, which had lost faith in Hekmatyar's ability to deliver a pro-Pakistan government in Kabul, had looked to form a new, Pushtun force recruited from both Afghanistan and from Pushtun regions of Pakistan, including the refugee camps.[8] The architect of this had been Major-General Naseerullah Babar, Benazir Bhutto's Interior Minister and rival of the ISI. The Taliban themselves claimed they had emerged as followers of Mullah Mohammed Omar, a Pushtun from Ghilzai who had wanted a 'pure' Islamist movement to 'cleanse' Afghanistan of war, corruption and debauchery. This interpretation would conveniently conceal the Taliban's motive of seizing power for itself. Mullah Omar was certainly ambitious. He courted foreign diplomats without the approval of the Rabbani government and moved columns of men to Kandahar, often with Pakistan's support. In fact, although Pakistan denied any connection, it was a ruse they had used in Kashmir. Whilst there were attempts to recruit Afghans by appealing to their grievances, the majority of the initial 80,000 personnel were Pushtuns from astride the Pakistani border.[9] Pakistan raised funds, assisted with recruitment, planning, ammunition, fuel and equipment. Some 30 trucks of combat supplies were crossing the border every day. Even aircraft were made available.

Pakistan's reason for supporting the Taliban was to resurrect the idea of protecting its western border in the event of a war with India. When the Taliban were secure in power, it is perhaps no coincidence that the Pakistan army felt confident enough to challenge India in the Kargil Conflict of 1999. A stable Afghanistan, however, also raised the possibility that an oil and gas pipeline could be built from Central Asia, with all the attendant profits of providing terminals on the coast of the Indian Ocean. Furthermore, the Taliban offered the chance to turn the tables on Afghanistan's calls for the establishment of 'Pushtunistan'. Instead of such a state being built at the expense of Pakistan, the new state would be superimposed on Afghanistan, thus diverting or satisfying Islamist and Pushtun aspirations at home. But such a policy was not without its risks. Once in power, Pakistan had precious few means to control its protégé. If the Taliban found the means to be financially independent, there would be no way of influencing their policies at all, and this was precisely the problem in 2001.

The Taliban was a militaristic organization, eager to turn the clock back to an idealized version of Islamic society. Yet such sentiments suggest something conceptually constructive in their ethos and this is misleading. The recruits to the Taliban were disaffected and angry young men, leavened by war veterans of the Soviet occupation. They were Sunni Pushtuns, but augmented with significant numbers of foreign volunteers from across the Middle East, Africa and Europe. Repudiating politics, Omar referred to himself as Amir Al-Momineen ('leader of the faithful') and sought exclusive power, which was legitimized as a 'divine right'. There could be no power-sharing since that would assume that Allah's will was divisible. Omar also made use of the props and rhetoric of Islam, impressing his followers with a dignified piety, but in reality ruling with an oligarchy of friends, who included Osama bin Laden.

The Taliban made use of their ISI and Pakistan military contacts, but they also relied on the support of drug barons and provincial governments. For recruits and for influence beyond the country they made use of networks of Deobandi *Madrassehs* in Pakistan.[10] These religious colleges politicized Islam into a 'fundamentalist' creed and attracted young men. A certain momentum was generated by this flow of recruits and they found themselves amongst idealistic friends who shared radical ideas and were fed a heady cocktail of religious dogmatism and militarist doctrine. This spawned several hydra-like heads: supporters for the radical Jamiat-e Ulema-i Islam party of Pakistan, terrorist personnel for groups like Sipah-i Sahaba (Army of Companions) and Lashkar-e Jhangvi (Army of Jhangvi) and militia soldiers for the Taliban and Harakat ul Ansar that operated in Kashmir.[11] This model of recruiting has also been used by groups that associate with al-Qaeda, although there is a more discerning selection process of the recruits. The delivery of a fiery and uncompromising *Weltanschauung* helps to identify those who are most enthusiastic and likely to join up. Private interviews with a strong emphasis on the value and prestige the individual could accrue then take place before access to specialized training.

In 1996 the Taliban were not fully in control of the country. Massoud still held the north-east, the Hazarajat was relatively untouched and Dostam controlled the area around Mazar. Having failed to secure any deal with the Taliban, Dostam allied himself with Massoud, Rabbani and the Shia leader Mohammed Kharim Khalili on 10 October. This group was joined by Mohseni's Harakat and Sayyaf's Ittehad and adopted the title of Jabha-i Mutthad-e Islami Milli bara-i Nejat-e Afghanistan (National Islamic United Front for the Salvation of Afghanistan), more commonly known as the 'Northern Alliance'. It was significant that all these Afghan groups were united against the Taliban, a Pakistan-inspired organization.

The Taliban, however, engineered a split in Dostam's forces by recruiting Malik Pahlavan as a rival, a move that led to fighting in Mazar, from which Dostam fled in May 1997. Almost immediately, Pakistan announced that it recognized the Taliban as the legitimate authority in Afghanistan, but it was premature. Malik Pahlavan's men clashed with Taliban fighters as they entered Mazar and locals joined in against the 'outsiders'. The battles took on a vicious ethnic dimension as prisoners were slaughtered on both sides. Dostam then returned and repulsed a second Taliban offensive. The Taliban had already forced 200,000 people out of the areas to the north of Kabul to be sure that their operations would not be hindered by civilian insurrection.[12] Nevertheless, in August 1998 the Taliban overran Mazar and massacred large numbers of civilians, mainly Hazaras, in revenge for the deaths of their men the previous year.[13] Survivors state that the killing went on for three days and was led by foreign Taliban fighters under the direction of Mullah Omar's associate, Mullah Abdul Manan Niazi. Several were boiled or asphyxiated by being locked in metal containers in the sun. Thirty patients in a hospital were murdered in their beds. Firing squads toured the streets, and decrees forbade the inhabitants from moving or burying the bodies. Eyewitnesses spoke of dogs tearing at the corpses.

The Hazaras were in fact the target of the Taliban's next offensive, starting with Bamian on 13 September 1998. The city was recaptured by Wahdat in April 1999, but the Taliban retook it in May, and, as at Mazar, killed hundreds of civilians in reprisals. Their advance through the Hazarajat was marked by episodes of great brutality fuelled by fear of insurrection, ethnic hatreds and sectarianism. At Yakaolong, 300 Hazaras were killed, including a large group of civilians who had sheltered in a mosque and which was subjected to rocket fire. Anti-Taliban forces briefly retook Bamian again on 13 April 2001, but they were quickly overrun and the whole region remained terrorized until the fall of the Taliban later that year.[14]

Nevertheless, the anti-Taliban forces of Massoud were the most successful in defying Mullah Omar's expansionism, an important feature in keeping anti-Taliban resistance alive. A series of pitched battles were fought in the Shomali Valley, north of Kabul, in the years 1996–9, and the Taliban resorted to the 'ethnic cleansing' tactics they had practised against Mazar. Crops and buildings were destroyed and populations systematically uprooted. Fearful of uprisings as they spread themselves across the country, the Taliban were eager to assert their control more firmly during these campaigns.

'Security' was the Taliban's primary objective. They claimed to be asserting Sharia law and restrictions on private and public life in order to 'protect' the Afghan people. They expressed a desire to continue the Jihad until there were no opponents left, and they aimed for a 'strong'

Afghanistan that would be 'weapons-free' (that is, not in the hands of any agencies other than their own). Afghans quietly described the means by which this was enforced as *Wahshat* (Terror).[15] Whilst the Koran states that there is no compulsion on belief, the Taliban made sure their laws were strictly enforced often by a 'religious police', the Amr bil-Maroof wa Nahi An il-Mukir (Department for the Promotion of Virtue and Suppression of Vice). Brutal and bigoted, the religious police were ideologically motivated, dishing out summary justice 'pour encouragez les autres'. Television was banned and radio tolerated only as a means of propaganda, prayers and for the broadcast of new decrees. Music, dancing, drumming and all visual representations of animals and people were outlawed. On 10 March 2001 the Bamian Buddhas were destroyed and artefacts in the Kabul museum systematically vandalized. International opinion, already angered by the cultural destruction, soon focused on the Taliban mistreatment of women. Denied employment, many war widows were left destitute. Those who fell foul of the religious police in Kabul could be stoned to death or executed publicly by firing squad. When the United Nations protested, the Taliban claimed that their Koranic law was derived from Allah and therefore could not be criticized or challenged. Islam had been hijacked to serve the interests of a totalitarian despotism, namely the personal rule of Mullah Omar.

Omar revealed a staggering ignorance of international realities in his dealing with the West. When the United Nations refused to accept Taliban delegates in place of Rabbani's representative, Omar condemned the UN as a tool of the West. When energy corporations approached the Taliban, hoping that the new regime in Kabul might ensure stability and enable them to build oil and gas pipelines through the country, Omar expected the corporations to pay for the entire reconstruction of Afghanistan.[16] The talks failed and Omar grew contemptuous of all UN and NGO personnel in the country. Despite UN appeals, the Taliban continued with their economic blockade of the Hazarjat, causing untold human suffering. Staff of NGOs were harassed and it was becoming clear that Omar wanted them all to leave.

Nevertheless, Omar's greatest miscalculation was in his protection of Osama bin Laden. Bin Laden, who inherited considerable wealth, had been influenced as a young man by Dr Abdullah Azzam, a Palestinian radical. During the Soviet occupation of Afghanistan, bin Laden put his beliefs into action, setting up a guest house for Arab fighters and establishing links with Hekmatyar and Sayyaf. In 1989 he established a base at Jaji and founded al-Qaeda, but at the war's end he returned to Saudi Arabia. Azzam's assassination fuelled bin Laden's hatred of all 'Jews', which, in his mind, included all of the United States, but Azzam's poison had already done its work long before his death.[17] What confirmed bin Laden's rage was the stationing of Western troops on Saudi soil during the Gulf War, and, travelling to Afghanistan and Pakistan, he settled in Sudan in late 1991. Osama bin Laden believed that, if the USSR had been defeated by guerrilla action, the same could be done to the West, not appreciating, of course, that the Soviet Union and the United States were two entirely different polities. With no experience of the West, his paradigmatic views were based entirely on the assumption that religious zealotry alone could bring down a super-power. Convinced of his own delusions, bin Laden returned to Afghanistan in 1996 to orchestrate his campaign of terrorism.[18]

Osama bin Laden's presence had an effect on the Taliban. Some were suspicious of the Arab outsider, but many were carried along by the radicalism that he, and other foreign fighters, brought with them. Mullah Omar was concerned that bin Laden issued murderous *fatwas* without authority, although this was likely to have been jealousy since he himself did the same. He must also have known about his reputation for international terrorism after the bombing of the World Trade Center in New York in 1993. Omar, however, felt a certain obligation to host bin Laden because of his previous service against the Soviets and also because of his offer to assassinate Massoud. Moreover, the Pushtun tribal custom of sheltering renegades, *Paktunwali*, could not be overlooked if he was to maintain his own prestige. Finally, it was a question of money. The Taliban were in receipt of Arab money and bin Laden was one of the main benefactors.

Afghanistan thus became a springboard for the training of al-Qaeda and the masterminding of terrorist operations. On 7 August 1998 suicide car bombs were detonated outside the US embassies in Kenya and Tanzania. America retaliated by launching cruise missile strikes against al-Qaeda camps which killed a number of Taliban. Taliban assets in the United States were frozen and the United Nations followed up with sanctions, demanding that Osama bin Laden should be handed over to the United States. In December 2000 the pressure mounted when military sanctions were imposed. Pakistan claimed that sanctions were having a detrimental effect on humanitarian grounds, a view that UN investigators found to be groundless – it was a drought that was causing problems. In December 1999 the Taliban assisted a group of hijackers on board Indian Airlines Flight IC814 to escape, and there were a number of assassinations of moderate Afghans. In May 2001, reminiscent of the Nazis, all non-Muslims were ordered to wear a yellow patch and more statements were issued advocating global jihad. Fresh attacks were launched against the Northern Alliance, usually spearheaded by the fanatical 'foreign' Taliban. On 9 September a group of al-Qaeda, posing as journalists, packed a camera with explosives, and, during an interview with Massoud, they detonated it. Massoud died in the blast. Two days later, an even more spectacular suicide attack was launched on the United States.

WAR ON TERROR AND THE FALL OF THE TALIBAN

The attacks on New York cost the lives of 2,893 people. A further 233 died in the attack on the Pentagon and on board United Airlines Flight 93, which crashed in Pennsylvania. The world was stunned. Captured on television, the event was as vivid and spectacular as it was horrific. For millions who had never directly experienced the concept of terror, it was a frightening and heartbreaking event. Many journalists expressed the view that the 'world had changed'. There was also a widespread expectation that the United States would react with overwhelming force.

There were indeed strong currents of anger and nationalist pride in America, but the strategy their armed forces developed was sophisticated, even if the political agenda was somewhat vague. Many were puzzled what a 'war on terror' entailed. What were the strategic objectives or 'war aims'? Was it possible to eradicate all terrorists, and how was this to be effected: by military, police or judicial action? In more tangible terms, it involved the closer cooperation of international security services to track down al-Qaeda members or their associate groups. It also involved the creation of a world coalition that would force nations that harboured terrorist groups to close them down. President George W. Bush described an 'Axis of Evil' that included the pariah states of Iraq, Iran and North Korea, although some countries that had tolerated extremists were not mentioned. Syria, Saudi Arabia and Pakistan, for example (the latter two American allies), were not listed. Critics argued that the focus on terrorists was in danger of being lost by taking on Iraq, although the proliferation of weapons of mass destruction into the hands of terrorists through Saddam Hussein (who had used poison gas on his own people in 1988) was a major concern to the Western powers.[19]

In the short term, the objective was to neutralize Osama bin Laden by defeating the obdurate Taliban. The NATO allies were quick to announce that they were in support of the United States when it came to military action. Uzbekistan was enlisted as a location from which operations might be mounted, and 1,000 US troops were sent there in September. United Arab Emirates and Saudi Arabia were pressured to end their support for the Taliban too, and a carrier fleet was moved into the northern part of the Indian Ocean. The United States made contact with the Afghan United Front/Northern Alliance, and Special Forces were despatched to assist in the co-ordination of air and ground operations. The key to the whole campaign, though, was Pakistan. After what was effectively an ultimatum, President Pervez Musharaff declared himself in favour of American-led action in Afghanistan. Since Pakistanis had died in the attacks on the World Trade Center in New York, Musharaff was able to distance himself from the Islamist extremists. He was prepared to enforce this new direction in policy publicly. When the ISI Director, Lieutenant General Mahmood Ahmed, failed to get the Taliban to hand over Osama bin Laden after a visit to Kandahar, Musharaff sacked him. At this point, however, as Operation Enduring Freedom got underway on 7 October 2001, Musharaff must have realized that Pakistan's policy of creating a friendly power on the western border had failed spectacularly.

The chief characteristic of this phase of the fighting in Afghanistan was the overwhelming effect of American air power. In the first wave, B52 and B1 'Stealth' bombers, along with 25 strike aircraft, launched a bombardment on training camps, radar installations and known Taliban positions. Fifty cruise missiles were fired from British and American submarines to augment the attack. The air offensive utterly destroyed the capacity of the Taliban to operate in the air and seriously affected their ability to move and fight on the ground. Special Forces directed further bombing of Taliban positions in front of the Northern Alliance, whilst AC130 gunships provided close air support. Some 12,000 bombs and missiles were deployed in the space of a few weeks, and even seasoned Taliban veterans broke under the intensity of the attacks. Many fighters later explained that they could not even see the aircraft that attacked them. Especially feared was the 15,000-pound BLU-82 'Daisycutter', which, although only dropped on four occasions, had a devastating impact. The CBU-103 'Combined Effects Munitions', colloquially known as a 'Cluster bomb', was also highly effective, although the debris of unexploded ordnance attracted media criticism in the West. Despite fears of indiscriminate bombing, 6,700 of the weapons used were precision-guided and Special Forces were able to lay down carpets of explosions a few hundred metres in front of their own positions with confidence. On a comparatively few occasions were targets inaccurately selected, but media critics tended to draw attention to these isolated cases in their efforts to present a balanced account of the conflict.[20] The Taliban invited Western and Middle Eastern journalists into hospitals filled with civilian casualties, knowing that the cameras would feed greedily on graphic images.

The collapse of the Taliban was incredibly swift when it came. Over four days in November 2001, all the major urban centres fell. Mazar was the first to be taken, as Dostam secured his old power base. Those that had tolerated the Taliban now found reason to defect, and, after a spree of looting in Kabul on 13 November, they abandoned the capital. Musharaff hinted that, perhaps, Taliban moderates might be able to join an Afghan government in the future, but American disapproval soon silenced the suggestion. Nevertheless, the fact that a Special Forces raid in the south on 19 October failed to achieve the element of surprise led to suspicion that ISI had tipped the Taliban off. Given the fact that so many of the Taliban had been Pushtuns, there were rumours that Pakistan had arranged to fly out many of the fighters. How many of these there were, and whether the United States gave tacit consent to such a move, has not been established. By November, though, resistance was ebbing away. In Mazar, a large group of Taliban prisoners attempted to overwhelm their captors, but a prolonged fire-fight suppressed the revolt. The last real resistance was at Kunduz, where a large number of 'foreign' Taliban had entrenched themselves. The town fell to the Northern Alliance after a sustained air bombard-ment on 26 November. On 9 December 2001, amid scenes of jubilation, Hamed Karzai entered the capital and brought the war to a close.

The Taliban had fallen for several reasons of equal magnitude. Pakistan withdrew its financial and military support, and Islamist extremists were unable to send reinforcements because of the speed of the US-led operations. The air bombardment was so intense that few Taliban could endure it. From a political perspective, though, the Taliban simply did not have any legitimacy to govern. They had demonstrated that they were just as ruthless and uncompromising as previous regimes, all of which had managed to alienate substantial sections of the Afghan people. By 2001 the Taliban were thoroughly hated and the drought that affected the south further undermined their base of support. The foreign involvement was, unlike the Soviet effort, welcomed as liberation. In 1979 Afghanistan was not, as Soviet strate-gists believed, in 'crisis', but in 2001 it was not just in crisis, it was in a catastrophic state. When Mullah Omar fled Kabul, he spoke in terms of an approaching apocalypse, but this narrow-minded individual really had nothing else to offer, and he was bundled unceremoniously out of the land he had ruined.

The Bonn Conference of 3 October 2001 marked the beginning of a long and difficult process of reconstruction. Six neighbouring coun-tries plus the United States and Russia (known as the Six plus Two) agreed that Afghanistan should enjoy a multi-ethnic, freely elected government. Nevertheless, at the subsequent meeting of Afghans that December, Dostam, former Taliban leaders and Zahir Shah were not present. Even so, a 'road map' for peace, starting with the formation of an interim administration (not a government), was agreed upon. Provision was made for an Emergency Loya Jirga led by a Chairman, a Supreme Court, banking and currency arrangements, UN assistance, a Human Rights commission and agreements on the return of the refugees. It was a good start. In addition, an international peace-keeping force, ISAF (International Security and Assistance Force), was to be deployed under the command of a British officer, Major-General John McColl. This had the task of restoring confidence in the cities and it protected the leaders of the new administration from terrorists. Meanwhile, British and American Special Forces continued to hunt down al-Qaeda activists, including Osama bin Laden.

What was encouraging about the peace process was the early steps taken to hand over authority to the Afghans. There was no question of occupation, but nor was there an opportunity, as had occurred in 1989, for Pakistan to intervene in Afghan politics for its own ends. The presence of ISAF was crucial, though. Without their detachments there would be too great a temptation for some warlords to resume their campaigns.

Afghanistan, however, faces a difficult future. The ideal form of government will have to include a degree of devolution, since so much of the conflict from 1978 onwards was a reaction to centralizing tendencies by successive governments in Kabul. Karzai hopes that a willingness to devolve will build trust, but this will take time. Afghanistan still needs to bring together the militias and military factions in one army and civil police force, essential if the rule of law is to be re-established. Only 7,500 police had been recruited by 2004, although there is a need for an estimated 40,000.[21] Above all, Afghanistan needs to feel the effects of material prosperity as a peace dividend. In March 2004 Afghan delegates arrived in Berlin to lobby for $27.6 billion in aid, which works out at $164 per Afghan (a figure considerably lower than the estimated $336 per Iraqi estimated for the Second Gulf War of 2003). The Afghan government raised $300 million in 2003, but 94 per cent of its needs that year were externally supplied. Even if the 20 per cent economic growth of 2002–3 could be sustained at a steady 9 per cent, Afghanistan cannot hope to be financially independent until 2016. Tragically, opium generates $2.3 billion each year, but there is understandable foreign pressure to eradicate the narcotics industry. Outside Kabul, there is still a great deal of lawlessness and tax farming. Of the 10.5 million voters, only 1.5 million had registered in 2004, largely the result of inaccessibility from the capital but also because of pressure from warlords and regional leaders. A comprehensive disarmament programme is needed for the 45,000 former fighters not serving the government, but that requires the supervision of UN or ISAF forces, and there are really too few of them to be effective.

Afghanistan is a case example of the consequences of both state collapse and uninhibited state power. The revolutionary process that had begun in 1978 had resulted in the gradual erosion of the Afghan state. Those that propagated ever more radical solutions were, like so many revolutionary zealots, consumed by the monster they had unleashed. Without consent, radicals were forced to turn to state terror to enforce their new Utopia, and the result was brutality, coercion and atrocities. The Taliban, backed by their external allies, were themselves part of this flux. Convinced of the righteousness of their own ideology, they perpetrated the very crimes they claimed to have come to eradicate. The politicization of Islam, with all its moral certainties, has produced a fundamentalism that stands in contradiction to the religious liberties and political freedoms of the rest of the world. Whilst the Islamists convinced themselves that these were Western values to be destroyed, they have, in fact, proved to be the essential requirements for social groups to coexist. As the world has developed linkages, accelerated by the improvements in global communications, the Islamists, with their atavistic desire to enforce an exclusive, mono-ethnic hegemony in the Middle East and elsewhere, seem ever more out of touch with reality. The Islamists are therefore forced to retreat into a world of delusion, reinforced with a conviction that they are in defence of a victimized culture. Their solution is to adopt the 'last resort' of their faith, violence through terror, but this is really only an excuse to reject the modernity of the globe, avoid dialogue and escape into a fantasist realm that gives them prestige. Al-Qaeda found themselves a haven of this nature in Afghanistan, with dire consequences for the Afghans. Some critics of the United States have argued that America needs to 'engage with the rest of the world' because of an arrogant foreign policy and intrusive economic culture.[22] In fact, the consequences of American isolationism would indeed be severe – at the end of the twentieth century America actually engaged far more with the rest of the world than at any previous time in its history. It is not the United States therefore that needs to take a global view and 'engage with the world', but the Islamic extremists who propagate their narrow doctrines of hatred and murder indiscriminately.

Chapter 10

Insurgency, Terror and Peace-Making

Conflict in South Asia is more than 'war' between states, and any definition should include civil conflict, and perhaps even violence on the micro scale as well.[1] Whilst the limits of available space here prevents the encyclopaedic cataloguing of all forms of conflict, from industrial or land disputes to full-scale war, it should be acknowledged that there are significant stresses within South Asian societies that threaten to develop into more widespread or serious confrontations. The unrest in East Pakistan, for example, escalated into a conflict between civilians and sympathetic Bengali soldiers on one side and the West Pakistan Army on the other, before widening into a war between Pakistan and India. Similarly, the testing of Pakistan's nuclear weapons in 1998, and the confrontational response by India, strongly influenced the Pakistan's army to 'up the ante' in Kashmir, and this led directly to the Kargil Conflict of 1999.

Other than the confrontations between state governments, there are four areas that have the potential to create conflict in South Asia: ethnic, national and sub-national identities; identities reinforced by religion; ideological convictions; and economic-political disputes. These factors have been the source of conflict since 1947 in a number of flashpoints across the region.

In Assam, for example, the fear that an influx of 'foreigners' into the state would dilute the local population and subordinate them economically to outsiders set off one of India's most serious insurgencies. The 'foreigners' in Assam were, in many cases, refugees from the repression in Bangladesh and they arrived in such large numbers that they threatened to outnumber the local Assamese. Against a background of rising oil prices, which made the local oil reserves more attractive to outsiders, and a contrasting feeling amongst locals that infrastructure and welfare had been neglected, the Assamese began to strike, riot and then murder Bangladeshi migrants. In 1983 the world's media was alerted to the problems of this remote region by the image of corpses floating down the tributaries of the Ganges and Brahmaputra.[2] This was soon followed by the creation of the United Liberation Front of Assam (ULFA), which aimed for independence through armed struggle. Guerrilla bases were concealed successfully in the remote jungle and inside Bangladesh. The Indian Army was forced to react when its initial attempts to contain the insurgents failed. Launching a series of large-scale operations, such as Operation Rhino (1991), the army forced ULFA's leaders into hiding. The local government offered talks aimed at reconciliation, but ULFA split on the issue and some hardliners pledged to continue the struggle.

Meanwhile, in neighbouring Nagaland, tribesmen who had never trusted any central authority waged their own intermittent guerrilla campaign from 1947, but this intensified when Myanmar's army launched a massive offensive against the Muslim tribesmen of the country's north-west. Tens of thousands of refugees poured over the border into Nagaland, Manipur and Mizoram. The Indian government was thus faced with the problem of sheltering and feeding thousands of people whom the local population resented. Although Myanmar and India reached an agreement on repatriation in 1992, many of the refugees refused to go back to face the Burmese troops.

The example of India's north-east illustrates the complexity of factors that led to conflict and the difficulties that face any government in trying to resolve it. Ethnic, religious, economic, political and sub-national identities were all involved to a greater or lesser degree. The complex nature of the insurgency, however, should not preclude a clearer definition of terrorism and guerrilla warfare in South Asia. Indeed, the clarity of definition may be imperative, since a universal treatment of insurgent enemies has led, in the past, to prolonged conflict when solutions were otherwise obtainable.

The virus of political terrorism in South Asia has developed from a variety of historical germs. Western notions of nationalism and revolution, which themselves began as concepts of political and social liberation through the collective 'will of the people', have empowered the civilian to challenge authority with armed force. The important point here is not so much that Western ideas have been imported into South Asia, but that political murders could be legitimized by a claim to represent others, or to be the 'true voice' of a chosen group. These concepts differed from earlier peasant rebellions where there might be popular backing for armed insurrection in defence of land, rights or religion. In the nineteenth century, alongside the religious conviction of earlier epochs, rose a set of new, secular, mobilizing ideologies such as nationalism, revolutionary socialism and communism. Each shared the characteristics of an exclusive *Weltanschauung*: those that did not fit into the vision of a new utopian social order were to be suppressed or exterminated. In the name of these ideologies, men and women were willing to go to their deaths or to kill in savage ways.

The definition of terrorist and guerrilla is all too often and conveniently blurred when it serves a political purpose, but there are important distinctions. Terrorists will use indiscriminate violence against both civilians and state security personnel to generate a climate of fear and thus specifically compel a change in policy. Guerrillas are essentially trying to pursue a conventional war but are forced into an asymmetrical stance by the power of their opponents. Their political aim, though, remains unchanged: the achievement of liberation or the acquisition of sovereignty. Put simply, guerrillas have a single objective – to liberate their homeland from a foreign occupation. Guerrillas aim for popular support, tend to exist in larger, mass organizations, and are only partially clandestine. The responses by conventional armies to terrorist or guerrilla warfare need to be distinct if they wish to avoid turning terror gangs into the focus of a popular cause.

Operating in small, cell-structured groups of highly secretive members, the terrorists aim to coerce authorities into a change of policy, and will target civilians in order to generate fear and thus put pressure on otherwise robust governments. Terrorists sometimes follow less rational agendas: terror may be an expression of anger, frustration, a desire to punish or simply intimidate. There is generally little attempt to win over populations, to control territory or even to take power. The chief difficulty for conventional forces is how to detect insurgents who are concealed as civilians. Counter-insurgency easily degenerates into reprisals against civilians suspecting of harbouring or sympathizing with terrorists.

Responses to actions by guerrillas and terrorists can change the nature of the initial engagements. With guerrillas, negotiations may well be desirable since the aim would be to find a political solution. Since both sides seek mass support, a common agenda could bridge the gap between them. If negotiation is likely to lead to an unacceptable compromise, state security forces resort to propaganda, the 'beheading' of guerrilla leadership, or try to inflict such heavy casualties as to deter further resistance. By contrast, since terrorists harbour an exclusive world view that enables them to justify civilian casualties, many governments believe that negotiation is not desirable. The risk of a hard-line strategy, however, is alienation of the civilian population through a reign of terror. This is likely to be counter-productive, as has been shown in Kashmir. In fact, collaboration from much of the civilian population is crucial and assists in building an intelligence picture of the enemy. India has gone to great lengths to recruit former Separatists and informers amongst the Kashmiri population.

Intelligence, supplied by a civilian population that feels its security is best served by cooperation with the authorities, can build up an accurate picture that peels away the camouflage provided by the modern urban environment. Once some personnel are located, further observation and monitoring will eventually yield networks and contacts. Terrorists, like all military forces, require resources to function. They need manpower and therefore they must find communication channels to recruit – a point when they are vulnerable to detection. They require funds, arms, ammunition and propaganda organs (although the mass media may inadvertently supply some of this): all of which, again, make the terrorist 'visible'. The severing of these resources, and the ability to 'turn' weaker cell members, is often the solution.

The politicization and militarization of Islam since the 1970s has given certain terror gangs the advantage of religious conviction to motivate their members and a tool to win over mass support, thus turning themselves into the spearhead of a revolutionary guerrilla movement.[3] Their interpretation of Islam, however twisted, has the effect of driving a wedge between its intended enemies and the *Ummah*, the rest of the Muslim world. It causes moderate Muslims to question their identity and loyalty to a 'secular' state authority, whilst spreading fear throughout the world. Two events sparked this current regeneration: the invasion of Afghanistan by the Soviet Union in 1979 and the Iranian Revolution by the followers of Ayatollah Khomeini the same year. Momentum was added to the sense of 'Islam in danger' by the periodic flaring of conflict between heavily armed Israelis and Palestinian rioters, by the struggle between secular government and Algerian 'fundamentalists' from 1962, and by the Russian operations against Chechnya.

Islamist organizations in Pakistan are not immune from these global influences. Ramzi Yousef, for example, the bomber against the World Trade Center in 1993, was not an Iraqi as first believed, but a Pakistani (his real name was Abdul Karim Rind and he was from Baluchistan). Yousef was influenced by the militancy of Mosque-Madresseh complexes that favoured radical preaching, demanded utter obedience and inspired its protégés with a strong sense of 'other worldly' mission. The Markaz Dawa Al Irshad (Centre of Preaching) of Pakistan, to which Osama Bin Laden contributed 10 million rupees, supported its own militant organization Lashkar-e Toyeba, which has carried out terrorist operations in Kashmir and in India against perceived 'infidels' who 'oppress' Muslims, following the classic militant model. The Lashkar is now Pakistan's biggest Jihadi organization and has had regular contact with a certain Abu Aziz, a *Kuniat* or code name for Bin Laden. It should be noted, however, that there is a far older historical root to this idea of pan-Islamic revival in South Asia. In 1897 millenarian clerics (some self-appointed) promised paradise for those who would take up arms and die fighting against the infidel on the North-West Frontier of India.[4]

It is interesting to note that guerrilla armies have often needed the support of regular forces to ensure that their struggle continues. Those that lack external backing usually fail. In Afghanistan, at first the Mujahideen struggled until substantial supplies flowed in from Pakistan and the United States. The latter's Stinger SAM missiles had a significant effect on the Soviet use of close air support by Hind helicopter gunships out of all proportion to the numbers actually deployed.[5]

The proliferation of weapons that are more mobile but have a more devastating effect, from Semtex explosive to bio-warfare (where a few droplets of certain agents or toxins can contaminate large volumes of food or water supplies), make terrorism more, not less likely in the future. A more globalized world, facilitated by faster and less regulated means of communication such as the Internet, will almost certainly offer the terrorist more opportunities to propagate an exclusive world view in an attempt to exploit conflicts over environmental, ideological or resources issues. Globalization, however, may also provide the means for detection and closer cooperation against the terrorist, and foster the idea of an inclusive and integrated world that will ultimately starve them of their resources.

One unconventional development of terrorism related to globalization is Cyber Warfare. This is perhaps unsurprising when terrorism and guerrilla movements are so dependent on communication.[6] Already there are organized groups who make use of the full range of modern technology to plan and execute terrorist operations, and in 2003 the *Times of India* reported on the increased cyber terrorist traffic between India and Pakistan.[7] Worms, Trojan Horses, data theft and Blogs were initiated by groups in Pakistan such as AIC (Anti-India Crew) and G-Force. Indian groups have responded in kind by defacing Pakistani websites and practising a similar kind of 'hackivism'. Of the 20 terror groups that maintain websites worldwide, five are located in South Asia.[8] Whilst these sites may be the organs that spread their brand of extremism, it may also be the case that, by encouraging this space for dialogue, marginalized groups feel it is preferable to fight with words than with bombs and guns.

It is, however, easy to underestimate the determination of terrorist organizations. The characteristic of the Muslim extremists in Pakistan and the Hindu-oriented LTTE (Liberation Tigers of Tamil Eelam), both of which produce suicide bombers (which they euphemistically refer to as 'martyrdom operations'), is strict discipline and organization, lubricated with a heady dose of utopian idealism. Such convictions will make it harder to deter the terrorists in Kashmir, even when the supplies of arms and money are denied them. As has been shown elsewhere in the world, even impoverished regions can generate significant guerrilla activity.

Equally, it would be wrong to focus only on religious movements in South Asia, since religion, although capable of mass mobilization, is very often only one factor amongst many. Religion is easily recognizable as a badge of identity and therefore appears to be the most important element, but more nebulous political or socio-economic issues may be the real root cause of conflict. The Mukti Bahini of Bangladesh were motivated by an ideology of nationalism that had been stimulated by perceived political and economic inequalities imposed by West Pakistan: they fought against their co-religionists alongside Indian troops in 1971. Similarly, in Afghanistan, whilst religious rhetoric could be invoked to win popular support, ethnic rivalry could play a just as important, if less easily identifiable role in the conflict. Indeed, religion was less important as a cause or sustaining feature of the civil war, even though the Taliban made much of their 'mission'. Their sponsors, the ISI, were motivated by the *realpolitik* of dominating the region on Pakistan's western approaches, rather than the 'other-worldly' concerns of spiritual purity.

The problem of classification of resistance to a central authority is particularly poignant when it comes to Baluchistan in 1973. Although condemned as 'miscreants' and even 'traitors' by the Pakistani government, the Baluchis were, in fact, trying to defend a traditional autonomy under threat from Zulfikar Ali Bhutto. Bhutto, shaken by the resistance of the Bangladeshis which had led to their independence, aimed to break the back of rival groups so as to centralize power and decision-making in the country. He set up the Federal Security Force (FSF), a paramilitary organization initially concerned with bodyguard duties but quickly extending their remit to include the intimidation of political leaders.[9] In a classic example of 'state terror', the FSF turned into an instrument of oppression against ordinary citizens. Reacting to this development, but also to directives from the capital, the Baluchi provincial government challenged Bhutto and called for the preservation of rule by local headmen or Sardars, and of the tribal order. When Bhutto tried to remove the provincial government, the Baluchis believed they were under attack, and they mobilized against the FSF and other agents of the Pakistan Peoples Party. Bhutto sent the regular army in, and air power played a crucial role in dispersing the insurgents. The sparse population, and arid and mountainous conditions, gave the fighting a different character from that in East Pakistan just two years before, but it was, nevertheless, a second civil war. General Tikka Khan, who had led the 'crackdown' in Bangladesh, commanded the forces in Baluchistan against the 'insurgents', and the tribesmen were driven into the hills along the Afghan border.

Bhutto condemned the Baluch Liberation Front and talked of a possible threat to the nation from a Baluchi-Pushtun axis, backed by Soviet forces via Afghanistan. He talked of national defence, but it was a thinly veiled attempt to secure power in a state that was thoroughly divided. In the face of perceived opposition, Bhutto extended his reign of terror, even arresting members of his party. Murder, torture, false imprisonment and the seizure of property followed. As any popular support ebbed away and the regime became dependent on coercion, Bhutto turned to the clerics to create a social cement through Islam. When India detonated its first nuclear weapon in 1974, Bhutto stepped up the rhetoric of nationalism. But his efforts to centralize power in his own hands did not prevail and he was 'hoisted by his own petard'. It was a combination of the army and the ISI who removed him: the very instruments Bhutto had used to extend his rule.

CHANGES IN THE PARADIGM OF TERRORISM

Until the 1970s, preventing, controlling and investigating acts of terrorism were considered as part of the responsibilities of the civil police. It had the leadership role in counter-terrorism, particularly in intelligence collection, or investigation and crisis management after a terrorist attack. In India, the intelligence collection cells of the police such as the Special Branch (SB) and the Criminal Investigation Department (CID), which followed the British model of police administration, were the most important in the prevention of terrorism. The role of the armed forces and the national intelligence agencies was confined to providing support to the police. The ethos of dealing with terrorism was based on the view that terrorism was a phenomenon that had to be tackled through consensual governance, the redress of grievances, better communal and inter-religious relations, better physical security and better police-community relations.[10]

The nature of terrorism has, however, changed. There has been an escalation in the tactics used by terrorists: the hijacking of civilian aircraft, hostage-taking, blowing-up planes in mid-air, and car or truck bombings to intimidate the civilian population and to project the state as an institution incapable of protecting them. India has been the victim of a number of terrorist incidents carried out by Sikh and Islamist groups since 1981. The most publicized development has been the advent of suicide bombing starting from the 1980s, emulating the anti-Israel and anti-Western Jihadi terrorist organizations of the Middle East. It has also been the case that terrorist groups have had access to increasingly sophisticated arms and ammunition, including explosives, detonators, timers and communication tools, much of which came from the large stocks supplied to the Afghan Mujahideen for use against the Soviet troops in Afghanistan.

Alongside the more advanced weaponry, which has placed greater military power in the hands of ever-smaller groups over the last half-century, terrorists have begun to adopt improved communications systems, and to carry out research into alternative weapon systems. This is a particularly important development since al-Qaeda advocates mass-casualty terrorism and is unconcerned with the effect its actions have on world opinion. They have expressed a desire to use weapons of mass destruction (WMD) to achieve their objectives. Al-Qaeda, and the groups inspired by its example, advocate terrorism as punishment of their enemies rather than seeking any specific political objective, although traditional territorial designs are common to all the Islamists. Bin Laden has encouraged a trans-national networking of Jihadi terrorist organizations and promotes the transfer of funds from innumerable sources to support extremist organizations.

Terrorism is shifting the traditional interpretation of war. War is regarded as a phenomenon that is, given certain laws of combat, predictable. Linearity of the system is assumed since it imparts stability to the analysis. In other words, a direct and proportional connection is established between each cause and effect. This has often led to the study of war as a closed system not susceptible to perturbations from its surroundings. Synchronization is regarded as a sacrosanct feature of command and control, especially in joint operations. The evolution of terrorist groups, however, requires an adjustment of the definition and also the response to the new type of warfare emerging.

Three main attributes of changing terrorist activities are in organization, strategy and technology. In organization, the terrorists have abandoned hierarchical structures in favour of cells. Following the model of Islamist groups in Pakistan and Afghanistan, the organization is controlled and supported by a council that is located at the centre of a star network. Cells are connected to the network, but the disruption of one section cannot defeat the whole organization completely. In the war in Afghanistan in 2001, the coalition dealt a heavy blow to the central council and its command and control, but remnants of the old network have survived.

The terrorists strategy may be to cause systemic disruption as much as target destruction. Terror can create a disproportionate effect on the delicate and vulnerable threads of society. In Kashmir, a few acts of terrorism caused the flight of thousands of Hindus. There may have been a secondary economic motive for the bomb attacks in Bombay (Mumbai) in 2001 too: trying to replicate the financial chaos caused by the destruction of the World Trade Center in New York. In the future terrorists are likely to use advanced information technologies for offensive and defensive purposes to a far greater extent, and this will involve economic warfare.

As terrorism has evolved, so have the counter-measures. Counter-intelligence in its traditional sense was defined as pre-empting efforts at intelligence collection, subversion and sabotage by other states. Now, counter-intelligence aims to frustrate the attempts of terrorist organizations, from the region or outside, to recruit and train new volunteers and acquire high tech skills and equipment. This demands a willingness to cooperate with other countries against terrorist alliances, such as the International Islamic Front (IIF). Counter-measures may have once focused on the disaffected economic groups of a state, but the uncompromising line of Islamic extremists makes negotiation virtually untenable.

Counter-terror intelligence is therefore concerned with neutralizing terrorist cells at three levels: strategic, tactical and psychological. At the strategic level, there is an analysis of the organization of the terrorists, the identity of their leaders, their aims, *modus operandi*, source of funds, weapons and explosives at their disposal, and contacts with external elements, including foreign intelligence agencies. At the tactical level, there is an attempt to uncover their specific plan of action. This 'preventive intelligence' enables the state to frustrate the terrorists' plots. Finally, at the psychological level, there is an effort to neutralize the propaganda of terrorists. Information about the terrorists, which enables the state to mount its own psychological war against them, is critical. This could include clues suggesting discontent with the leaders of terrorist gangs, the use of coercion in the recruitment of volunteers, or the enlistment and misuse of children for terrorist operations. The government of Sri Lanka was able to show that the LTTE had conscripted children, and the Government of Nepal has argued that Maoist guerrillas in the kingdom have compelled people to take part in demonstrations at gunpoint.

There have been a number of 'intelligence failures' in South Asia which suggests faults with counter-measures in the region. The assassination of Rajiv Gandhi by the LTTE in Chennai (Madras) in south India in May 1991, the explosions in Mumbai (Bombay) in India in March 1993, the explosions in Coimbatore in South India in 1998, and the terrorist incidents in Delhi and Mumbai (namely the attack on the Indian Parliament in December 2001 and the twin blasts in Mumbai in August 2003) seem to indicate failures of the counter-terrorism agencies. They were either unable to prevent these incidents due to a lack of precise intelligence or of follow-up action when such intelligence was available.

It should be noted, however, that for every successful operation there are many more that are thwarted. Intelligence collection, physical security and crisis management are the three components of the counter-terrorism strategy. If the intelligence machinery fails to provide early warning about an intended act of terrorism, the physical security apparatus should be effective enough to check the terrorists. In the event of both the intelligence and the physical security mechanisms failing, the crisis management infrastructure can contain the damage, reassure the public, reduce casualties and obtain valuable forensic evidence.

Occasionally, India has benefited from the failures of the terrorists themselves. There was an abortive attempt to kill Rajiv Gandhi at Rajghat in Delhi in 1987, and terrorists failed to make an arms drop from the air at Purulia in December 1995. The attack on Parliament House at Delhi in December 2001 was badly co-ordinated, lost the element of surprise and was defeated by the physical security of the guards on duty. Nevertheless, intelligence agencies prefer to obtain preventative information through communication intercepts or a person who has penetrated the terrorist organization. 'Moles' may be one option, but terrorists who have been 'turned' are far more useful because of their experience. With the development of new forms of communication, the interception of couriers is less common, and the terrorists of South Asia are waking up to the vulnerabilities of the Internet, cell phone and fax. After the Americans successfully captured al-Qaeda operatives in Pakistan using TECHINT (technical intelligence), terrorists avoided using their own names, use code words extensively and avoid attracting any attention (formerly done by the issue of *fatwas* or other propaganda).

There is a pressing need in South Asia for greater intelligence cooperation, and India has already taken the lead. Inspired by the Counter-Terrorism Center in the United States (which brought together experts from different agencies under a Director of the CIA), and responding to the United Nations Resolution 1373 to act against terrorist organizations, India has established a working relationship with Myanmar.[11] In November 2003 the two countries committed themselves to strengthening bilateral mechanisms, and considered additional ways to intensify efforts to prevent, counter and suppress the activities of terrorist groups. The unrest on the border has long been an issue that both countries share concern about and it was inevitable they would need to cooperate. They agreed that training programmes of

Myanmar personnel in Indian institutions should be increased and there should be a joint plan on border security.

GUERRILLA WARFARE: THE MAOISTS IN NEPAL

The situation in Nepal illustrates many of the characteristics of guerrilla warfare in South Asia, but also the failures of effective counter-insurgency. Maoist rebels, the CPN-Maoist (Communist Party of Nepal), began their 'People's War' on 12 February 1996 against the constitutional monarchy. Their aim is to establish a Maoist people's 'democracy', but this aspiration comes at a cost. Some estimates give the total deaths from this insurgency at 1,600, but others range up to 8,000. Although the casualties include security forces and guerrillas, a large number of civilians have been killed by both sides. The police are accused of extrajudicial killings in captivity, and some disappeared whilst in custody. On the other side, civilians have been kidnapped, executed and killed in bomb blasts by the insurgents.[12]

The insurgency has radiated from five mountain districts: Rolpa, Rukum and Jajarkot in the mid-west, the western district of Gorkha and an eastern district of Sindhuli. However, 68 of Nepal's 75 districts are now affected. Put another way, the insurgency has directly impacted upon the lives of roughly two-thirds of the 24 million people of Nepal. The Nepalese government admits that 32 districts are virtually under the control of the guerrillas. In these they organize mass meetings openly. In January 2001 the Maoists actually declared the formation of provisional revolutionary district governments in Rolpa, Rukum, Jajarkot and Sallyan. There is a growing realization in government circles that, if the guerrillas continue to expand their zone of influence at the current rate, they will be able to overwhelm the state within a few years.

Despite their territorial gains, however, the Maoists seem to have achieved little politically. It is true they have established parallel governments in a number of locations, collecting taxes and meting out punishments, but they really only control through fear and they have no permanent base of operations – unlike the LTTE in Sri Lanka. If their avowed aim is the overthrow of the monarchy, then they have failed so far. If they aim to take over the state, then by this criterion too they have failed. There is also evidence to suggest the Maoists have been less effective since 2002. The retraining of the Nepal security forces has put the rebels under pressure. Video footage of a Maoist ambush at Krishna Bhir in Dhading on 16 November 2002 suggests that the rebels are less than competent, if well informed on the movements of security personnel. Indeed, since 2002, the Maoists have been attacking more 'soft' targets (such as empty government buildings), which may indicate relative weakness compared with the security forces. There have been fewer casualties and fewer terrorist incidents in the last two years. Some of the Maoist military leaders now believe that a 'spectacular' terrorist attack, or a tangible military 'victory', is needed before the movement can begin negotiations.

The government's response to this threat has been to increase coercion. A National Security Council has been established and it has created a paramilitary force comprising 15,000 men (to be increased to 25,000 in the coming months). Although the Royal Nepali Army (RNA) has not been officially ordered against the guerrillas, the government has decided to establish six new military bases at battalion level around districts affected by the insurgency. Twenty-five district headquarters are now under RNA protection. Most operations to contain the Maoists, however, have been carried out by the police. 'Operation Romeo', 'Kilo Shera Two' and 'Jungle Search Operation' are three examples of a classic counterrevolutionary warfare 'search and destroy' methods. In many places the policy has backfired because of the number of civilian casualties and the lack-lustre attempts at winning 'hearts and minds' by the police.

There are no accurate figures on the strengths of the insurgents because they occupy remote and inaccessible jungle areas of Nepal, but it is estimated that the number of full-time guerrillas under arms is about 2,000, with an additional 10,000 irregulars armed with homemade weapons. There are some indications that the Maoists enjoy a certain degree of popular sympathy. The area the insurgents control is perhaps the most backward and least accessible of Nepal. It is here that the ordinary citizens have grown disaffected by government instability and corruption. The money allocated for development often does not get converted into tangible improvements. Government planners apparently ignore a large number of villages in the remotest regions. There are very few schools, no roads, no electricity and no medical facilities. At the local and at the national level, unemployment is increasing at an alarming rate. Rural youths have neither a job nor a school to attend and their prospects are demoralizing. It is for this reason that the Maoists have enjoyed greater success than previous Communist movements. Although there are still nineteen Far Left parties, there is a substantial popular participation in the movement as a whole, particularly amongst the 'untouchable' castes such as Kami, Sarki and Damai. What is striking is that the left-wing parties that have participated in the experiment in People's Government in 1990 are doing less well than those that advocate a hard line. Another new characteristic of Maoist movement is the number of women in the guerrilla ranks. Some estimate that as many as 30 per cent of the fighters are female.

The effect of that popular support is clear. The co-ordination and precision of guerrilla attacks mounted against the Security Forces show that the Maoists are better informed about the deployment and the weaknesses of the police than vice versa. It is clear that Nepali strategic planners need to find a way to prevent people giving sanctuary to guerrillas. This could be done by means of massive economic development package. However, the relief package that the government has allocated so far is a case of 'too little, too late'. The number of civilian casualties has destroyed faith in the government. Moreover, corruption amongst government agents has further damaged its reputation. The Maoists also deliberately target projects designed to assist the people in order to discredit the regime.

The effects on the people are tragic. There are at least 300,000 internally displaced persons in Nepal and many thousands from Western Nepal have fled across the border to India, depriving the country of vital manpower. Young men in rural areas abandon their villages for fear of harassment from the security forces or abduction by the Maoists. Land prices have increased, and the influx of rural migrants has swollen Kathmandu's overcrowded population to three million. In some cases rural schools have been abandoned and the only new urban schools are those catering for the better off. The effect of these changes on the agriculture of the country will be entirely negative. But, above all, the atmosphere is one of increasing fear. In the space of a few weeks in 2004, Maoists attacked buses (5 November), abducted civilians (16 November and, on 28 November, 1,500 people from across eight districts), detonated bombs in schools that killed and maimed children (6 and 10 November), gunned down young men without any known cause (10 and 13 November), including an eight-year-old child (20 November), 'executed' civilians suspected of spying for the security forces (27 November), and lobbed bombs at a peace rally (7 December). In seeking to establish a Communist world order through armed struggle, the Maoists seem to be following in the footsteps of the Khmer Rouge.

Despite the opportunity to demonstrate how brutal the Maoists really are, the government's handling of the media has been clumsy. The media rights group Reporters Without Borders said that press freedom had been 'one of the great victims' of the state of emergency imposed in November 2001. The security forces arrested more than 100 journalists and some of them were beaten up. Although a degree of press freedom returned with the lifting of the state of emergency in August 2002, there was a wave of attacks on media workers by both sides in the conflict. The Maoists have done themselves little favour in this regard. Aside from their rhetoric of revolution, their extreme measures have caused fear and distrust. They abducted more than 80 teachers from various schools in Udaypur and Sindhupalchowk districts in 2002. The aim seemed to have been to involve them in Communist education programmes.[13] Such coercion is counter-productive, and Nepal's educated and political elite is alienated by the archaic slogans against the bourgeoisie and property, and, of course, by the violence of their campaign.

The government of Nepal has complained that the Maoists are seeking shelter in India. They believe that the insurgents are supplied by gun-running into the Terai border area, but, in fact, the main source of arms and ammunition is that captured from the Security Forces during raids on their posts. Furthermore, the Nepalese allege that Maoist leaders and their cadres continue to use India as a safe haven and that many injured Maoists manage to get medical treatment from doctors there. In fact, India has every reason to cooperate with the government of Nepal on this matter. The Maoists of Nepal want nothing short of world revolution in the classic Marxist-Leninist model. They state: 'Because of the distinct conditions of this region, it becomes clear that it is inevitable for the communist revolutionaries to devise an integrated strategy against the Indian ruling classes of the monopoly bourgeoisie and their agents in the various countries.'[14] The networking of the Maoists in Nepal with other international groups is typical of guerrilla warfare and they have links with Communist parties not just in South Asia (such as Sri Lanka, Bangladesh and Afghanistan), but also in the wider world. Curiously, relations with China are not strong, although some of the other Communist parties in Nepal have closer links.[15]

India defends its own national interests by arresting guerrilla leaders of Nepal whom it captures on its side of the frontier. At Siliguri in India on 8 April 2004 the Maoist leader Mohan Baidhya was charged with 'waging war against India'. Speaking of his activities and his attempts to recruit support across the border, Baidhya told the *Annapurna Post*: 'I activated, I am activating and will continue to activate in order to establish republicanism in Nepal'.[16] To defeat the insurgents, the government of Nepal will need to be just as committed and just as active, and only a coherent and combined military, political and economic strategy will prevail in the end.

INSURGENCY AND STATE TERROR IN MYANMAR (BURMA)

The chief characteristic of Mynamar since 1962 has been the struggle between ethnic minorities in the provinces and the authoritarian government in Rangoon. As such, it provides a clear example of state terror and how insurgency is sustained. There has long been ethnic tension between the Burmans (who represent about 50 per cent of the population), the Karens and Shan (about 10 per cent each) and the other ethnic groups, but the minorities simply aim for autonomy and a significant voice within a united Burma. They want to see an end to the oppressive rule of the SLORC (State Law and Order Restoration Council), a front for the army that seized control of the country in 1988. The military government abolished civilian administration and massacred thousands of unarmed pro-democracy demonstrators in Rangoon and since then has unleashed a reign of terror across the country.[17] Without a resolution to the question of local autonomy and national power sharing, resistance struggles that have flared and simmered for decades cannot easily be resolved. But, without peace, there is little chance for grassroots economic development, which itself is a cause of grievance with the government.

The repressive strategy of the SLORC has attracted international criticism. Whilst it has negotiated cease-fires with most armed ethnic opposition groups, it has waged fierce assaults against others. The Muslim Rohingya people were targeted in 1991, and more than 250,000 fled to neighbouring India and Bangladesh. At least 140,000 more Karen, Karenni and Mon people from eastern Burma are refugees in Thailand following intense Burmese Army offensives from 1984 onwards. It is estimated there are a further 600,000 internally displaced persons (IDPs) who receive no international assistance. However, there is another side effect to the cease-fire agreements. The Burmese army's deals include permission to carry out opium cultivation and the right to trade without interference. The result has been a sharp increase in heroin production and smuggling from Burma and a concurrent worldwide rise in the use of heroin. Some groups are now also engaged in large-scale illicit manufacture of methamphetamines.

The military junta has exploited divisions within and among ethnic groups to bolster its rule. In 2000 the relocation of thousands of Wa farmers into traditional Shan areas has raised tensions and sparked fighting among those groups. Nevertheless, it is repression that maintains the government in power. Amnesty International believes that 'torture has become an institution' in Burma.[18] Reports by the United Nations, Human Rights Watch and many other groups have repeatedly detailed a sickening litany of abuses, including murder, torture, rape, detention without trial, massive forced relocations and forced labour. Severe violations of human rights, especially against the minorities, continue, including arbitrary executions and the conscription of villagers as military porters in combat zones. Children have been particularly hard hit, both as direct physical victims of military abuse and as members of affected families. In 2001 conditions in Shan State and Karen State deteriorated as the government launched wide-scale military operations. Hundreds of thousands of people in those areas have fled their homes. Some of the worst forced labour abuses have been reported from south-eastern Burma, where a billion-dollar pipeline is being developed by a consortium of America's UNOCAL and France's TOTAL oil companies and the Burmese regime. People have even been forced to work on tourism development projects too. In March 1997 the European Union withdrew Burma's trade privileges because of the prevalence of forced labour and other abuses.

Press censorship, restrictions on broadcast media and attacks on religious groups are also common. Muslims are continuing targets for army attacks. Dozens of mosques were destroyed as anti-Muslim riots, reportedly instigated by the Burmese military, flared in several Burmese cities in March 1997, and a new spate of attacks in the Arakan region was reported in late 2000. But no minority group is safe. It was estimated that, in 1998, nearly 300,000 Burmese were refugees in Thailand, Bangladesh and India.

The Burmese army claims to be trying to cut away the base of support for insurgents using a 'Four Cuts' strategy. Each campaign is designed to deny armed opposition groups access to food, money, information and recruits. It is often enforced through mass relocations and widespread destruction of communities, accompanied by killings and other brutality. Major offensives in 1997 and early 1998 forced tens of thousands of Karen, Mon and Shan people to abandon their villages and move into army-controlled 'strategic hamlets'. Some people have been chased from their homes to allow for logging operations or the creation of state farms, where military discipline can be imposed. Moreover, entire communities have been forced to move to new 'satellite towns' that often lack services or communications and are sometimes located on disease-prone and infertile lands.

The army has been expanded to meet the demands of this totalitarian control. About 40 per cent of the national budget is absorbed by the armed forces – the highest in the region.[19] The army, despite the absence of any significant external threat, has grown to more than 400,000 men. A consequence of this military expansion is that already limited financial resources are diverted from crucial areas such as health and education. Most of the resources for this expanding internal security force have come from China. The exact value of the arms shipments is difficult to determine, especially since some Chinese weaponry has reportedly been bought at 'friendship prices' or acquired in barter deals, but some estimates exceed $2 billion. It is also suggested that the arms purchases may have been financed to some extent by proceeds from heroin sales on the international market.

Myanmar's growing reliance on China is having unsettling effects in the region.[20] Repeated border incursions from Burma, including fierce battles in February 2001, have raised fears in Thailand that Burma's increasing military power will make its government more belligerent. Across South Asia, there is anxiety that China's People's Liberation Army is gaining access to intelligence gathering and naval port facilities on the Bay of Bengal as part of a greater drive to expand Chinese political and military influence throughout the Indian Ocean. Burma is seen as an important bridgehead in that effort, particularly since the Burmese and Chinese high commands enjoy close relations. The desire to tempt Myanmar from Chinese influence was an important consideration in the decision by the Association of Southeast Asian Nations (ASEAN) to admit Burma to the organization in July 1997. It is also a crucial factor for India as it sought to improve relations from 1999. The two countries are now cooperating militarily to suppress guerrilla activity along both sides of their common frontier and are seeking to increase commercial ties through bilateral trade. At the same time, India urges Myanmar to consider a national reconciliation process and transition to democracy.

Any hopes that Myanmar might make the transition to democracy were dashed in November 2004 when hardliners were selected to replace the military leaders most likely to favour progress. General Khin Nyunt, the Prime Minister who had opened negotiations with some ethnic groups and who had drawn up a seven-point road map to democracy in August 2003, was 'permitted to retire for health reasons' – a euphemism for being sacked. Five other Cabinet ministers were replaced. Lieutenant-General Soe Win, the officer responsible for the crackdown on Aung San Suu Kyi and a bitter enemy of the National League for Democracy, claims that he will honour agreements with the minorities of Myanmar, but there seem preciously few guarantees for this.

In the meantime, Myanmar's neighbours continue to support the status quo for their own national interests. Thailand has offered a 10 billion baht loan through the Export-Import Bank of Thailand in the expectation that this will lead to democracy, although commercial interests seem more likely as the overriding motive. China also wants to maintain its influence. The Chinese Vice-Premier, Wu Yi, stated in November 2004 that 'Burma remained a true friend' and that its 'internal problems must be solved by Burma itself'.[21] Even India feels that cross-border security must take a higher precedence than the domestic politics inside Myanmar.

Myanmar remains unpredictable in the region's security calculations. The regime in Rangoon depends on a pervasive and costly military intelligence apparatus (aided by China) to suppress domestic dissent. But this, with an expansion of the army to contain resistance to military rule, spurs a regional arms race. This rivalry diverts resources desperately needed for development. Myanmar is thus another example of a 'failed state' whose leaders resort to repression to maintain their rule. State terror has merely ignited a costly guerrilla war which itself holds back development, increases unrest and therefore fuels the conflict. Only substantial political reform there can break the cycle of violence.

MAKING PEACE: SRI LANKA

South Asia provides examples of long and intractable disputes, but there are also cases of successful peace-making. There are myriad factors at work and it is difficult to draw generalized conclusions across the region without losing a sharp focus. Guerrilla movements, however, whilst united against a government, often find it more difficult to sustain that unity after a cessation of hostilities. Since the war of independence in 1971, for example, internal divisions have beset Bangladesh. Similarly, Kashmiri Separatists have found it difficult to maintain any unified policy despite the existence of the All-Party Hurryiat Conference. A good example of peacemaking, however, comes from Sri Lanka, where political dialogue was restored through international mediation, despite the failure of India to establish a long-term peacekeeping presence in the country.

The Tamil Tigers and the Sri Lankan Army brokered a cease-fire in 2002, using Norwegian intermediaries. The Sri Lankan government that called for peace has since been ousted by the electorate, but despite the divisions between the Sinhalese, there has been a strong commitment to ending the violence. On the Tamil side, a split in the LTTE in 2004 meant that the cease-fire has held there too. In a bid to take over the leadership of the Tigers, Colonel Karuna, the commander of eastern Tamils (who bore the brunt of the fighting), led a campaign against the movement's overall leader and northern commander, Prabhakaran. Karuna alleged that Prabhakaran was offering too many concessions, especially to the Muslims who had moved in on lands vacated by Hindus after they had fled to India as refugees.[22] Despite this potential for communal violence and a new civil war between the members of the LTTE, Karuna's support dwindled even amongst his own followers. Ramesh, the newly installed Tamil Tiger leader in the east, called for the meeting with the Sri Lanka Army to confirm that the guerrilla war was over, and, as such, represents a victory for the moderates over the hardliners. Both sides appear to be sticking by their pledges of 2002: the Tigers agreed to drop calls for independence and settle for autonomy, whilst the government offered to share power. In 2004 the LTTE website reported that the Tigers were in the process of returning all child soldiers in the east back to their parents as a commitment to peace: 269 fighters were recently released, and nearly 150 of them were under 18. Tamil businessmen originally from the north were also slowly returning and reopening their shops.

However, the end of the split in the Tamil Tigers and the resumption of talks is only the first step in a much longer process. President Chandrika Kumaratunga still has the difficult task of fulfilling her election pledge to restart the stalled peace negotiations with the Tigers, and thus create a lasting peace.[23] Moreover, disagreements over policy between the then Prime Minister, Ranil Wickremasinghe, and the President on the eve of the 2004 elections did not assist the continuation of the dialogue. Six rounds of talks, however, starting with those in Thailand in October 2002, have made tentative steps towards a new administration. Indeed, the return of refugees, the reconstruction of zones affected by the conflict and the withdrawal of military forces on both sides have been the first tangible improvements on the ground, which suggests that both sides are now committed to peace. Nevertheless, reconciliation is a long business. It will take years for the scars of war to heal: the economic losses caused by the fighting, the loss of tourist revenue and the deaths of 64,000 Sri Lankans have been major dislocations.

For many there has been no peace dividend. The new government, a coalition of Sri Lankan Freedom Party, some minority groups and the JVP (People's Liberation Front), seems unable or unwilling to make progress on peace, despite the offer of $4 billion from international donors to restart a process stalled in April 2003. As a result, money promised by the Sri Lankan government for the reconstruction of homes was held back during 2004 (although the World Bank made available $75 million for 40,000 homes). The government estimates that 2.5 million, some 13 per cent of the population of Sri Lanka, has been seriously affected by the fighting. Amongst the casualties, the LTTE itself lists some 241 suicide bombers and 17,648 other fighters deaths on its website. All these deaths and injuries represent a loss to Sri Lanka's economic potential. The effects are often insidious. The UN's World Food Programme estimates that malnutrition is spreading rapidly through LTTE-controlled areas, with one in five children now affected.

Most chilling is the defiant rhetoric that periodically resurrects old fears. In a speech in October 2003, the LTTE, whilst using the vocabulary of peace, argued that it would retain all its arms and naval units, refuse to merge with the Sri Lankan Army, and insisted that, in its own areas, it would insist on political primacy – and that other parties would have to accept that. President Kumaratunga wants the creation of an ISGA (Interim Self-Governing Authority) in the north and east to be a result of the LTTE's meeting certain conditions for peace, but the LTTE insist that the establishment of ISGA has to come first, on the basis of the Palestinian Authority. The LTTE also demand that the ISGA would also be able to conduct its own foreign affairs – an area India has already objected to. India wants to see an end to the instability and the establishment of the full integrity and sovereignty to the Sri Lankan government. The last thing it wants is a victory for the terrorists and separatists, lest it inspire similar movements in India. Indian analysts urge a firm hand, and draw analogies with the Indian Army's suppression of Assam and Mizoram insurgents in the 1970s and '80s. They share the concerns of many Sinhalese that the LTTE continues to recruit fighters, and, in November 2004, Prabhakaran caused a wave of speculation and anxiety when he stated that further delays in the peace process would mean 'we will have no alternative than to advance the freedom struggle of our nation'.[24]

Vacillation on the Sinhalese side can only have strengthened the LTTE position, but it has also been the cause of other frustrating delays. Instead of presenting a united front to the LTTE, the political parties have been divided over how best to deal with the Tigers. Wickremasinghe himself also made four tactical mistakes as Premier. First, to further his own position, it appears that he sought to deny any meaningful role for the country's President in the political process. Second, in his eagerness to initiate talks, he embarked on a peace process without first establishing a 'road map' that would be acceptable to the Sinhalese majority. As a result, his negotiating style was reactive and it looked as though the LTTE were dictating terms. He even failed to explain the position of his government on the LTTE's detailed proposal for an ISGA. This tended to alienate the electorate. Third, he ignored violations of the cease-fire by the Tigers lest it made the LTTE even more recalcitrant than it was. Fourth, he believed, mistakenly, that international pressure on the LTTE would make it more amenable for a compromise.

The anxieties of the rank and file in the LTTE caused by the stalled peace process led to an upsurge in political murder in mid-2004. Some commentators fear that, despite the compromises of the political leaders, their efforts may come too late. The failure of Wickremasinghe suggests that the patience of Sinhalese and Tamils may be exhausted, which will lead to widespread violence again. Nevertheless, perhaps the significance of the civil war will, in the end, be judged on how it was ended, and how it sets an example to others in the region.

Finally, in the wake of the Tsunami of 26 December 2004, the Sri Lankan government and LTTE have been eager to control the distribution of aid as a way of demonstrating their authority to the people. Even in the midst of a natural disaster of epic proportions, neither side lost the opportunity to deploy their military forces and politicise the relief effort.

The negotiations between India and Pakistan in January 2004 were universally described as 'historic'. By co-operating, President Pervez Musharaf and the Indian Prime Minister, Atal Bihari Vajpayee, removed the Separatists' means to continue the struggle at its previous level of intensity, proving just how important it is for guerrillas or terrorists to have external support. Under the terms of the agreement, Musharaf promised to crack down on the militants, ending their cross-border attacks on Indian forces. In turn, Vajpayee agreed to begin unconditional negotiations with Pakistan on the status of Kashmir. Naturally, guerrilla fighters who have been hardened by the conflict wish to continue the struggle. One Separatist, a bearded fighter in his early twenties called Saifullah, argued: 'We will not allow Musharaf to sell out the blood of our martyrs . . . We will continue the jihad no matter what.'[25] Nevertheless, there are a significant number who seem war-weary. These men talk of betrayal but believe they have no choice but to return to their homes. Rifaat Hussain, a defence specialist at Islamabad's Quaid-i-Azam University, stated: 'It's the beginning of the end of the Kashmir jihad.'[26]

Unlike previous offers to curb the activities of the militants, Musharaf has gone beyond ordering a halt to operations across the Line of Control. Two serious assassination attempts in December 2003, one by a suicide bomber belonging to the Jaish-e-Mohammed organization, and the change in the international community's attitude to terrorism in light of 9/11, has focused the President's mind. Along with the diplomatic offers, Musharaf has brought an end to the artillery exchanges on the frontier, but it is the cessation of financial or military aid to the insurgents that will make the biggest difference. The security forces are instead making searches of Pakistani cities to locate extremists, and a limited operation was launched against militants, including former Taliban, in Waziristan in 2004. Talaat Masood, a retired officer, predicts that the link between militant Islam and the Pakistan armed forces, exploited for political reasons by General Zia, is coming to an end since they now realize that the jihad strategy is 'counter-productive'.

The end of Pakistan's support is likely to be greeted with relief by the Kashmiris. It is estimated that as many as 60,000 lives have been lost. Moghli Begum lost seven members of her family and believes, not untypically, 'the gun has destroyed my life'. In Srinagar, there are signs of recovery. There are more people on the streets, and fewer Indian troops. Trains have started running across the border and nearly 200 Kashmiri Hindu families who fled the valley because of fighting have returned to their homes. There are talks on transport, communications, trade and water rights, but there are still grounds for caution. According to Indian intelligence sources, not all of the Separatists' camps inside Pakistan have been put out of business. If the Indian Army can be persuaded to reduce its presence in Kashmir, it may be possible to demilitarize the situation sufficiently to restore civil policing: a method that has been used successfully in other insurgency conflicts. To some extent, the solution is not military at all. A lasting peace depends on the political will in Delhi to grant Kashmir greater autonomy, and the survival of a moderate line of policy in Islamabad. Nevertheless, the growth of international terrorism may come at the precise moment that Kashmir stands on a truly historic breakthrough for peace, since Pakistan may have lost control of its Islamist protégés.

PAKISTAN AND THE GLOBALIZATION OF TERRORISM

As a long-term ally of the United States, Musharaff was obliged to collaborate in the war on terror after 9/11, particularly since Pakistan had been the sponsor of the Taliban. India immediately pointed out that Musharaff himself had been the mastermind behind insurgents in the Indian Punjab and in Kashmir. In fact, India had largely quelled the unrest in the Punjab in 1995 and it is debatable how much Pakistan was involved. Terrorism in Kashmir is a different matter and the involvement of a large number of foreign mercenaries trained, armed and infiltrated by Pakistan's Inter-Services Intelligence (ISI), and the surviving remnants of al-Qaeda and the Taliban, threatens to extend the conflict.

Between 1989 and 1993 Pakistan's military-intelligence establishment relied largely on indigenous Kashmiri organizations for promoting terrorism in the Indian part of the state. But armed personnel from a number of Pakistani organizations, mainly from the Punjab, intensified and prolonged the fighting. The more prominent of these Pakistani organizations included: Harkat-ul-Mujahideen (HUM), which was an offshoot of the Harkat-ul-Ansar (HUA); Lashkar-e-Toyeba (LET), the militant wing of the Markaz Darwa al-Irshad (Centre of Preaching) – a foundation funded by Bin Laden; Jaish-e-Mohammad (JEM); Harkat-ul-Jihad-al-Islami (HUJI); and al-Badr.

Of these, the oldest is al-Badr, which was armed and equipped by the ISI through the intermediary of Jamaat-e-Islami (JEI) in East Pakistan before 1971. ISI used the organization to massacre a large number of Bengali Muslim intellectuals that year, in a crude attempt to neutralize political opposition. After the birth of Bangladesh, al-Badr returned to West Pakistan and was amongst the organizations used by the ISI against the Soviet troops in Afghanistan in the 1980s. In a similar way, HUM, LET and HUJI came into being in the 1980s and played a role in the guerrilla war against the Soviets. The final group, JEM, was formed in the beginning of 2000 after a split in the HUM. All of these groups have now focused on Kashmir, describing their objective as the 'liberation' of Muslims of India and the creation of two more 'Muslim homelands' in South Asia.

Their aims, however, are not limited to one small region of South Asia. They describe Western-style liberal democracies as anti-Islam since democracy suggests that sovereignty lies with the people. According to these organizations, sovereignty lies in God and the clerics, as the interpreters of Islam, claim a decisive role in legislating through directives. They look upon the successful functioning of democracy, especially in India, as a corrupting influence on Pakistan's civil society. All of the militant groups reject the concept of national frontiers and they recognize only the frontiers of the *Ummah*. They assert the right of Muslims to wage a *jihad* in any country where, in their perception, Muslims are suppressed, even if it is a 'Muslim' country. More chillingly, they describe Pakistan's atomic bomb as the *Ummah*'s weapon, the technology of which should be available to any Muslim country that needs to protect itself. Indeed, they believe Muslims have a religious obligation to acquire and even use weapons of mass destruction, if necessary, to protect their religion. They believe they have to wage an unlimited global war to achieve their objectives.

All of them look upon the United States, India and Israel as the principal enemies of Islam and, with the exception of al-Badr, they are members of bin Laden's International Islamic Front, which was formed in 1998. To this end, they have imported suicide terrorism in Kashmir, a phenomenon that was unknown in the state before the middle of 1999. The only important Kashmiri organization, which is still carrying on a campaign of terrorism, is the Hizbul Mujahideen, the militant wing of the Jamaat-e Islami (JEI) of Kashmir, itself a wing of the JEI of Pakistan.

According to the Pakistani media, about 6,000 trained terrorists of these organizations, the largest component of them belonging to the HUM and the HUJI, were killed in the operations of the American-led coalition in Afghanistan. The surviving remnants, estimated to be more than 40,000, entered Pakistan from Afghanistan along with the surviving remnants of al-Qaeda and the Taliban. Indian sources believe they sought sanctuary in the tribal areas of Baluchistan, the North-West Frontier Province (NWFP) and the Federally Administered Tribal Areas (FATA) of Pakistan, but have since spread over to other parts of the country away from the Pakistan-Afghan border, including Azad Kashmir and the Northern Areas (namely Gilgit and Baltistan). This dispersal became evident during the capture of Abu Zubaida, stated to be the number Three in al-Qaeda, along with nineteen other members of the organization, by the Pakistani security forces, when they were tipped off by American intelligence. It was reported that they had been given shelter there by LET.

The harbouring of terrorists by Pakistani-based organizations, or their transit from the border areas, seems plausible. Densely populated urban areas, such as Karachi, offer the perfect hiding place. Fazal Karim, a terrorist of the Lashkar-e-Jhangvi (LEJ), told his investigators: 'Our Arab friends hosted us in Afghanistan when we were on the run; now it's our turn to pay them back.'[27] Moreover, the terrorist incidents in Pakistan since 2001 bear all the hallmarks of al-Qaeda. Recent attacks were characterized by detailed planning, the targeting of Westerners and, in two attacks, suicide bombing. The grenade attack on Christian worshippers in an Islamabad church on 17 March 2002, in which five people, including the wife and daughter of an American diplomat, were killed, and the car bomb in Karachi on 8 May 2002, in which eleven French nationals died, suggest a change from previous violence in the city.

The role played by the Lashkar-e-Toyeba at Muridke, near Lahore, in facilitating the movement of al-Qaeda cadres to and from Afghanistan was highlighted by the *Friday Times* of Lahore.[28] The paper stated:

> Muridke, a city within a city, was built with Arab money . . . Its [LETS] contact with the Wahabi camps in Kunnar in Afghanistan has never been disowned although Muridke carefully mutes its obvious connections with the Arab warriors in Afghanistan. Its connections with Osama bin Laden have also been carefully hidden although news appearing in the national press have linked the two.

In a subsequent report, the same paper noted:

> Sources say that when Dawatul Irshad [Usually titled Markaz Dawa al-Irshad and since renamed as *Jamaat al-Dawa*], parent organization of the now banned Lashkar Tayyaba [Lashkar-e-Toyeba], shifted its activities to Azad Kashmir, it took with it many non-Pakistanis suspected of links to Al Qaeda. All these organizations were loosely affiliated and their activists moved across organizations and cells with a great degree of ease.[29]

In its report on 'Patterns of Global Terrorism 2000', released on 30 April 2001, the Counter-Terrorism Division of the US State Department had warned: 'Taliban-controlled Afghanistan remains a primary hub for terrorists and a home or transit point for the loosely-organized network of "Afghan alumni", a web of informally linked individuals and groups that were trained and fought in the Afghan war.' However, since the fall of the Taliban in Afghanistan, Pakistan, including Azad Kashmir and the Northern Areas, has become the new primary hub for terrorists and a transit point for terrorists operating against the Karzai government in Kabul, India, the United States, Bangladesh, Myanmar, Singapore, Malaysia, Indonesia, the Philippines, China, the Central Asian Republics,

Russia and Europe. India is anxious that the international community recognize this point and they accuse Musharaff of insincerity in his counter-terrorism measures.

After the attack on the Indian parliament in December 2001, Musharaf announced a series of measures to tackle the terrorist organizations in Pakistan and their supporters. He froze the bank accounts of organizations, which were named by the UN and the Americans as terrorist or suspected terrorist organizations. This was followed by the arrest of 2,000 leaders and activists of LET, JEM, Sipah-e-Sahaba Pakistan (SSP) – a Sunni extremist organization, Tehrik Jaffria Pakistan (TJP) – a radical Shia group, and Tehrik-e Nifaz-e Shariat-e Mohammadi (TNSM), a guerrilla organization based in the FATA. Each of these groups was also banned.

The measures, however, were not as effective as they could have been. Since the terrorist organizations learned in advance of the impending freeze on their accounts, they withdrew or transferred funds to other accounts in different names. The two accounts of HUM, for example, yielded a total of only 4,742 rupees (US $70), while the al-Rashid Trust, which handled the accounts of the Taliban and LET, had 2.7 million rupees (US $ 40,000). Ayman al-Zawahiri, the notorious activist of al-Jihad in Egypt who operated the accounts of al-Qaeda, had just US $252 confiscated. Moreover, some of the people arrested did little more than run the offices of the organizations in small towns, collected funds in streets and distributed pamphlets. Most of them were released after three months on the grounds that there was no evidence of their involvement in terrorism. In fact, it seems there were no arrests of trained terrorists. Moreover, although some groups were banned, this did not apply to HUM or HUJI, which are thought to enjoy close links with the Pakistan Army. India also feels aggrieved that twenty terrorists, fourteen of them Indian nationals, have not been extradited as requested.

The net result of this apparently inept treatment of radical groups is that India fears that there will not be an end to the Kashmir insurgency yet. Extremists groups are unlikely to surrender, even if the local population and the Kashmiri Separatists accept an agreement between India and Pakistan. The situation for Musharaff may be akin, in the end, to the story of Frankenstein's monster.

Chapter 11

Conclusion: Points of Conflict in South Asia

Conflict is, tragically, endemic in South Asia. The images of dismembered bomb victims, pitiful refugees or bereaved relatives wailing for their dead are depressingly common. It is impossible to ignore this human dimension of conflict. Apart from all the analyses and headlines, we are reminded that war and terrorism have a terrible cost. War is a tragic, wasteful and unsatisfactory aspect of human history that retards economic development in South Asia, and causes untold misery for its people. The types, causes and effects of these conflicts are briefly examined in this final chapter. This sections also looks at the global influences and attempts at conflict resolution in the region. The chapter concludes with some tentative remarks about potential future conflicts.

There are four categories of conflict in South Asia. These are: inter-state conflict, intra-state conflict (including insurgencies), communal or sectarian conflict (which may or may not be confined within national borders) and terrorism. Not all these types are unique to the region, but the deep roots of rivalry between sections of South Asian society and the long history of conflicts over certain areas (such as the fertile Indus Valley and the arid mountain zone to the north-west) are aspects peculiar to the subcontinent. The causes of war generate a great deal of debate. There may be a commonality of factors that could be identified across time and space in any region, but there are some that are specific to South Asia since 1947.

Ethnic tensions are especially prominent. South Asia is a region of immense diversity and great population density. The close proximity of many peoples of different linguistic, cultural and ethnic backgrounds makes the success of Indian democracy remarkable, but there have been significant problems. On the north-eastern border of India, for example, the Assamese opposed 'foreigners' who moved into border regions and were aggrieved by their own economic inferiority compared with the relative prosperity of Indian migrants from further west. In the remotest parts of the north-east, tribal territory was jealously guarded. Sikhs aspired to territorial and political autonomy in India's Punjab in the west. In the South of India, many Tamils still distrust the central authority of New Delhi, and particularly the chauvinist policies of the recent BJP government on the question of languages and education. For many minorities, the election of 2004 was decided on the issue of poverty, leavened by this fear of the Hindu radicalism of the BJP. In Pakistan, many provincial tribal groups resent or actively resist the Punjabi-dominated government. In the last decades there have been serious conflicts in Baluchistan, Waziristan and, most famously, in the former East Pakistan, now Bangladesh.

Perhaps the most serious ethnic conflicts have been in Sri Lanka and Myanmar. The Tamil–Sinhalese struggle drew in India, albeit in a peace-keeping and mediation role, and it led to the deaths of thousands in a bitter and dirty war. In Myanmar, the majority Burman population is sometimes pitted against other ethnic groups, although the military government frequently uses the minorities against each other in forced relocations and land redistribution initiatives. The long-term effects of these divisive policies are difficult to predict, but they have failed to provide the government with any lasting peace.

Religion remains a potent source of conflict in South Asia, a fact often underestimated in the West. The destruction of a mosque at Ayodhya in 1992 by a group of 500 Vishwa Hindu Parishad Hindus (a wing of BJP) led to rioting in Bombay and other cities, thousands of deaths and the reciprocal destruction of ancient Hindu temples in Pakistan and Bangladesh.[1] In response, a group of Hindu extremists called Shiv Sena (Shiva's Army) called for a more determined application of a militant Hindutva ('Hinduness') policy in India. In Pakistan, Muslim fundamentalism has spawned a militant brand of Islam and provides thousands of recruits for radical movements. For example, Lashkar-e-Toyeba, although now banned, still has underground cells willing to be martyred in a *jihad* against Indian and Western targets. Cities like Karachi also provide a useful hiding place for the extremists. In fact, Karachi is a city wracked by sectarianism. Clashes between Shias and Sunnis are common and extremely violent. Those groups with a Wahabi orientation are just as doctrinaire in their sectarianism and they reserve almost as much loathing for the more spiritualist Sufis as they do for Christians and Jews.

Ideologies are also the source of conflict in South Asia. National sovereignty, for example, is the key to the Kashmir dispute. Since independence in 1947, both India and Pakistan have been eager to assert their sovereign will, citing self-determination or a legal transfer of power as their points of reference. Ironically both seem opposed to the idea of Kashmiri independence. Indeed, within the two countries there are minorities who favour either autonomy or independence, but, so far, only Bangladesh has achieved this (with India's assistance, hence Pakistan's fears). The Sikhs of the Punjab, for example, hankered after greater autonomy in the 1980s and some still want full independence, especially after Mrs Gandhi's 'crackdown' in Operation Bluestar in Amritsar. In Pakistan, many Pushtuns of the North-West Frontier Province seek an independent Pushtunistan. In Sri Lanka, the LTTE once argued for an independent state but now talk of autonomy, whilst in Burma, tribal guerrilla forces of the Karen continue to oppose the Far Left government in Rangoon in the hope of independence. In Nepal, Communist ideology is the motivation for the Maoists, although the majority of the Nepalese who sympathize with them do so for two reasons: economic improvement and greater democratization.

The legacy of previous wars can make it easier for new conflicts to break out. The governments of India and Pakistan find it difficult to compromise over Kashmir because of the amount of blood that has been spilt. More than 24,000 have died in the conflict. Pakistan, for example, has expended a great deal of money, many lives and much effort in support of insurgents. It has fought difficult campaigns, often against the odds, in 1947–8, 1965, 1971 and 1999. So far it has not achieved a lasting strategic advantage from any of them. It sponsored the Taliban in Afghanistan, only to see them ousted by a Western-backed coalition. It armed the Separatists in Kashmir, but it is no nearer seeing the creation of an 'Azad' (free) Kashmir beyond the Line of Control. Despite the recent euphoria over Musharaff's negotiations with India, these defeats, coupled with a rise in militant Islam, may foster a feeling of bitterness and irredentism in the army and the Islamist hardliners that makes conflict more likely in the future. In the same way, observers are cautious about the future of Sri Lanka. Tens of thousands died in the fighting and hardliners seem determined to continue the struggle, despite the success of the dialogue that began in 2002.

Other than in the causes of conflict, there are patterns in the nature of the fighting in South Asia too. Across the region there are many examples of chronic mismanagement and corruption by state officials. The Congress Party in India has promised to 'wage war' on corruption because of the way that it undermines authority and fuels unrest. In Nepal, this has been one of the most important reasons for the Maoist insurgency, and, indeed, sustains the fighting by providing the insurgents with an important propaganda weapon. In addition, the fact that Nepal does not enjoy a free and unlimited democratic constitution creates more unrest. India has been fortunate that its army is governed by an ethos of service to the state, and it is taken as axiomatic that Indian democracy is more at risk from its politicians than its soldiers. This was borne out by the years in which Mrs Gandhi ran the country under a state of emergency, and her reactions to Sikh demands for autonomy need to be seen in the context of this political climate. The Sikhs did not, perhaps, cause the Indian government to take a hard line; it was rather that the Indian government was already moving in that direction and this coloured their response to the unrest in Amritsar.

Military intervention in government is an unfortunate reality in Pakistan, Bangladesh and Burma. The reason cited for these interventions is, again, corruption and mismanagement by civilian authorities. Nevertheless, the consequence is that the army will invariably opt for a military system of decision-making. Martial law, hierarchical administration and a tough line against dissent are the characteristics of militarized states. Afghanistan under the Taliban reflected this pattern, although a religious intolerance also characterized the regime. Interestingly, Pakistan found that its military rule did not help in the conflict with India in 1971. Indeed, it was a positive hindrance as commanders tried to contend with civil as well as military demands in a time of crisis. The Taliban, despite the scale and extent of their military force, proved incapable of preserving their rule unchallenged too. The Burmese government faces much the same sort of problem. The response of military governments, which are incapable of achieving consensus by their very nature, is therefore to impose state terror. In Myanmar, this has reached excessive proportions and the international community almost universally condemns the Rangoon government.[2]

Conventional armed forces in South Asia already employ more paramilitaries as a cheap alternative to standing armies, but the risk is a greater militarization of society. Certainly there are legal difficulties with these units in Kashmir: they are forces that are less accountable to the civilian authorities. For India this has, to some extent, been counterproductive. The civilian population resents the security forces and fears them as much as the Separatists. Nevertheless, it is difficult to protect vulnerable lines of communication, man borders, offer military aid to the civil power and patrol areas affected by insurgency with relatively small numbers of regular soldiers who are expensive to train. The economic reality of 'policing' an insurgency or containing a terrorist threat is an expansion of militias and paramilitary formations, although that does not necessarily presuppose they can act above the law.

There are also similarities in South Asian states on the issue of poverty and demography. The demographic profile of South Asian states, in contrast to the West, has a large proportion that can be considered 'young' and therefore eligible for military service. India, for example, has a population of approximately 1 billion and growing. The Indian Army now stands at 1.1 million men and is the world's second largest. Pakistan fields armed forces 510,000 strong, which is proportionately far higher than India. Pakistan also commits twice as much to its armed forces as India in its budget, some 30 per cent of its revenue. Since the liberalization of the Indian economy begun by Rajiv Gandhi (and launched by Manmohan Singh, the new Prime Minister in 2004), India has enjoyed a growth in GDP of some 6 per cent, and, in 2003–2004 a growth of 8.4 per cent. As the 2004 election results show, however, the electorate is disenchanted with the slow rate of development in rural areas and consumer prices have risen by 3 per cent in the last year. Crippling poverty has the potential to increase civil unrest and communal violence as disaffected Indians seek to vent their frustration with rival economic groups. A slowing of growth, as occurred in the early 1990s, or stagnation could cause massive problems for India.

Failed states, and the impoverished victims of war, have turned to the lucrative production of narcotics to sustain their domestic economies. Farmers in Afghanistan can make far more from opium than traditional produce, and the Burmese government virtually encourages heroin production as a way to boost its own flagging economy and offer minority groups a last lifeline of support. This situation has major implications for the international community. It would be a short-sighted policy to try to stop drug-trafficking on the borders of developed nations since only by tackling the source of supply can the problem be truly contained.

The effects of conflict in South Asia can be detected in other, tragic ways. Across the region, there are tens of thousands of people displaced by war and insurgency.[3] Refugees from Myanmar can be found on the borders with Thailand, Laos, Bangladesh and India. There are still refugee communities of 'Biharis' in Bangladesh. Thousands of Sri Lankan Tamils reside in southern India. There are Afghan camps in Pakistan's NWFP, in the Central Asian republics and inside Iran. Conditions in these camps are primitive, although the host states do their best with limited resources. In almost every case, refugees place enormous strain on local economies, create tensions (sometimes religious or ethnic in nature) with the indigenous population and act as breeding grounds of discontent amongst young men of military age. From an economic perspective, refugees deprive the original states of valuable manpower and business entrepreneurs. Young Afghan men, for example, have in some cases grown up knowing only the camps and the business of war: they have missed out on their apprenticeship in agriculture or trade, which is crucial in the re-establishment of a peace-time economy.

Prolonged war hardens attitudes just as often as it creates war-weariness. Separatists and nationalists, religious idealists and Communist ideologues deepen their convictions in the crucible of war. They become determined to avenge, to promote martyrdom and to seek 'total' solutions – victory or death, paradise or *Götterdammerung*. In the teeth of these extremist positions, India and Sri Lanka and, to a lesser degree, Bangladesh have remained committed to consensual politics and democracy. Nepal, Myanmar, Pakistan and Afghanistan are under pressure from international opinion to establish greater democratization. This development could be sustained only with a series of trust-building initiatives, economic improvements at grass roots and the subordination of the armed forces to civilian, constitutional bodies. It is not clear, however, whether military rule is a cause or a consequence of internal unrest. So-called democratic politicians have shown themselves to be just as extreme as doctrinaire groups like the Separatists, nationalists, theocrats and Communists. In Nepal, Myanmar and Pakistan there is ample evidence that civilian leaders squandered opportunities for power-sharing and caused so much disaffection that the army felt compelled, as a national duty, to step in.

Terrorists in South Asia are also widespread. In the last thirty years many groups have become more ruthless and, at the beginning of the twenty-first century, there are now terrorists who favour mass casualties, 'punishment' attacks and absolute exclusivity in their philosophy. In addition, their capabilities have increased. New communications and greater population mobility enable the terrorist to have a 'global reach'. In attacks, there is a trend towards systemic disruption as well as 'spectacular' devastation. The methods of kidnapping, hijacking, car and truck bombs, and assassination, will soon be supplemented by 'information age' offensives in cyberspace, attacks on energy supplies, mass contamination, more emphasis on secondary effects caused by mass panic, and, should they obtain them, the use of WMDs. These attacks will not be limited to South Asia, but may emanate from flashpoints in the region as terror is 'globalized'.[4]

Many of the conflicts in South Asia have been subject to global influences. The superpowers, the United States, the Soviet Union and China, were able to pressure regional states. India and Pakistan both calculated on weapons supply and the speed of international intervention when they planned operations in 1965 and 1971. India severely under-estimated the willingness of China to uphold its version of the Sino-Indian border in 1962, a miscalculation mirrored by the Taliban leadership in 2001 about America's determination to neutralize training faculties by means of an air and ground assault. During the Cold War, South Asian states tried to remain outside the East–West confrontation by joining the Non-Aligned Movement. After 1971, however, this neutrality looked like an empty gesture as India and Pakistan moved closer to the USSR and the USA respectively, and Burma moved into the Chinese orbit.

After the collapse of the Soviet Union, India and Pakistan have had more room to manoeuvre, and both sides see an advantage in courting American patronage. India is eager to demonstrate that Pakistan is an untrustworthy ally for Washington: it backed the Taliban and promoted insurgency in Kashmir. The logic of the 'War on Terror', India argues, is to root out the nest of vipers inside Pakistan. Islamabad is eager to gain American approval as a means for survival. Dollars, and the restraining effect of the United States on India, are required, and Musharaff has tried hard to demonstrate his commitment to international order in the teeth of domestic public opinion. Confronted with irrefutable evidence by Western intelligence, he exposed his own atomic-bomb-making expert, Dr Abdul Qadeer Khan, for selling nuclear secrets to Iran, Libya and North Korea.[5] This was a severe blow to Pakistan's national prestige, but Musharaff distanced himself successfully from Khan's activities in a television broadcast. Islamic extremists have also been the target of Musharaff's new policy, especially after two assassination attempts, but he cannot risk alienation of all of them and he will proceed cautiously against them.

The international community has a role to play in containing or resolving conflict in the region, but there are limitations in trying to impose a settlement externally. The United States has, in the past, placed restrictions on arms sales. In 1971 America suspended its military support of India (which had begun in 1962 after the border war with China) and despatched a fleet into the Bay of Bengal. This caused enormous resentment and persuaded India to seek military support from the Soviets. President Carter's threats to limit uranium supplies to India, after the detonation of its first nuclear weapon, failed to persuade India to sign a Non-Proliferation Treaty. Indeed, cutting off military aid cannot guarantee compliance since the supply of arms can be made by other powers. Moreover, whilst high-tech weapons or aid donations may be limited and thus starve the protagonists of their ability to conduct conventional operations, it is far harder to influence insurgency in this way.

The South Asian states are eager to assert their sovereignty because of their colonial legacy. India has favoured an independent line of diplomacy ever since Nehru's ministry of 1947–65. This was another reason for the Non-Aligned Movement of 1961, which the South Asian states embraced. This tradition, however, makes it harder for the West to pressure Indian and other regional governments. The desire for strategic security has also been evident in the thinking of South Asian statesmen. As with the Soviet occupation of Afghanistan during the 1980s, so there is resentment of the American presence there amongst many Pakistanis. Amongst Islamic militants, there is a strong desire for revenge against a 'puppet' regime. Hamed Kharzai has struggled to extend his jurisdiction beyond Kabul and the border with Pakistan is not secure. India fears that this will lead to the 're-Talibanization' of Afghanistan and therefore the return of safe havens for terror groups that will target Delhi and other Indian cities.[6]

Oil in Central Asia will add a further complication to international interests in the region. Pipelines will be needed to exploit this vast new reservoir. China has attempted negotiations with Kazakhstan, but, to the West, the instability in the Caucasus makes it desirable to route new lines through Afghanistan, Pakistan, Iran or Iraq. India is concerned about the empowerment of these former rivals.

There is of course an assumption that the international community will have the will to intervene to prevent conflict in South Asia. In fact, the United Nations and the Western powers have appeared reluctant to tackle the Kashmir dispute head-on. On the other hand, if limited war escalates into nuclear confrontation, as demonstrated by the Kargil Conflict in 1999, there has been a greater willingness to take action. The permanent five members of the UN brought diplomatic pressure to bear on India and Pakistan to end the weapons testing. Norway too has shown its desire to offer the sort of 'good offices' used by the United Nations to start negotiations in Sri Lanka. The UN missions to Afghanistan at the end of the Soviet era were widely proclaimed as a model for future conflict in the region. There appears, however, to be little progress on Myanmar. The 'Westphalian Doctrine', whereby the international community avoids intervention in the domestic disputes of sovereign nation states, is being challenged, but after difficult and protracted operations in Iraq, or interminable talks without success between Israel and the Palestinians, there is some doubt about the readiness of Western states to get embroiled in conflict-resolution or 'regime change'. American analysts predict that, after 2015, there will be greater world instability and rivalry for the United States, which may affect its ability to effect change.[7] Moreover, there is also the question whether regional states can be influenced if they become economically, or militarily, more independent, thus negating the methods used by the United States in 1965 and 1971.

Conflict resolution may be achieved by war (by conquest or defeat), through direct negotiation, by negotiation through a third party, by external pressure or by the collapse of insurgent or terrorist groups. In South Asia, all these have been evident. The Civil War in Afghanistan was ended by an international coalition in support of the United Front /Northern Alliance which routed the Taliban. India and Pakistan have made attempts to resolve the Kashmir dispute by direct negotiations. Sri Lanka's protagonists have made use of a third party's mediation, although the erosion of civilian support for the insurgents also had a part to play. The decline of support for Assamese guerrillas and Sikh Separatists amongst civilians was an important factor in reducing violence in two regions in India. Insurgency and terrorism are certainly adversely affected by attrition, an erosion of will and a loss of popular backing amongst civilian sympathizers. Their abandonment by foreign backers can be just as dramatic. Conversely, the politicization of conflict and the resentment of perceived state terrorism can fuel insurgency.

In the future, there are four areas that are likely to cause conflict in South Asia: resources, the challenge to India's regional hegemony, perceived cultural threats and environmental crises. For states struggling to exploit resources for economic growth, and to increase food production to feed their teeming cities, there is a distinct potential for conflict. Although India was able to negotiate new water management arrangements with Nepal and Bangladesh in the early 1990s, there has been little progress to date with Pakistan over the Punjab. As population growth continues in the region, a Malthusian disaster may be averted by the exploitation of new GM crops, but energy needs will increase and threaten to outstrip the resources available.[8]

To some extent India has assumed the mantle of paramount power in the subcontinent bequeathed by the British, but it is a position of regional hegemony resented by all its neighbours. India's armed forces did not perform well in the India–China border war of 1962, its air forces suffered heavy losses in 1971 and the army had major difficulties containing insurgents in Sri Lanka in the late 1980s. Whilst it is an economic giant, it is still weak in comparison to the global leaders in the West and in East Asia. There is a strong possibility that India's neighbours will try to assert themselves against India, as Pakistan and China have done in the past. Indeed, the centrifugal forces of separatism in India, and in Pakistan, may increase rather than subside in this century.

There has been a long history of communal violence in South Asia, and minorities are eager to assert their identities by force when they feel threatened. The Sikh Separatists, like many other groups, have used terrorism to further their cause. Suicide bombing by LTTE and by Muslim extremists is an established tactic and may appear elsewhere. More powerful 'hand-held' weapons technology will also be developed. Acts of sabotage, bombings, kidnap, assassination and terror are therefore likely to increase in the future rather than decrease.

Pressure on states caused by the displacement of refugees was evident in the Bangladesh War of 1971 and as a result of fighting in Myanmar and Afghanistan, but environmental crises may make this more common in the future, and generate conflict. Flooding of the Gangetic delta is more likely according to those that predict climate change. In India, erratic changes in the monsoon, caused by the India Ocean version of the El Niño, may give rise to famines, as they did in the 1870s and 1960s, but on a more frequent basis. Unless GM crops and other improvements prove a success in South Asia there may be problems of land exhaustion. There is already a threat of 'overpopulation' pressure on the land, despite a massive migration to the urban centres of the subcontinent. All have the potential to rupture social relations and lead to conflict, especially if the consequence is a scarcity of food supplies.

The most likely pattern of conflict in South Asia is a continuation of limited warfare, especially insurgency, terrorism and state countermeasures. One aspect that lies outside the scope of this study will be the transfer of South Asian conflicts to communities living around the world. Ethnic and sectarian violence between South Asians or those descended from them has already been a concern for police forces in the United Kingdom. However, it is the globalization of terrorism that will undoubtedly draw more attention to the region. It is to be hoped that this international interest will also mean a greater willingness to assist, mediate and resolve existing regional conflicts. The consequences of neglecting them will mean a repetition of the tragedies that have affected so many thousands already, and that, surely, would be a crime against humanity.

References

Chapter 1: The Significance of Conflicts in South Asia

1 Giles Kepel, 'The Origins and Development of the Jihadist Movement: From Anti-Communism to Terrorism', *Asian Affairs*, XXXIV/2 (July 2003), pp. 91–108.
2 Tariq Mahmud Ashraf, 'Global Trends, 2015: South Asia', *Strategic Vision*, III (January–February 2004), p. 22.
3 Jeremy Black, *Why Wars Happen* (London, 1998), p. 15; see also Bertrand Taithe and Tim Thornton, *War: Identities in Conflict, 1300–2000* (London, 1998), pp. 1–12.
4 Black, *Why Wars Happen*, p. 20.
5 For an interesting study of this phenomenon, see Tan Tai Yong, 'Maintaining the Military Districts: Civil Military Integration and District Soldiers' Boards in the Punjab, 1919–1939', *Modern Asian Studies*, XXVIII (1994), pp. 883–74.
6 Jihadists also define the threat in traditional territorial terms, referring to the occupation of Muslim *Ummah* (homelands) by powerful forces of unbelievers. This has had some influence on the Jihadists' perception of the Kashmir dispute.
7 See M. G. Chitkara, *Combating Terrorism* (Delhi, 2003).
8 Robert Bradnock, *India's Foreign Policy since 1971* (London, 1990), p. 23.
9 Cited in Stanley Wolpert, *A New History of India*. 6th edn (Oxford, 2000), p. 453; Mohan Malik, 'The Stability of Nuclear Deterrence in South Asia: The Clash between State and Anti-State Actors', *Asian Affairs*, XXX/3 (2003).
10 Wolpert, *New History of India*, p. 349.

Chapter 2: Conflicts in India

1 Larry Collins and Dominique Lapierre, *Freedom at Midnight* (London, 1975), p. 188.
2 Robert W. Bradnock, *India's Foreign Policy since 1971* (London, 1990), p. 16.
3 *The Independent*, 15 April 1989.
4 K. Subramanyam, 'India and the Soviet Union', *India's Foreign Policy: The Nehru*

Years, ed. B. R. Nanda (Delhi, 1976), p. 171.

5 *The Independent*, 4 February 1989.

6 Stanley Wolpert, *A New History of India*, 6th edn (Oxford and New York, 2000), p. 351.

7 Bradnock, *India's Foreign Policy*, n. 25, p. 118.

8 Subramanyam, 'India and the Soviet Union', p. 103.

9 R. Litwak in T. George, *India and the Great Powers* (Aldershot, 1984), p. 115.

10 See George Blyn, *Agricultural Trends in India, 1891–1947: Output, Availability and Productivity* (Oxford and Philadelphia, PA, 1966).

11 *India Today* (30 June 1989).

12 Government of India's *Economy Survey, 1988–9*.

13 *India Today* (Delhi, 1985), p. 61.

14 *Far Eastern Economic Review* (4 January 1990), pp. 50–2.

15 P. J. S. Duncan, *The Soviet Union and India* (London, 1989), pp. 78–9.

16 For a typical criticism of the United States, see R. K. Sharma, *The Economics of Soviet Assistance to India* (New Delhi, 1981), pp. 3–4.

17 Cited in A. Appadorai, *The Domestic Roots of India's Foreign Policy, 1947–1972* (Delhi, 1981), p. 100.

18 *Current* (Bombay), (16 May 1987), p. 12.

19 *The Economist* (8 July 2000), p. 84.

20 *Pakistan Yearbook, 1986–7* (Islamabad, 1986).

21 Duncan, *The Soviet Union and India*, pp. 74–7.

22 Romila Thapar, *Early India: From the Origins to AD 1300* (London, 2002), pp. xxiii and 13ff.

23 Wolpert, *India*, p. 381.

24 M. Tully and S. Jacob, *Amritsar: Mrs Gandhi's Last Battle* (London, 1985).

25 Wolpert, *India*, p. 453.

Chapter 3: Conflicts in Pakistan, Bangladesh, Sri Lanka, Nepal and Myanmar

1 Yunas Samad, 'Reflections on Partition: A Pakistani Perspective', *14th European Conference on Modern South Asian Studies Conference: Copenhagen, August 1996*.

2 K. B. Sayeed, 'Pakistan in 1983', *Asian Survey* (1984), p. 1084.

3 Hasan-Askari Rizvi, *The Military and Politics in Pakistan, 1947–86* (Delhi, 1988), p. 242.

4 Oliver Roy, 'Islam and Foreign Policy', in *A History of Pakistan and its Origins*, ed. Christophe Jaffrelot, trans. Gillian Beaumont (London, 2002).

5 *Dawn Overseas Weekly* (Karachi), (14 December 1988).

6 H. I. Malik, *State and Civil Society in Pakistan: Politics of Authority, Ideology and Ethnicity* (Basingstoke, 1997).

7 *Dawn Magazine* (Karachi), (11 September 1992), cited in Ian Talbot, 'Military Intervention in Pakistan', paper delivered to the *New Military History of South Asia*

Conference: Cambridge, 1997.

8 Hasan-Askari Rizvi, 'The Legacy of Military Rule in Pakistan', *Survival*, XXXI/3 (May–June 1989), p. 266.

9 S. Ahmed, 'The Military and Ethnic Politics', in *Pakistan 1995*, ed. C. H. Kennedy and R. B. Rais (Boulder, CO, 1995), p. 125.

10 See, for example, Rajat Kanta Ray, *Social Conflict and Political Unrest in Bengal, 1875–1927* (New Delhi, 1984).

11 See Anthony Mascarenhas, *The Rape of Bangladesh* (New Delhi, 1972).

12 Subhash Kapila, 'Bangladesh's Domestic Political Violence by Islamic Jehadis' and 'Bangladesh Emerges as Alternative Base for Pakistan's Proxy War Against India' (11 May 2004), South Asia Analysis Group: http://www.saag.org

13 Kumari Jayawardena, *Ethnic Conflict in Sri Lanka* (Colombo, 1985).

14 Coalition To Stop the Use of Child Soldiers, *Child Soldiers Global Report* (2001), p. 342; Rohan Gunaratna, 'LTTE Child Combatants', *Jane's Intelligence Review* (July 1998); Rachel Brett and Margaret McCallin, *Children: The Invisible Soldiers* (Radda Barnen, 1998), pp. 93 and 98. The case study was conducted for the UN Study on the Impact of Conflict on Children, prepared by Graça Machel and presented to the UN in 1996.

15 Jonathan Gregson, *Blood Against the Snows: The Tragic Story of Nepal's Royal Dynasty* (London, 2002).

16 Deepak Thapa and Bandita Sijapati, *A Kingdom Under Siege: Nepal's Maoist Insurgency, 1996–2004* (London, 2004).

17 Interview, 28 May 2001, cited in Steven C. Baker, 'Nepal's Maoist Insurgency', FrontPageMagazine.com (25 July 2003).

18 Christina Fink, *Living Silence: Burma Under Military Rule* (London, 2001)

19 Aung San Suu Kyi, *Letters from Burma* (London, 1997).

Chapter 4: Global Influences on South Asian Conflicts

1 A. Appadorai and M. S. Rajan, *India's Foreign Policy and Relations* (New Delhi, 1985), p. 18.

2 G. W. Chowdhury, *India, Pakistan, Bangladesh and the Major Powers: Politics of a Divided Subcontinent* (New York, 1975), p. 8.

3 S. Chawla, 'The Foreign Relations of India', in *Comparative Foreign Relations*, ed. D. O. Wilkinson and L. Scheinman (Encino, CA, 1976), p. 95.

4 See T. George, R. Litwak and S. Chubin, *India and the Great Powers* (Aldershot, 1984), pp. 142–3.

5 P. J. S. Duncan, *The Soviet Union and India* (London, 1989), p. 112.

6 See Dulip Bobb, *India Today* (15 December 1988), p. 14.

7 William J. Barnds, *India, Pakistan and the Great Powers* (New York, 1972), pp. 47–8.

8 Robert Bradnock, *India's Foreign Policy since 1971* (London, 1990), p. 16.

9 R. C. G. Thomas, *Indian Security Policy* (Princeton, NJ, 1986), p. 10.

10 Pran Chopra, *India's Second Liberation* (Delhi, 1973), p. 201.

11 Cited in R. L. Hargrave and S. A. Kochanek, *India: Government and Politics in a Developing Nation*, 4th edn (San Diego, CA, 1986), p. 289.

12 Bradnock, *India's Foreign Policy*, p. 102.

13 *The Independent* (9 August 1989).

14 See R. P. Cronin, *The United States, India and South Asia: Interests, Trends and Issues for Congressional Concern* (Subcommittee on Asian and Pacific Affairs, Committee on International Relations, Washington, DC, 1978), p. 11.

15 See M. S. Rajan, V. S. Mani and C.S.R. Murphy, *The Nonaligned and the United Nations* (New Delhi, 1987).

16 R. M. Bell and D. Scott-Kemmis, *Indo-British Technical Collaboration since the Early 1970s: Change, Diversity and Foregone Opportunities* (University of Sussex Policy Research Unit, 1984), p. 6.

17 See *Far Eastern Economic Review Yearbook 1989*, p. 185.

18 Cited in Bradnock, *India's Foreign Policy*, p. 62.

19 See Neville Maxwell, *India's China War* (London, 1970).

Chapter 5: The Kashmir Dispute, 1947–2004

1 US Secretary of State, Press Conference on the Crisis in South Asia, Palais de Nations, Geneva, 4 June 1998.

2 Sumit Ganguly, 'Nuclear War Between India and Pakistan?', Center for Defense Information (13 December 1999), www.cdi.org/adm/1214/transcript.html

3 Judith M. Brown, *Modern India: The Origins of an Asian Democracy*, 2nd edn (Oxford, 1994), p. 237.

4 D. George Boyce, *Decolonisation and the British Empire, 1775–1997* (London, 1999), p. 105.

5 Boyce, *Decolonisation*, p. 99.

6 S. Das, *Communal Riots in Bengal, 1905–1947* (Delhi, 1991).

7 Gulab Singh also ensured, by the treaty of Amritsar, that the British recognized his annexation of Ladakh (1834). The agreement of 1846, however, specified that Gulab Singh was not to extend his territory any further, which prevented another conflict with the Tibetans, the claimants of Ladakh. Alistair Lamb, *The China–India Border: The Origins of the Disputed Boundaries* (London, 1964), p. 64.

8 The principal trade had been in silk, jade, hemp, salt and wool. For British trade there, see John Keay, *Where Men and Mountains Meet* (Oxford, 1977), pp. 17–47.

9 G. J. Alder, *British India's Northern Frontier, 1865–95* (London, 1963), p. 100.

10 Human Rights Watch: Behind the Kashmir Conflict (September 1994 and May 1996).

11 Harinder Baweja, 'New Disenchantment', *India Today* (Delhi), (31 December 1995).

12 Human Rights Watch, Interview (19 October 1998).

13 Gunaratna Rohan , 'Will Kashmir Trigger the Bomb?', *Jane's Intelligence Review* (1 August 1998). The Indian Embassy in the United States estimates the figure to be nearer 200,000.

14 Cited in Barry Bearak, 'Kashmir a Crushed Jewel Caught in a Vise of Hatred', *New York Times* (12 August 1999).

15 US Secretary of State, Press Conference on the Crisis in South Asia, Palais de

Nations, Geneva, 4 June 1998. See also Norman Dixit, *India–Pakistan in War and Peace* (London and New York, 2002), pp. 327–50.

16 General Pervez Musharaff, cited in *The Economist* (29 January 2000), p. 81.
17 Cited in Bearak, 'Kashmir', *New York Times* (12 August 1999).
18 Peter L. Bergen, *Holy War Inc.* (London, 2001), pp. 235–6.
19 *The Economist* (29 July 2000), pp. 67–8.
20 *The Economist* (29 July 2000), p. 67.
21 *The Economist* (12 August 2000), p. 63.
22 See *The Economist* (14 April 2001).
23 See *The Economist* (26 May 2001), p. 78.
24 Lawrence Ziring, *Pakistan at the Crosscurrent of History* (Oxford, 2003), pp. 298 and 303; Stanley Wolpert, *A New History of India* (New York and Oxford, 2000), p. 454.

Chapter 6: The India–China Conflict of 1962

1 Girilal Jain, *Panchsheela and After: Sino-Indian Relations in the Context of the Tibetan Insurrection* (Bombay, 1960), p. 8.
2 See *Indian Press Digests*, no. 1 (University of California, 1956), pp. i–ix.
3 *Report of the Officials of the Governments of India and the People's Republic of China on the Boundary Question* (New Delhi, 1961), pp. CR–101.
4 *Prime Minister on Sino-Indian Relations* (New Delhi, 1961), I, i, pp. 184–5.
5 Michael Brecher, *Nehru: A Political Biography* (London, 1959), p. 458.
6 Walter Crocker, *Nehru: A Contemporary's Estimate* (London, 1966), p. 87.
7 S. S. Khera, *India's Defence Problems* (Bombay, 1968), p. 187.
8 D. M. Mankekar, *Guilty Men of 1962* (Bombay, 1968), p. 138.
9 Neville Maxwell, *India's China War* (London, 1970), p. 81.
10 *Notes, Memoranda and Letters Exchanged and Agreements Signed between the Governments of India and China: White Paper, Ministry of External Affairs, Government of India* (New Delhi, 1959–63), vol. I, p. 26.
11 *Notes, Memoranda and Letters*, vol. I, p. 51.
12 Maxwell, *India's China War*, p. 105.
13 *Notes, Memoranda and Letters*, India's note (26 April 1959), vol. I, p. 68.
14 *Notes, Memoranda and Letters*, India's note (27 August 1959), vol. I, p. 44.
15 *Times of India* (31 August 1959).
16 *Times of India* (24 October 1959).
17 Nirad Chaudhuri, *The Continent of Circe* (London, 1965), p. 109.
18 Karunakar Gupta, *India in World Politics* (Calcutta, 1969), p. 163.
19 *Prime Minister on Sino-Indian Relations*, I, i, p. 210.
20 Indeed, there was also a legal precedent for not negotiating. The Supreme Court ruled that it had been unlawful for the government to hand over a few villages at Berubari to Pakistan in 1958. Nehru could not therefore cede any territory without changing the constitution and for that he would need a two-thirds majority in the Lok Sabha: but this was not a popular issue for changing the constitution at all. Supreme Court Reports, 1960, III, pp. 250ff.

21 *Times of India* (6 October 1959).

22 Maxwell, *India's China War*, p. 161.

23 Maxwell, *India's China War*, p. 185.

24 Lieutenant General B. M. Kaul, *The Untold Story*, (Bombay, 1967). pp. 41, 317–18.

25 Maxwell, *India's China War*, p. 228.

26 Kaul, *Untold Story*, pp. 300–01.

27 Maxwell, *India's China War*, pp. 222–3.

28 Maxwell, *India's China War*, p. 254.

29 *Prime Minister on Sino-Indian Relations*, I, ii, [AQ: vol/, part?]p. 102; *Notes, Memoranda and Letters*, vol. VII, p. 37.

30 Brigadier J. S. Dalvi, *Himalayan Blunder* (Bombay, 1969), p. 134.

31 Maxwell, *India's China War*, p. 310.

32 *Notes, Memoranda and Letters*, vol. VII, pp. 80, 83–4.

33 *Statesman*, 20 October 1962. For the Chinese repercussions, see Bruce A. Elleman, *Modern Chinese Warfare* (London and New York, 2001), pp. 267–8.

Chapter 7: The India–Pakistan Wars of 1965 and 1971, and the Bangladesh War of Independence

1 J. N. Dixit, *India–Pakistan in War and Peace* (London, 2002), p. 146

2 Dixit, *India–Pakistan*, p. 147.

3 Dixit, *India–Pakistan*, p. 156.

4 Dixit, *India–Pakistan*, pp. 158–62.

5 Lawrence Ziring, *Pakistan at the Crosscurrent of History* (Oxford, 2003), p. 8.

6 Ziya-ul-Hasan Faruqi, *The Deoband School and the Demand for Pakistan* (Bombay, 1963); Ishtiaq Husein Qureshi, *Ulema in Politics* (Karachi, 1974).

7 Dixit, *India–Pakistan*, p. 165. The figures for the Indian Army personnel include paramilitaries such as the BSF (Border Security Force), but note that Dixit claims, erroneously, that Pakistan had acquired more than 1,400 tanks.

8 Stanley Wolpert, *A New History of India* (New York and Oxford, 2000), p. 386; Helal Uddin Ahmed, 'Armed Resistance in the War of Independence', *The Independent* (31 July 2002).

9 The Bangladeshi perspective on the origins of the resistance can be found in Major Rafiqul Islam, *A Tale of Millions: Bangladesh Liberation War, 1971* (Dhaka, 1995).

10 Robert V. Jackson, *South Asian Crisis: India, Pakistan and Bangla Desh* (London, 1975), p. 81.

11 Richard Sisson and Leo E. Rose, *War and Secession: Pakistan, India, and the Creation of Bangladesh* (Berkeley, CA, 1990), pp. 145 and 209.

12 Dixit, *India–Pakistan*, p. 182.

13 John H. Gill, *Atlas of the 1971 India–Pakistan War: the Creation of Bangladesh* (Washington, DC, 2004), p. 12.

14 Dixit, *India–Pakistan*, pp. 190–208.

15 Brigadier Shahdullah Khan, *East Pakistan to Bangladesh* (Lahore, 1975), p. 110.

16 Major-General Rahim Khan, Commander of 39 Division, *The Herald* (September

2000), cited in Gill, *Atlas*, p. 17.

17 Major-General Lachhman Singh Lehl, *Victory in Bangladesh* (Dehra Dun, 1991), p. 61.

18 Dixit, *India–Pakistan*, p. 209.

19 Gill, *Atlas*, pp. 23–4.

20 Gill, *Atlas*, p. 26.

21 Brigadier H. S. Sodhi, '*Operation Windfall*': *Emergence of Bangladesh* (New Delhi, 1980), p. 280.

22 Lehl, *Victory in Bangladesh*, p. 55.

23 Wolpert, *New History of India*, p. 390.

24 Major-General Rao Farman Ali Khan, *How Pakistan Got Divided* (Lahore, 1992), pp. 119–20.

25 Lieutenant-Colonel Mukhtar Ahmad Gilani, 'Lost Opportunity – A Military Analysis 1971', *Defence Journal* (January 2003); Major Agha Humayun Amin, 'The Western Theatre in 1971: A Strategic and Operational Analysis', *Defence Journal* (February 2002).

26 Gill, *Atlas*, p. 62.

27 Gill, *Atlas*, p. 64.

28 Ziring, *Pakistan*, p. 132.

29 Dixit, *India–Pakistan*, p. 226.

Chapter 8: Afghanistan: The Soviet Occupation, 1979–89

1 Cited in Edward R. Giradet, *Afghanistan: The Soviet War* (London, 1985), p. 108.

2 Noor Ahmed Khalidi, 'Afghanistan: Demographic Consequences of War, 1978–87', *Central Asian Survey*, X/3 (1991), p. 107.

3 Henry S. Bradsher, *Afghanistan and the Soviet Union* (New York, 1985), p. 28.

4 William Maley, *The Afghanistan Wars* (London and New York, 2002), p. 26.

5 Maley, *The Afghanistan Wars*, p. 28.

6 Giradet, *Afghanistan*, p. 121.

7 *K polozhenii v 'A'*, P176/125, cited in Maley, *The Afghanistan Wars*, p. 33.

8 Bernard Lewis, *The Political Language of Islam* (Chicago, 1988), p. 72.

9 Maley, *The Afghanistan Wars*, pp. 63–4.

10 Hasan Kakar, *Afghanistan: The Soviet Invasion and the Afghan Response, 1979–1982* (Berkeley and Los Angeles, 1995), p. 117.

11 Marvin G. Weinbaum, *Pakistan and Afghanistan: Resistance and Reconstruction* (Boulder, CO, 1994), p. 32.

12 Maley, *The Afghanistan Wars*, p. 77.

13 Tom Carew, *Jihad! The Secret War in Afghanistan* (Edinburgh and London, 2000), p. 44.

14 Mohammed Yousef and Mark Adkin, *The Bear Trap: Afghanistan's Untold Story* (London, 1992), p. 77.

15 Maley, *The Afghanistan Wars*, p. 92.

16 Giradet, *Afghanistan*, p. 126.

17 Fahima Nassery, cited in 'Une femme torturée', in *Femmes en Afghanistan*, ed.

Bernard Dupaigne (Paris, 1986), p. 11.

18 Maley, *The Afghanistan Wars*, p. 109.
19 Antonio Giustozzi, *War, Politics and Society in Afghanistan, 1978–1992* (London, 2000), p. 209.
20 Mark Urban, *War in Afghanistan* (London, 1990), p. 207.
21 BBC *Summary of World Broadcasts* FE/0292/C/1 (26 October 1988).
22 Giustozzi, *War, Politics and Society*, p. 168.
23 Henry S. Bradsher, *Afghan Communism and Soviet Intervention* (Karachi and Oxford, 1999), p. 277.
24 Sarah Mendelsohn, *Changing Course: Ideas, Politics and the Soviet Withdrawal from Afghanistan* (Princeton, NJ, 1998), pp. 37–8.
25 Maley, *Afghanistan Wars*, p. 133.
26 Maley, *Afghanistan Wars*, pp. 139–40.
27 Anatoly S. Chernyaev, *My Six Years with Gorbachev* (University Park, PA, 2000), pp. 161–2.
28 Maley, *Afghanistan Wars*, p. 151.
29 Mark Galeotti, *Afghanistan: The Soviet Union's Last War* (London, 1985), p. 153; Maley, *Afghanistan Wars*, p. 165.

Chapter 9: Afghanistan: The Civil War, 1989–2001

1 'Passing the Hat Round for the Rebuilders', *The Economist* (1 April 2004).
2 Barnett R. Rubin, *The Fragmentation of Afghanistan: State Formation and Collapse in the International System* (New Haven, CT, 1995), p. 152.
3 Henry S. Bradsher, *Afghan Communism and Soviet Intervention* (London and Karachi, 1999), p. 346; Mohammed Yousaf and Mark Adkin, *The Bear Trap: Afghanistan's Untold Story* (London, 1992), p. 227.
4 William Maley, *The Afghanistan Wars* (London and New York, 2002), p. 179.
5 Najibullah was subsequently captured by the Taliban and executed, his remains being strung up for public display. Maley, *Afghanistan Wars*, p. 218.
6 Barnett R. Rubin, 'Women and Pipelines: Afghanistan's Proxy Wars', *International Affairs*, LXXIII/2 (1997), p. 287.
7 Amnesty International, *Afghanistan: International Responsibility for Human Rights Disaster* (London, 1995), pp. 62–5.
8 Maley, *Afghanistan Wars*, p. 220.
9 Ahmed Rashid, 'The Taliban: Exporting Extremism', *Foreign Affairs*, LXXVIII/6 (1999), p. 27.
10 Mohammed Qasim Zaman, 'Religious Education and the Rhetoric of Reform: The Madrassa in British India and Pakistan', *Comparative Studies in Society and History*, XLI/2 (1999), p. 322; S.V.R. Nasr, 'The Rise of Sunni Militancy in Pakistan: The Changing Role of Islamism and the Ulama in Society and Politics', *Modern Asian Studies*, XXXIV/1 (2000), p. 179.
11 S.V.R. Nasr, 'International Politics, Domestic Imperatives and Identity Mobilisation: Sectarianism in Pakistan, 1979–1998', *Comparative Politics*, XXXII/2 (2000), p. 179.

12 Peter Marsden, *The Taliban: War and Religion in Afghanistan* (London and New York, 2002), p. 51.
13 Marsden, *The Taliban*, p. 55.
14 Ahmed Rashid, *Taliban: Militant Islam, Oil and Fundamentalism in Central Asia* (New Haven, CT, 2000), pp. 67–79.
15 Maley, *Afghanistan Wars*, p. 233.
16 Rashid, *Taliban: Militant Islam, Oil and Fundamentalism*, pp. 157–82.
17 Barnett Rubin, 'Arab Islamists in Afghanistan', in *Political Islam: Revolution, Radicalism, or Reform?*, ed. John L. Esposito (Boulder, CO, 1997), p. 196.
18 Peter L. Bergen, *Holy War Inc.: Inside the Secret World of Osama bin Laden* (New York, 2001), p. 102.
19 'The Next Phase', *The Economist* (13 October 2001).
20 Barry Bearak, 'In Village where Innocents Died, Anger Cannot Be Buried', *New York Times* (16 December 2001).
21 *The Economist* (1 April 2004).
22 George Soros, 'The Bubble of American Supremacy', *The Atlantic On-line*: http://www.theatlantic.com/issues/2003/12/soros.htm

Chapter 10: Insurgency, Terror and Peace-Making

1 See Jeremy Black, *War and the New Disorder in the 21st Century* (London and New York, 2004), pp. 26–68.
2 Stanley Wolpert, *A New History of India* (Oxford and New York, 2000), p. 411.
3 Samuel P. Huntington, *The Clash of Civilisations and the Remaking of World Order* (New York, 1997), p. 110–13.
4 R. O. Christiansen, 'Conflict and Change Among the Afridis and Tribal Policy 1839–1947', unpublished PhD Thesis, University of Leicester, 1987.
5 William Maley, *The Afghanistan Wars* (London and New York, 2002), p. 80.
6 Alex Schmid and Jenny de Graaf, *Violence as Communication* (London, 1982).
7 Sandeep Joshi, 13 November 2003.
8 Harkat ul Mujahideen (HUM), Jammu and Kashmir Liberation Front (JKLF), Liberation Tigers and Tamil Eelam, Lashkar-e-Toyeba/Tayyiba, Mujahideen-e Khalq: www.firstmonday.org/issues/issue7_11/Conway/index.html.
9 Lawrence Ziring, *Pakistan at the Crosscurrent of History* (Oxford, 2003), p. 141.
10 B. Raman, 'Intelligence and Counter-Terrorism', South Asia Analysis Group, 21 April 2004: http://www.saag.org See also B. Raman, 'Mumbai Blasts Target: The Indian Economy': http://www.saag.org/paper8/paper771.html
11 On 28 September 2001, the Security Council unanimously adopted resolution 1373 under Chapter VII of the UN Charter. This established a body of legally binding obligations on all member states. Its provisions require, among other things, that all member states prevent the financing of terrorism and deny safe haven to terrorists. States were asked to review and strengthen their border security operations, banking practices, customs and immigration procedures, law enforcement and intelligence cooperation, and arms transfer controls. All states are required to increase cooperation and share information with respect

to these efforts. The Resolution also called upon each state to report on the steps it had taken, and established a committee of the Security Council to monitor implementation.

12 Chitra K. Tiwari, 'Maoist Insurgency in Nepal: Internal Dimensions', South Asia Analysis Group, 20 January 2001: http://www.saag.org.

13 Nepalnews.com, 31 May 2004.

14 B. Raman, 'Nepal Maoists, India & China', South Asia Analysis Group, 2003: http://www.saag.org.

15 The Maoists continue to receive support from members of the Revolutionary Internationalist Movement (RIM), the headquarters of which are believed to be based in the USA. Amongst the members of the RIM are: the Ceylon Communist Party (Maoist), the Communist Party of Afghanistan, the Communist Party of Bangladesh (Marxist-Leninist), the Communist Party of Nepal (Maoist), the Communist Party of Peru, the Communist Party of Turkey (Marxist-Leninist), the Haitian Revolutionary Internationalist Group, the Maoist Communist Party (Italy), the Marxist-Leninist Communist Organization of Tunisia, the Proletarian Party of Purba Bangla (PBSP) in Bangladesh, the Revolutionary Communist Group of Colombia, the Revolutionary Communist Party of the USA and the Union of Communists of Iran (Sarbedaran).

16 *Annapurna Post* (Kathmandu), (9 April 2004), p. 1.

17 William Carpenter, *Asian Security Handbook: An Assessment of Political Security* (New York, 1996).

18 Amnesty International, *Myanmar: The Institution of Torture* (London, 2000).

19 Andrew Selth, *Burma's Defence Expenditure and Arms Industries* (Canberra, 1997).

20 Andrew Selth, *Burma and the Strategic Competition between Burma, China and India* (Canberra, 1996).

21 C. S. Kuppuswamy, 'Myanmar: The Shake Up and the Fall Out', South Asia Analysis Group, 9 November 2004: http://www.saag.org

22 B. Raman, 'Split in LTTE: The Clash of the Tamil Warlords', South Asia Analysis Group, 8 March 2004: http://www.saag.org

23 BBC News, 15 April 2004.

24 Jonathan Steele, 'Sri Lanka Talking with Tamil Tigers', *The Guardian*, cited in The Himalayan Times Online, 22 December 2004: http://www.thehimalayantimes.com

25 Zahid Hussain, Ron Moreau and Sudip Mazumdar, 'The End of Jihad', *Newsweek International* (9 February 2004), p. 24.

26 Hussain, Moreau and Mazumdar, 'The End of Jihad', p. 24.

27 B. Raman, 'Kashmir & the Pro-Bin Laden Terrorist Infrastructure in Pakistan', South Asia Analysis Group, 17 June 2002: http://www.saag.org

28 *Friday Times* (14 –20 December 2001).

29 *Friday Times* (1–7 February 2002).

Chapter 11: Conclusion: Points of Conflict in South Asia

1 BBC, 6 December 1992; the views of Vishwa Hindu Parishad at http://www.ayod-

hya.com (2002); The BJP's interpretation of events is at
http://www.bjp.org/history/ayodhya.htm

2   *The Daily Telegraph* (15 May 2004).

3   See, for example, Amnesty International, ASA 31/046/2004 on Nepal's Maoist
kidnappings; the human rights abuses by the Jammu and Kashmir authorities
at AI Index: ASA 20/034/2003 (Public), News Service No. 274 (3 December 2003);
The Wire, XXXIV/6 (July 2004), listed 1 July 2004 and human rights abuses, 21
May 2004, ASA 33/013/2004; AI official visit to Myanmar, 16/037/2003 (22
December 2003) at http://web.amnesty.org

4   B. Raman, 'Escalation of Jihadi Terrorism', 1 August 2004:
http://www.saag.org/papers11/paper1074.html

5   *The Sunday Times* (8 February 2004), p. 21.

6   'Heavy Fighting against Taliban', 4 August 2004:
http://www.indiamonitor.com/ A similar process is feared in Bangladesh: Bert
Lintner 'Bangladesh: A Cocoon of Terror', *Far Eastern Economic Review* (4 April
2002); Dr Subhash Kapila, 'Bangladesh Government in Denial Mode on
Country's Talibanisation': http://www.saag.org/papers11/paper1058.html

7   Jeremy Black, *War and the New Disorder in the Twenty-First Century* (London and
New York, 2004), p. 163-9.

8   Black, *War and the New Disorder*, pp. 30-41.

Selected Further Reading

Books

Ahmed, Ishtiaq, *State, Nation and Ethnicity in Contemporary South Asia* (London, 1996)

Amnesty International, *Myanmar: The Institution of Torture* (London, 2000)

Appadorai, A., *The Domestic Roots of India's Foreign Policy, 1947-1972* (New Delhi, 1981)

——, and M. S. Rajan, *India's Foreign Policy and Relations* (New Delhi, 1985)

Aung San Suu Kyi, *Letters from Burma* (London, 1997)

BAAG (British Agencies Afghanistan Group), *Return and Reconstruction* (London, 1997)

Bajwa, Major-General Kuldip Singh, *The Falcon in My Name: A Soldier's Diary* (New Delhi, 2000)

Barnds, William J., *India, Pakistan and the Great Powers* (New York, 1972)

Beckett, I.W.F., *Modern Insurgencies and Counter-Insurgencies* (London and New York, 2001)

Bergen, Peter L., *Holy War Inc.: Inside the Secret World of Osama Bin Laden* (New York, 2001)

Birgisson, Karl Th., 'United Nations Good Offices Mission in Afghanistan and Pakistan', in *The Evolution of un Peacekeeping: Case Studies and Comparative Analysis*, ed. William J. Durch (New York, 1993)

Black, Jeremy, *War and the New Disorder in the 21st Century* (London, 2004)

——, *Why Wars Happen* (London, 1998)

Bradnock, Robert W., *India's Foreign Policy since 1971* (London, 1990)

Bradsher, Henry S., *Afghanistan and the Soviet Union* (Durham, NC, 1985)

——, *Afghan Communism and Soviet Intervention* (Karachi, 1999)

Brecher, Michael, *Nehru: A Political Biography* (London, 1959)

Burke, S. M., and Lawrence Ziring, *Pakistan's Foreign Policy*, 2nd edn (Karachi, 1990)

Burki, S. J., *Pakistan under Bhutto* (London, 1988)

Candeth, Lieutenant-General K. P., *The Western Front: The Indo-Pak War 1971* (New Delhi, 1984)

Chitkara, M. G., *Combating Terrorism* (New Delhi, 2003)

257

Chowdhury, G. W., *India, Pakistan, Bangladesh and the Major Powers: Politics of a Divided Subcontinent* (New York, 1975)

Cloughly, Brian, *A History of the Pakistan Army: Wars and Insurrections* (Karachi, 1999)

Cohen, Stephen P., *The Pakistan Army* (Berkeley and Los Angeles, 1985)

Collins, Larry, and Dominique Lapierre, *Freedom at Midnight* (London, 1975)

Dixit, J. N., *India-Pakistan in War and Peace* (London and New York, 2002)

Duncan, P. J. S., *The Soviet Union and India* (London, 1989)

Fink, Christina, *Living Silence: Burma under Military Rule* (London, 2001)

Galeotti, Mark, *Afghanistan: The Soviet Union's Last War* (London, 1995)

Ganguly, Sumit, *Conflict Unending* (Washington, DC, 2001)

—, *The Crisis in Kashmir: Portents of War, Hopes of Peace* (Cambridge, 1997)

George, T., R. Litwak and S. Chubin, *India and the Great Powers* (Aldershot, 1984)

Gill, John H., *An Atlas of the 1971 India–Pakistan War* (Washington, DC, 2004)

Giradet, Edward R., *Afghanistan: The Soviet War* (London, 1985)

Gregson, Jonathan, *Blood Against the Snows: The Tragic Story of Nepal's Royal Dynasty* (London, 2002)

Guistozzi, Antonio, *War, Politics and Society in Afghanistan, 1978–1992* (London, 2000)

Gupta, Karunakar, *India in World Politics* (Calcutta, 1969)

Gupte, Pranay, *Mother India: A Political Biography of Indira Gandhi* (New York, 1992)

Hall, D.G.E., *A History of South East Asia*, 4th edn (London, 1981)

Horn, R. C., *Soviet-Indian Relations: Issues and Influence* (New York, 1982)

Hosking, Geoffrey, *A History of the Soviet Union* (London, 1990)

Huntington, Samuel P., *The Clash of Civilisations and the Remaking of World Order* (New York, 1997)

Islam, Major Rafiqul, *A Tale of Millions: Bangladesh Liberation War, 1971* (Dhaka, 1995)

Jaffrelot, Christophe, ed., *A History of Pakistan and its Origins* (London, 2002)

Jalal, Ayesha, *The State of Martial Rule: The Origins of Pakistan's Political Economy of Defense* (New York, 1990)

—, *Democracy and Authoritarianism in South Asia* (Cambridge, 1997)

Jayawardena, Kumari, *Ethnic Conflict in Sri Lanka* (Colombo, 1985)

Juergensmeyer, Mark, *Terror in the Mind of God: The Global Rise of Religious Violence* (Berkeley and Los Angeles, 2000)

Kakar, Hasan, *Afghanistan: The Soviet Invasion and the Afghan Response, 1979–1982* (Berkeley and Los Angeles, 1995)

Kapur, Rajiv A., *Sikh Separatism: The Politics of Faith* (London, 1986)

Kennedy, C. H., and R. B. Rais, eds., *Pakistan 1995* (Boulder, CO, 1995)

Khan, Brigadier Saadullah, *East Pakistan to Bangladesh* (Lahore, 1975)

Khera, S. S., *India's Defence Problems* (Bombay, 1968)

Klevemann, Lutz, *The New Great Game* (London, 2003)

Kux, Dennis, *The United States and Pakistan, 1947–2000: Disenchanted Allies* (Washington, DC, 2001)

Lehl, Major-General Lachhman Singh, *Victory in Bangladesh* (Dehra Dun, 1991)

Mahmud Ali, S., *The Fearful State: Power, People and Internal War in South Asia* (London, 1993)

Maley, William, *Fundamentalism Reborn? Afghanistan and the Taliban* (London, 1988)

——, *The Afghanistan Wars* (London and New York, 2002)

Malik, H. I., *State and Civil Society in Pakistan: Politics of Authority, Ideology and Ethnicity* (Basingstoke, 1997)

Marsden, Peter, *The Taliban: War and Religion in Afghanistan* (London and New York, 2002)

Mascarenhas, Anthony, *The Rape of Bangladesh* (New Delhi, 1972)

Maxwell, Neville, *India's China War* (London and New York, 1970)

Mazari, Shareen M., *The Kargil Conflict, 1999* (Islamabad, 2003)

Mohan, Ram, *Sri Lanka: The Fractured Island* (London, 1989)

Nanda, B. R., ed., *Indian Foreign Policy: The Nehru Years* (New Delhi, 1976)

Nath, Major-General Rajendra, *Military Leadership in India* (New Delhi, 1990)

Nojumi, Neamatollah, *The Rise of the Taliban in Afghanistan: Mass Mobilisation, Civil War and the Future of the Region* (New York, 2002)

Prasad, S. N., ed., *History of the Indo-Pak War, 1971* (New Delhi, 1992)

Praval, Major K. C., *Indian Army After Independence* (New Delhi, 1990)

Rajan, M. S., V. S. Mani and C.S.R. Murthy, *The Non-Aligned and the United Nations* (New Delhi, 1987)

Rashid, Ahmed, *Jihad* (New York, 2002)

——, *Taliban: Islam, Oil and Fundamentalism in Central Asia* (New York, 2000)

Rizvi, Hasan-Askari, *The Military and Politics in Pakistan 1947–86* (Delhi, 1988)

Roy, Oliver, *Islam and Resistance in Afghanistan* (Cambridge, 1986)

Rubin, Barnett R., *The Fragmentation of Afghanistan: State Formation and Collapse in the International System* (New Haven, CT, 1995)

Sar Desai, D. R., and Anand Mohan, eds, *The Legacy of Nehru* (New Delhi, 1992)

Selth, Andrew, *Burma's Defence Expenditure and Arms Industries*, Strategic and Defence Studies Centre, Working Papers, 309 (Canberra, 1997)

Singh, Major-General Sukhwant, *India's Wars since Independence*, 3 vols (New Delhi, 1998)

Sisson, Richard, and Leo E. Rose, *War and Secession: Pakistan, India and the Creation of Bangladesh* (Berkeley, CA, 1990)

Smith, Martin, *Burma: Insurgency and the Politics of Ethnicity* (London, 1991)

Tanham, George K., and Marcy Agmon, *The Indian Air Force: Trends and Prospects* (Santa Monica, CA, 1995)

Thapa, Deepak, and Bandita Sijapati, *A Kingdom Under Siege: Nepal's Maoist Insurgency, 1996–2004* (London, 2004)

Thomas, R.C.G., *Indian Security Policy* (Princeton, NJ, 1986)

Tully, Mark, and S. Jacob, *Amritsar: Mrs Gandhi's Last Battle* (London, 1985)

Urban, Mark, *War in Afghanistan* (London, 1990)

Weinbaum, Marvin G., *Pakistan and Afghanistan: Resistance and Reconstruction* (Boulder, CO, 1994)

Wolpert, Stanley, *A New History of India* (Oxford, 2000)

Yousaf, Mohammed, and Mark Adkin, *Afghanistan: The Bear Trap* (London, 1992)

Zaheer, Hasan, *The Separation of East Pakistan: The Rise and Realisation of Bengali Nationalism* (Oxford, 1994)

Ziring, Lawrence, *Pakistan at the Crosscurrent of History* (Oxford, 2003)

Articles

Ahmed, Samina, David Cortright and Amitabh Mattoo, 'Public Opinion and Nuclear Options for South Asia' *Asian Survey*, xxxxviii/8 (1998), pp. 727–44

Ashraf, Tariq Mahmoud, 'Global Trends 2015: South Asia', *Strategic Vision*, iii (January–February 2004)

Broxup, Marie, 'Afghanistan according to Soviet Sources, 1980–85', *Central Asian Survey*, vii/2–3 (1988), pp. 197–204

Evans, Alexander, 'Subverting the State: Intervention, Insurgency and Terror in South Asia', *War Studies Journal*, ii (1996), pp. 17–29

—, 'The Kashmir Insurgency: As Bad As It Gets', *Small Wars and Insurgencies*, xi (2000), pp. 69–81

Hollen, Christopher van, 'The Tilt Policy Revisited: Nixon-Kissinger Geopolitics and South Asia', *Asian Survey*, xx/4 (1980)

Huntley, Wade L., 'Alternative Futures after the South Asian Nuclear Tests: Pokhran as Prologue', *Asian Survey*, xxxix/3 (1999), pp. 504–24

Kepel, Giles, 'The Origins and Development of the Jihadist Movement: From Anti-Communism to Terrorism', *Asian Affairs*, xxxiv/2, (July 2003), pp. 91–108

Khalilzad, Zalmay, 'Afghanistan in 1995: Civil War and a Mini-Great Game', *Asian Survey*, xxxvi/2 (1996), pp. 190–95.

Khanal, Y. N., 'Nepal in 1997: Political Stability Eludes', *Asian Survey*, xxxviii/(1998), pp. 148–54

Malik, Iftikar, 'Pakistan in 2001: Starting Anew or Stalemate?', *Asian Survey*, xli/1 (2001), pp. 104–15

—, 'Pakistan in 2001: The Afghanistan Crisis and the Rediscovery of the Frontline State', *Asian Survey*, xlii/1 (2001), pp. 204–12

Marwah, Onkar, 'India's Military Intervention in East Pakistan, 1971–2', *Modern Asian Studies*, xiii/4 (1979), pp. 549–80

Mohan Malik, J., 'China–India relations in the Post-Soviet Era: The Continuing Rivalry', *China Quarterly*, cxlii (June 1995), pp. 317–55

—, 'The Stability of Nuclear Deterrence in South Asia: The Clash between State and Anti-State Actors', *Asian Affairs*, xxx/3 (2003)

Nasr, S.V.R., 'The Rise of Sunni Militancy in Pakistan: The Changing Role of Islamism and the Ulama in Society and Politics', *Modern Asian Studies*, xxxiv/1 (2000), pp. 139–80

Rajagopalan, Rajesh, 'Innovations in Counter-Insurgency: The Indian Army's Rashtraya Rifles', *Contemporary South Asia*, xiii/1 (March 2004)

—, '"Restoring Normalcy": The Evolution of the Indian Army's Counter-Insurgency Doctrine', *Small Wars and Insurgencies*, xi (2000), pp. 48–68

Rubin, Barnett R., 'Women and Pipelines: Afghanistan's Proxy Wars', *International Affairs*, lxxiii/2 (1997)

Sayeed, K. B., 'Pakistan in 1983', *Asian Survey*, xxiv (1984), pp. 219–28

Talbot, Ian, 'General Pervez Musharraf: Saviour or Destroyer of Pakistan's Democracy', *Contemporary South Asia*, xi/3 (2002)

——, 'Pakistan in 2002: Democracy, Terrorism and Brinkmanship', *Asian Survey*,
    XLIII/1 (2003)
Zaman, Muhammad Qasim, 'Sectarianism in Pakistan: The Radicalisation of Shi'i
    and Sunni Identities', *Modern Asian Studies*, XXXII/3 (1998), pp. 689–716

Current Affairs

Amnesty International Reports
BBC (London)
Dawn (Karachi)
Economist (London)
Far Eastern Economic Review
Friday Times (Lahore)
The Guardian (London)
The Independent (London)
Human Rights Watch Reports
India Quarterly
India Today
Nepal Times
New York Times
Newsweek International (New York)
SAPRA Security and Policy Risk Analysis (India)
SAAG South Asia Analysis Group (India): http://www.saag.org
Sunday Times (London)

Index